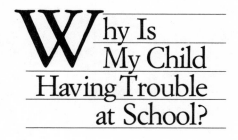

Why Is My Child Having Trouble at School?

Why Is My Child Having Trouble at School?

A Parent's Guide to Learning Disabilities

**BARBARA Z. NOVICK, Ph.D., and
MAUREEN M. ARNOLD, Ph.D.**

Villard Books   New York   1991

All rights reserved under International and Pan-
American Copyright Conventions. Published in the
United States by Villard Books, a division of Random
House, Inc., New York, and simultaneously in
Canada by Random House of Canada Limited,
Toronto.

Villard Books is a registered trademark of Random
House, Inc.

Library of Congress Cataloging-in-Publication Data
Novick, Barbara Z.
    Why is my child having trouble at school? : a
parent's guide to learning disabilities / Barbara Z.
Novick, Maureen M. Arnold—1st ed.
    p. cm.
Includes index.
ISBN 0-394-58509-7
    1. Learning disabilities—Popular works.
I. Arnold, Maureen M.   II. Title.
RJ496.L4N68   1991
618.92'85889—dc20   90-28508

Manufactured in the United States of America
9 8 7 6 5 4 3 2
First edition

DESIGNED BY BARBARA MARKS

ACKNOWLEDGMENTS

We wish to express our deepest gratitude to the many children with whom we have worked over the years for helping us to better understand the learning process and the many factors that affect it. We are also grateful to their parents. It was the challenging questions, repeated requests for a book that provides an up-to-date understanding of the brain's role in learning and a book that also serves as a guide to helping a child who is struggling at school, that provided the inspiration for this book. We thank Emily Bestler, our editor, and her co-workers at Villard Books for their expertise, encouragement, and support. Finally, we acknowledge a friend and colleague who introduced us to a new way of thinking about why children have difficulty with learning and how their frustration often shows itself.

CONTENTS

PART ONE

Things
You Need
to Know

INTRODUCTION

Learning disabilities, learning disorders that originate in the brain, affect one child in five. Do you
suspect that your child may be one of them? We can guess, because
you are reading this, that you do. We can also guess, for the same
reason, that you want to help your child in every way you can.

In over forty years of combined experience as professionals who
specialize in understanding the many factors that affect the way we
learn, we have worked with thousands of children who are struggling with learning. We have also helped scores of parents provide
their children with the special support they need. In this book, we
will give you the tools you need to see through the many "masks"
of a learning disability, provide you with a step-by-step action plan,
and serve as your personal guide in your efforts to help your child.

The first step in dealing effectively with your child's learning
difficulties is understanding what goes on in the brain as a child
learns, the patterns of normal development in children, and the
learning process itself. These are the topics of the six chapters that
make up Part One of the book.

A learning disability affects not only a child's ability to learn
but also his or her behavior and emotions. It affects the whole
family, too. Chapter 1 provides an overview of this complicated,
often painful, ripple effect. It also answers the questions that parents
ask most often about learning disabilities.

In Chapter 2, we describe the brain and its complex role in
learning. We'll answer questions such as: What areas of the brain
are responsible for which learning functions? How does the brain

receive information from the senses and interpret it to enable a child to master academic skills? What if the brain is not working as well as it should?

An inefficiency in the workings of even one small area of the brain can have a tremendous impact on a child's ability to meet the social and academic challenges he faces. If your child's brain has such an inefficiency, he needs your help. The better your knowledge of the brain and its workings, the more help you will be. Such knowledge will fine-tune your observational powers, and you will see your child's strengths and weaknesses with greater clarity. You will recognize more readily the signs of his disability and be able to move more swiftly to find the right professionals to work with him. At that point, your knowledge of the brain's role in learning will enable you to ask questions, offer observations, and make valuable suggestions. Rather than feeling passive, you will feel empowered. This strength will surely be transmitted to your child, who will benefit immeasurably.

Building on our picture of the working brain, we take you next through the childhood years, charting growth and skill development in the crucial areas of sensory-perceptual ability, motor and linguistic abilities, and thinking processes. We also discuss the factors that affect the pace and soundness of development. A clear sense of what constitutes average development is important for all parents, whether or not their child has a learning disability. What if a child's development isn't average? We focus next on the consequences that inefficiency in the brain's workings may have on the course of a child's sensory-perceptual, motor, linguistic, and thinking development.

Other important developmental areas are discussed in Chapter 5. Here we chart the stages of a child's social and psychological growth and the "tasks" he faces on his way to becoming a socially mature and psychologically healthy adult. We look also at the impact that neurological inefficiency may have on this process.

The first part of the book ends with a chapter on learning in school. Before you can truly appreciate how various disturbances can undermine learning, you need to understand how children learn and what factors affect the learning process. In turn, when you understand just how complex learning is, you will have a better feeling for what your child is going through as he struggles in school. This will affect your perception of your child, your relationship with him, and your ability to cope on a day-to-day basis. We also give you an overview of the developmental achievements and academic demands of the years from preschool on, which will help you gear your expectations to the potential of your child's growing mind and body.

Helping a child with a learning disability means, first of all, understanding the problem. Part One of the book lays that groundwork. Key concepts introduced there will be developed further in the chapters that follow.

CHAPTER 1

Learning About Learning Disabilities

Sarah had been an enthusiastic preschooler and an avid learner in kindergarten and first grade. But in second grade she started complaining about school, saying she was bored. This change came suddenly, and it upset her parents, especially her father, who still had vivid memories of his own struggles in school and had been pleased to see Sarah having an easier time. Sarah's mother was more angry than anxious. She had given a lot of thought to Sarah's schooling. In fact, she and her husband had chosen to live where they did because the local schools had such a good reputation. Could Sarah's teacher be to blame?

At a conference with the teacher, Sarah's parents were surprised and dismayed to learn that their daughter rarely participated in class discussions and was often seen staring out of the window. They were also told she had adopted a bossy, know-it-all facade and lacked interest in her work. When she did produce, her writing was sloppy —poorly formed letters, sometimes written backward or with upper- and lowercase confused, lines slanted toward the bottom of the page.

Following the conference, Sarah's father decided to make a real effort to work with her at home, so they practiced writing, keeping the letters uniform and neatly lined up. Sarah fought him, though, and his offers of help usually resulted in shouting matches and slammed doors. Then he noticed that Sarah was even having difficulty writing her own name—something she'd had ample opportunity to practice. Maybe repetition wasn't the answer. Maybe Sarah's willingness to make an effort, called into question so often lately, wasn't lacking after all. But what was wrong?

Driving to work in the car pool, Sarah's father mentioned his concerns to a friend. As it happened, the friend's son had experienced some of the same difficulties during his early school years and it had turned out that the boy had a learning disability. The friend urged Sarah's father to have his daughter tested. Acting on a referral from Sarah's pediatrician, Sarah's parents made her an appointment for a comprehensive psychological evaluation. And it turned out that Sarah did have a learning disability: her difficulty with writing was due to the inefficient workings of one of the areas of her brain responsible for writing, not because she was not bright enough to learn or was emotionally disturbed or physically handicapped in any way. In fact, because of inefficient brain workings, it was very difficult for Sarah to coordinate what her fingers were doing with what her eyes told her they should do. Her disruptive behavior and poor attitude about school were ways of dealing with this frustration. By acting on this information, Sarah's parents were able to get her the help she needed.

Sarah's story stands in marked contrast to Timmy's. He, too, had terrible difficulty learning to write. His classmates called him stupid, and he was the butt of all their jokes. He was also inattentive and impulsive in school and uncooperative at home. His teacher and his parents were convinced that he was lazy and uninterested in his schoolwork. Timmy assumed that he was just plain dumb. He grew to hate school, and the more he turned it off, the more disruptive his behavior became. He dropped out when it was legally possible and spent his days and nights hanging around street corners because he was unable to find a job without a high school diploma. If Timmy had been properly evaluated as a young child, it would have been clear that he was neither dumb nor lazy. Rather, he had a serious writing disorder. With proper intervention and support,

Timmy would have come to believe in himself and would have had a chance to experience academic success.

_____ SOME IMPORTANT POINTS

If you're reading this book, you probably sense that your child is not functioning up to his potential. Perhaps he lags behind his classmates academically, or his skills compare unfavorably with those of younger siblings. Could he be suffering from a learning disability?

Today, one child in five is affected by difficulty in learning. Learning disabilities strike 20 percent of the world's population, without regard to race, creed, or color, or economic, social, or cultural background. However, they do seem to discriminate on the basis of sex: boys are affected much more frequently than girls. The ratio ranges from five to one all the way up to seven to one. No one knows why. (Because of this sex difference, we've opted to use the pronoun "he" when referring to the child with a learning disability.) Learning disabilities have afflicted—or perhaps empowered—some of society's most notable inventors, thinkers, artists, and performers. Thomas Edison, the inventor of the light bulb, was a failure in school. Albert Einstein was a slow learner and socially inept for much of his early life. The sculptor Auguste Rodin was the worst student in his school and had great difficulty learning to read and write. In our own time, Cher talks about having a reading disability. So does Tom Cruise.

During the past ten years, there has been a remarkable proliferation of interest and research into the relationship between brain functioning and a child's ability to learn. This new information has forced professionals in a broad range of fields to alter their ideas about the children who struggle with learning. We now understand that children with learning disabilities are not bad, or lazy, or dumb. We know that exceptional intelligence and a privileged education provide no protection. We also know that a learning disability needn't be a ticket to lifelong failure.

As a loving, responsible parent, you have great concern for your child's development. Is he developing normally or not? Do you think that he may perhaps have a learning disability? If you've answered yes, then you need to become an educated observer. If your child needs help, there will be signs to tell you so, signs you can easily learn to read. A change in behavior at home, continued difficulty in performing tasks at school, a dive in emotional well-being, persistent avoidance of certain kinds of activities—all can signal a need for help. As a parent, you have an ear to the ground: important signs and symptoms won't escape you. You can learn to interpret what you're noticing, and we can help you. With guidance, you can proceed to the proper plan of action.

The more you know about learning disabilities, the earlier you'll be able to recognize the symptoms. Time is of the essence. Skills are built one on another, and failure to master one before the next is learned can prevent forward motion and start a downward spiral. Trouble with reading can lead to difficulty in learning to spell, and so forth. Even a minor learning disability can cause major trouble if it remains unattended for too long. Allowing a learning disability to run its destructive course without treatment or with inappropriate treatment can leave your child stranded in a maze not really of his own making. With prompt, appropriate treatment, you can help your child find his way around the obstacle in his path and proceed along the course of development. Again, early recognition of symptoms is the key.

There is, however, a difference between *recognizing the symptoms* and *defining the nature* of a learning disability. Parents may be able to recognize the symptoms—indeed, they may be the first to do so. But parents can't be expected to pinpoint the basis of the disability. This takes a specialist, a professional who can perform a comprehensive psychological evaluation.

Sometimes, the symptoms of a disability have no apparent connection with the area of primary difficulty. Take, for example, the case of nine-year-old James.

James was inattentive and disruptive in class. He passed notes to his friends, answered out of turn, and talked to his classmates instead of listening to the lessons. He also suddenly became uncooperative at home, something that was quite new. Acting on the school's recommendation, his parents sent him for psychological testing. A comprehensive psychological evaluation discovered a rather severe difficulty processing language, a difficulty whose basis was physical. Because of inefficient workings in the parts of the brain that underlie language, James had trouble understanding what was said to him and what he read.

Once the language difficulty was pinpointed, other behaviors, which had been less troublesome to other people and therefore largely ignored, took on new meaning. James's speech had been slow in coming, and, as a toddler, he had lagged behind his peers in adding new words to his vocabulary. He hadn't really "caught on" to reading until the second grade. And in third grade he got a C for reading because he often did not grasp the main ideas of the stories he read.

Since children develop skills at different rates, it's often hard to see the symptoms of a learning disability early on. These symptoms may not be noticed, or may not be taken seriously, until behavioral problems develop. This was the case with James: it was only after he had developed obvious behavioral symptoms, in reaction to his frustration with learning, that his parents and teachers became concerned. So for him, accurate evaluation came late—but not too late. With appropriate treatment, he found ways to lessen the impact of his language disability and, within a couple of years, was doing better, both academically and behaviorally.

As in James's case, proper evaluation must always precede attempts to help a child with a learning disability. Hiring someone to tutor your child in arithmetic will not help with the problem if its underlying cause is a language disability that affects his understanding of computations presented as "stories" ("If Tom has seven cents and loses a nickel . . ."). Scattershot attempts to "fix" a symptom without addressing its source can only lead to frustration, time lost, and possibly money wasted too. Every learning disability is complex; inept efforts to help further compound the problem. Already upset about his difficulty, your child tries hard to improve, but fails. He knows that he has disappointed those who love him. Typical reactions are to "act out" or to withdraw. Depression, frustration, and anger also develop. The emotional turbulence is like a storm cloud, overshadowing the whole family.

As a parent, you are your child's advocate, responsible for finding the best solution possible. What should you do? Seek professional help? Not right away. First you must educate yourself, because before you can attempt to deal effectively with your child's disability, you must understand just what is wrong. The second step is to relax. Without a constructive focus, your concern will only further disturb your youngster. He takes his cues from you as to how to regard himself and his prospects. He wants to feel hopeful. So relax, knowing that you have begun your efforts to do everything you can to help. You're reading this book and finding out what you need to know to become your child's best advocate.

_____ QUESTIONS PARENTS ASK ABOUT LEARNING DISABILITIES

A good place to start is with some straightforward answers to the most common questions about learning problems and learning disabilities—the questions that parents ask, time and time again, when they come to our offices. The answers should dispel some of your fears, but at the same time, they will ground you in the reality of a serious problem.

What is a learning problem? A learning problem is a difficulty with acquiring such skills as reading or arithmetic. It can be very subtle, so that it is hardly noticeable. Or it can be very severe, so that it really shackles the child in his attempts to learn.

A learning problem may have its roots in emotional factors. Excessive fearfulness or preoccupation, for example, may make it difficult for a child to learn. Or the basis of the problem may be environmental—perhaps a school setting that is too unstructured for a particular child—or biological. Often, more than one of these factors is involved. A comprehensive psychological examination is necessary to determine what root (or roots) a learning problem has, and what roles the various factors play in a child's difficulties.

Health problems may be responsible when the bases of a learning problem are biological. Or the biological bases may be inefficiencies in the workings of the brain. In that case, the learning problem is more properly called a learning disability. This is an important point, so we'll repeat it: "learning problem" is a general term that covers learning difficulties with a great variety of root causes. The term "learning disability" refers to one particular type of learning problem.

What is a learning disability? ·A learning disability is a learning problem that is attributable to inefficient workings of the brain. It is *not* attributable to limited intelligence, or severe emotional disturbance, or a handicap such as blindness or deafness. According to the current legal definition, a child with a learning disability is functioning two or more years below the expected level for his age and his assessed IQ. (A very bright child who is functioning at grade level, rather than well above, may also have a learning disability.)

Does my child have a subnormal intelligence? Is he retarded? One recognized way of describing a child's intelligence is in terms of his scores—at a particular time and in comparison with other children his age—on IQ tests. These tests assess numerous abilities (often broadly divided into two categories: verbal and nonverbal) that have been identified as necessary for academic and vocational success, such as defining words, analyzing visual materials, and so on. Factors such as artistic aptitude and creativity are not currently measured by intelligence tests. The tests do not assess a child's motivation, his emotional state, or his attitudes, all of which are vitally important in any area of achievement.

According to current diagnostic criteria, a child with a learning disability is not of subnormal intelligence or mentally retarded. He may in fact be extremely intelligent and more capable in some areas than other children.

Will he outgrow the disability? Right now, we do not know how to "fix" the inefficient workings of the brain that underlie a learning disability. But with a good evaluation leading to appropriate treatment, a child with a learning disability may learn how to get around his difficulties in a number of ways; by using alternative brain functions to do the work the inefficient ones can't handle.

In the process of learning how to deal with his disability, the child may also learn something else of value. Life is full of unexpected obstacles. By learning to overcome one such obstacle early on, he may gain the strength and resilience that will help him surmount other troubles encountered later in life.

Is my child's learning disability due to an emotional problem? No. As we said above, the root of a learning disability is inefficiencies in the workings of the brain. However, a child may have emotional problems in reaction to his learning disability, and these may require therapy. Low self-esteem, born of a child's deep sense of failure, can compound even the mildest disability with an emotional overlay that is hard to get through. Sometimes, by the time we get to see a child, he is knotted up emotionally by years of confusion, anger, and frustration. Then we may recommend psychotherapy before attempting remediation of the learning disability— or we may recommend that psychotherapy and remediation go hand in hand.

How long will treatment take? Every child's disability and his emotional reaction to it are different. The length of his treatment depends on a number of factors, including the nature and the severity of the child's disability, his intellectual strengths, the extent to which alternative brain functions can be used to bypass inefficient ones, the amount of support that relatives, teachers, and peers can give him, and his basic state of emotional well-being.

Can medication "cure" a learning disability? No known medication acts on the cause of a learning disability.

Could something be going on at home to cause the disability? Trouble at home—discord between parents, for example—is never the primary cause of a child's learning disability. Neither is a parent who is preoccupied or inattentive or away much of the time. But these factors can contribute to the effect the disability has on the child and how well he copes with it.

Is this disability inherited? Research suggests that some learning disabilities may be inherited and that others are not. Even if a person suffered from a learning disability as a child, it does not necessarily mean that his children will inherit the difficulty. If one of them does, however, it is important to keep in mind that the child will also "inherit" his parents' attitude toward the disability —simply by mirroring their reaction to it.

If you yourself had difficulty learning, you probably feel especially disturbed to witness your child going through the same thing. You identify strongly with his distress and sense of helplessness. However, better help is available for him now than was available for you as a child. Great strides in evaluation and treatment have vastly improved your child's chances of dealing effectively with his disability.

Does my child need placement in a special class or a special school better geared to his needs? The fact that a child has a learning disability does not necessarily mean that he needs special education. In certain cases, though, special arrangements need to be

made. Together with school personnel and other professionals, you
can decide on that course of action if it is warranted.

Most children with learning disabilities can be helped. And,
while no one can guarantee that treatment will succeed, we can say
with certainty that, if a child suffers from a learning disability,
neither his learning nor his emotional well-being is likely to flourish
over the long run without proper evaluation and treatment. Getting
your child the help he needs is something of a learning task in itself
—for you. But first, you must understand what learning is.

CHAPTER 2

The Human
Nervous System

Our nervous system mediates everything we do, from an action as basic as breathing to one as complex as writing a poem. To understand learning in general, and a child's learning disabilities in particular, you need to know something about the human nervous system—how it is structured, how it works, and how its various parts function in the learning process.

———— ORGANIZATION

The structures that make up the human nervous system are traditionally divided into two different systems, the central nervous system (CNS) and the peripheral nervous system (PNS). The brain and the spinal cord together make up the CNS. The PNS consists of the nerves branching out from the brain and the spinal cord, and parts of the autonomic nervous system (which we'll describe in a moment).

The organization of the nervous system into CNS and PNS is structural: these divisions have to do with the way the nervous system is put together. But the nervous system is also organized into functional divisions. Here again there are two systems, the somatic and the autonomic. The somatic system conveys and processes sensory information (such as light or sound) and mediates voluntary muscle movement—movements that we do purposefully, such as flexing an arm or raising an eyebrow.

The autonomic system sends commands to the glands, the smooth muscles of the skin, the blood vessels, and the internal organs (the heart and stomach, for example). It functions reflexively and automatically. Your heart goes on beating, day and night, without any conscious prompting. You don't have to think about passing food down your digestive tract—the muscles of the intestinal wall do their work automatically.

Doctors make a distinction between the sympathetic and the parasympathetic parts of the autonomic nervous system. Roughly speaking, the sympathetic system activates the body, putting it on emergency alert. It is what makes your heart pound and your mouth go dry when you narrowly avoid a car crash. The parasympathetic system, on the other hand, deals with body functions when you are "at peace": it keeps the heart rate and breathing steady, takes care of digestion, and permits sexual activity.

_____ THE NEURON

The basic unit of the nervous system is the nerve cell, or neuron. Neurons make up the bulk of the nervous system, communicating among themselves, as they do the system's work. Technically a neuron is a cell with a cell body, an armlike projection called an axon, and one or more dendrites. The branching dendrites increase the surface area of the neuron, making it more receptive to messages sent by other nearby cells (Figure 2-1).

Neurons communicate with each other across an infinitesimally small gap in the region between the dendrite of one neuron and the axon and cell body of another. There are countless billions of these points of contact in the nervous system. At the synapse, a chemical messenger (a neurotransmitter) is released, crosses the synaptic gap, and is picked up by the next neuron in the chain. The effect of the neurotransmitter on the next cell may be to stimulate it, so as to send the message on, or to inhibit it and so stop the nerve impulse from going further. (This part of the process is rather like the way a rumor spreads. When the story is interesting, it gets passed on;

FIGURE 2-1

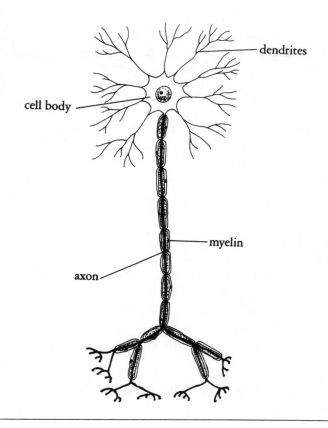

when it's not, it doesn't.) If the effect is stimulating and strong enough, the cell body will fire and the nerve impulse will be sent on. It is sent out along the axon to yet other neurons, or to a structure that responds to it, such as a muscle in your arm (Figure 2-2).

Many of the dendrites and axons are sheathed in a white fatty material called myelin. Regions of the nervous system where most of the tissues are sheathed in myelin are called white matter. Neurons that do not have myelin sheaths are grayish in color, and the

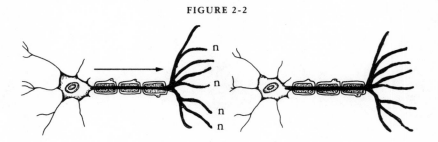

A nerve impulse moves down the axon. A neurotransmitter (n) is released into the synaptic gap between the neurons to be picked up by the next neuron. This process enables a nerve impulse to be passed from one neuron to the next.

regions where these neurons preponderate—the outer layer of the brain, for example—are called gray matter.

Neurons are not like other cells in the body, which are continually dying and being replaced. With the exception of the neurons of the nerve that is responsible for the sense of smell, neurons that die have no successors. Brain cells destroyed by alcohol or drug abuse are gone forever.

THE CENTRAL NERVOUS SYSTEM

The central nervous system (CNS)—the brain and the spinal cord —evolves from a hollow structure called the neural tube during the very early development of the embryo. Soon after conception, the head region of the neural tube begins to expand to form the brain, and the rest of the tube becomes the spinal cord.

By the time of birth, the brain has nearly all of the 20 million or so neurons that it will ever have. These cells, however, are simple and relatively isolated from each other. During the first year of life, the size of the neurons increases and so do the number of connections between them—each one develops from 1,000 to 10,000 connections with other neurons. The growth of the brain after birth also involves the laying down of myelin.

The Spinal Cord

This cylinder of white and gray matter—myelinated and unmyelinated fibers—is enclosed in the backbone and protected by it. Pairs of nerves that supply the limbs and torso pass out of the spinal cord in an orderly fashion: those that supply the lower parts of the body branch out from the bottom and those involved with upper parts branch out higher up. These spinal nerves belong to the peripheral nervous system, which we'll describe later.

The spinal cord is a two-directional pathway and relay system. It carries information from the senses *to* the brain and commands *from* the brain to the muscles. Damage at any level of the spinal cord interrupts sensory information coming from parts of the body supplied by nerves leaving the cord below the injury. And because the system is two-way, the damage also blocks impulses from the brain to the same areas. Someone who has had a severe injury and damaged his spinal cord at waist level will have no feeling in his legs and will not be able to move them, either.

As well as carrying sensory information in one direction and motor information in the other, the spinal cord mediates the spinal reflexes. Reflexive movement is automatic. You do not think about jerking your hand away from a hot stove. Nor do you plan a knee jerk when the doctor taps your leg just below the kneecap. The first behavior we exhibit is reflexive: a newborn's movements are based on a collection of reflex responses to the surrounding world. As a child grows, the ability to move purposefully gradually develops, but a number of reflexes stay with us all our lives.

The Brain

The brain is snugged into the skull, protected not only by a bony dome but by layers of membranes and a cushion of cerebrospinal fluid. It runs on oxygen and glucose, supplied by the bloodstream, and survives no more than four minutes or so if these fuels are cut off. The brain has four main regions: the cerebrum, the cerebellum, the deep structures, and the brain stem (Figure 2-3).

The Cerebrum

When people speak of the brain, they usually mean the cerebrum, the part of the brain that is so highly developed, and so large, in

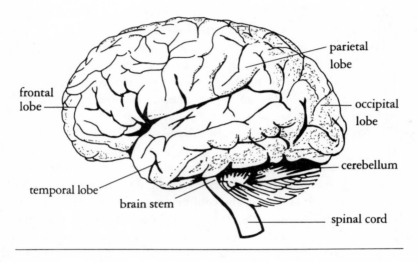

humans. Its cells are densely packed and its outer layer (the cortex) deeply convoluted, rather like the skin of a very dried apple. A noted researcher has estimated that we would have a brain the size of a basketball if its surface weren't convoluted.

A deep valley runs across the cortex from front to back, dividing it into two very similar halves, the two cerebral hemispheres. Other valleys and ridges subdivide each hemisphere into four regions or lobes: the occipital, temporal, parietal, and frontal lobes. The frontal lobes, not surprisingly, lie in the front part of the cortex; the others are in the back.

Posterior cerebral cortex. The back region of the cerebral cortex, containing the occipital, temporal, and parietal lobes (one of each in each hemisphere), is the sensory area of the brain. It is responsible for receiving and interpreting information from all the senses except the sense of smell. This it does in three zones into which the region is divided: the projection, association, and higher-association zones. (Each of the lobes in this region has both projection and association zones; the higher-association zones lie in the areas of overlap between the lobes.) To illustrate, let's follow the reception and processing of a bit of visual information—say, a colored light. First, the light stimulates the retina and a message is sent to the projection zones of the occipital lobes via a subcortical relay station called the thalamus. The occipital lobes receive and register the information: a light of some kind. Then the association zones take over. These are responsible for making sensory discriminations and for integrating the information so as to give it meaning. In our example, discrimination finds that the light is a red light, not a green one. Finally, in a higher-association zone, the visual information is integrated with information coming from other sources—for example, the areas that underlie language. Here, the object is given a verbal label: "red light" (Figure 2-4). The whole process happens so quickly that it seems instantaneous.

Just as the occipital lobes deal with visual information, the temporal lobes receive and interpret sound—auditory information. The language-dominant hemisphere (in right-handers and most left-handers, this is the left hemisphere) discriminates the sounds of speech; the right hemisphere processes nonverbal sounds such as music, explosions, or the rustling of leaves in the wind.

Somatosensory information (information provided by the sense of touch, for example) is dealt with in the parietal lobes. How much brain space is dedicated to the representation of any particular body part does not depend on how large the body part is, but how sensitive. The face and hands have the greatest representation, and the shoulders and back have less.

Information from three sensory areas—visual, auditory, somatosensory—is integrated in the higher-association zones of the posterior cerebral cortex. It is thanks to the higher-association zones in the language-dominant hemisphere that you can do such things as read this book and understand what is being said to you. The higher-association zones in the right hemisphere make it possible for you to deal with a visual-spatial challenge like finding a new route home from work. Right-hemisphere zones also enable you to appreciate the nuances of a musical composition.

Anterior cerebral cortex. The frontal lobes have this region to themselves. Here, both motor performance and behaviors that don't involve motor activity are planned, set in motion, evaluated, and modified. Like the posterior cerebral cortex, this area is divided into projection, association, and higher-association zones.

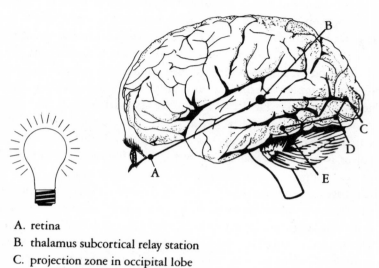

FIGURE 2-4

A. retina
B. thalamus subcortical relay station
C. projection zone in occipital lobe
D. association zone in occipital lobe
E. higher association zone in occipital-temporal area

The projection zones are responsible for the messages that control movements of the voluntary muscles—the ones that we use deliberately and consciously. The body parts most involved in finely controlled movement have the greatest representation in the brain. Motor association zones are responsible for integrating individual movements into larger working units—for example, integrating the fine motor control of individual fingers to tie a shoelace or button a coat.

The higher-association zones of this region of the brain perform an extraordinary variety of tasks. Among other things, they organize and carry out activities where step-by-step planning is a factor, such as writing a book report or solving a math problem. They are important in the mediation of our emotions. They also deal with the evaluation and modification of behavior. All in all, this region of the brain plays a crucial role in allowing you to think, learn, regulate your emotions, formulate ideas, and carry out plans.

Interhemispheric commissures. Complex tasks need information from both sides of the brain. For example, when children first learn to write the alphabet, the attempt to copy a letter begins with a visual analysis of its shape. This is a function of the right cerebral hemisphere. Motor control of the writing hand (in right-handers) is in the left hemisphere. To copy the letter, there has to be communication between the two sides. Information is transferred between the cerebral hemispheres by way of the interhemispheric commissures, large bundles of nerve fibers that connect major regions of the cortex.

The Cerebellum

Second in size to the cerebrum is the cerebellum, the "little brain," which lies beneath the cerebrum and behind the brain stem. The cerebellum is responsible for the control of body balance, muscle tone, and the precision and coordination of movements. Professional golfers and gymnasts are among those who owe their careers to a well-functioning cerebellum.

The Deep Structures

A number of structures associated with specific human behaviors are located deep within the brain, in what is known as the subcortical region. The thalamus, for example, acts as a relay station for all sensory information (except smell) transmitted to the cerebrum. The hypothalamus regulates appetite, sexual arousal, and emotional states such as anger.

Above the hypothalamus, and closely interconnected with it, are the subcortical structures collectively known as the limbic system. These complex circuits are involved with memory and emotion, and with behavior that is basic to the survival of the individual and the species: feeding and reproduction.

Also deep in the brain is a group of centers called the basal ganglia. These function as a processing station or bridge between the sensory and the motor systems. In combination with other structures in the brain, the basal ganglia influence our movements. For example, they are essential in maintaining normal posture and motor control.

The Brain Stem

The brain stem lies below the deep structures of the cerebrum, at the top of the spinal cord. The long nerve tracts that carry sensory information and messages about voluntary muscles to and from the brain pass through the brain stem. The brain stem also contains most of the cranial nerves (discussed below), which connect directly with the cerebrum; the reticular activating system, which is concerned with attention and arousal; and various important autonomic functions, such as those involved with breathing.

_____ THE PERIPHERAL NERVOUS SYSTEM

Cranial nerves, spinal nerves, and certain parts of the autonomic nervous system together make up the PNS. The cranial nerves carry messages to and from the head, the neck, and some of the body's internal organs. These nerves originate in the brain stem, except for the nerves that have to do with vision (the optic nerves) and with smell (the olfactory nerve).

We have already mentioned the spinal nerves, which branch out from the spinal cord, when we described the CNS. These nerves carry impulses from the somatosensory receptors to the brain and outward to both the muscles and the glands.

_____ THE DEVELOPMENT OF BRAIN FUNCTIONS

As we have seen, the brain has two sets of functions. First, it controls activities that are necessary for life, such as breathing, heart rate, and digestion. Second, it is responsible for receiving, integrating, and responding to the information that comes to it. These two sets of responsibilities are carried out in different brain regions that mature at different rates. The development of brain regions and their corresponding functions follows an expected timetable.

The first part of the brain to develop is the brain stem, where control of basic life functions such as breathing and digestion is located. This region begins to develop early on, and the functions it controls are in place before birth. The brain regions that control motor activity also begin to develop very early: the unborn child starts to move in the womb at about the twentieth week of gestation. Basic motor abilities are present at birth, as the baby's primitive reflexes show. Throughout infancy and early childhood, motor abilities continue to improve as the brain continues to develop.

Structures needed for the transmission of sensory information— for example, sight, sound, and touch—begin to develop a bit later than those that subserve motor activity and are fairly well developed at birth. During early infancy there is a dramatic development in sensory abilities. For example, although a newborn is able to tell the human voice from other sounds, he does not respond selectively to his caretaker's voice. But a three-month-old turns when he hears his mother or father speaking, because the requisite auditory discrimination abilities are now in place.

Those regions of the brain that mediate such behaviors as attention and emotion—the reticular activating system and the limbic system—develop while the baby is still in the womb. By contrast, the ability to form complex associations between pieces of information doesn't develop until a child is five to eight years old. This ability, central to the performance of academic skills such as reading and writing, is mediated by the late-developing higher-association zones of the posterior cortex. During the same period, communication between the two brain hemispheres by way of the interhemispheric commissures also becomes more efficient, increasing the brain's functional abilities.

A child of five or six has a growing ability to concentrate, formulate problems, make plans, and check results. By adolescence, the development of these skills (which is associated with the maturing of the association zones of the frontal lobe) is usually complete. For some, though, it continues into early adulthood.

_____ DEVELOPMENTAL LAG

In some children, the central nervous system matures at a slower-than-average rate. Why this happens is often unclear. Research, though, does indicate that such developmental lags are more frequently noted with boys than with girls. Delayed development of the CNS, particularly of the cerebral cortex, results in delayed development of a broad range of abilities. Among them are motor abilities, linguistic abilities, and thinking processes. The delay may affect all of these areas, or only one of them. A developmentally delayed child has the skills of a younger child—sometimes a much younger child—and is usually late in developing the abilities he'll need for learning in school.

There are two key points to be made about developmental lag. First, there is a difference between a child whose development is simply slow and a child whose development is slow *and* not normal.

For example, a sign of normal development in a four-year-old is the ability to talk grammatically. If a child of four isn't yet talking grammatically but does in general have the language abilities of a three-year-old, he is a slow developer. If he not only talks ungrammatically but also has a tiny vocabulary, says words oddly, and doesn't understand much of what is said to him, his development is slow *and* not normal. The second important point is this: a child with delayed development either catches up or he doesn't. If he doesn't, then it's clear—in retrospect—that his problem was not delayed development. Unfortunately, this is never clear *except* in retrospect.

_____ BRAIN FUNCTION—SOME GENERAL CONCEPTS

Cerebral Lateralization

Each of the cerebral hemispheres has its own specialized functions. The left hemisphere is specialized for language in all right-handed people and most left-handers, and is responsible for processing serial information. Because of its control of language, our most important intellectual possession, the left hemisphere is often known as the dominant hemisphere. The right hemisphere is specialized for tasks that involve making sense of what we see (this includes distinguishing one person's face from another's); nonverbal thinking (for example, analyzing visual patterns such as wallpaper designs); appreciating the nuances of music; and a number of language functions, such as the understanding and expression of the rhythm of speech.

Scientists disagree about how and when cerebral lateralization —the division of brain functions between the two halves—develops. There are two major viewpoints. One holds that the two hemispheres begin to acquire their different specialized functions while the baby is still in the womb. The other theory is that, at birth, the functions of the brain are controlled equally by both hemispheres. But as the brain matures, a number of these functions, notably language, shift to the left hemisphere, giving it a dominant role in later development.

Contralateral and Ipsilateral Transmission

As a general rule, the nerves that carry sensory information *toward* or *into* the CNS (the *afferent* nerves) transmit that information contralaterally—to the side of the brain opposite the stimulus. For example, if you stroke your cat with your right hand, the sensation of smoothness is registered in the left side of your brain. This is the case for almost all somatosensory information. Visual information is in part transmitted contralaterally, with the right field of vision of both eyes reporting to the left occipital lobe, and vice versa. Most auditory information is transmitted to the temporal lobe opposite the receiving ear, but some is transmitted ipsilaterally—to the same-side lobe.

The *efferent* nerves carry motor information *out* of the CNS to organs that become active when they are stimulated, such as your arm muscles. The bulk of these nerves also have contralateral representation in the brain. All this left-to-right and right-to-left switching is the result of the crisscrossing of nerve tracts in the brain stem.

_____ WHAT CAN GO WRONG

Almost without exception, one of the first questions parents ask when told that their child has a learning disability is "Why?" Why does their child have trouble learning? What caused the learning disability? Where did it come from? Were they in any way responsible? Medical science knows some of the answers to these questions, but not all. Nor is a great deal known about prevention. The current thinking is that all learning disabilities are associated with disturbance or inefficiency in brain functioning.

Doctors classify brain dysfunction as either "acquired" or "developmental." Acquired brain dysfunction is the result of damage to the brain after birth. Brain damage may be due to a head injury that fractures the skull and injures the brain. Or it may be due to environmental chemicals, such as pollutants in factory burn-offs, that are breathed in or absorbed and reach the brain by way of the bloodstream. Various viral and bacterial infections can produce a damaging encephalitis—inflammation of the brain. Brain damage can also result from a very high fever. Depending on the severity and the site of the damage, and the stage of brain development during which damage occurs, a child may have no subsequent difficulties or a whole range of problems.

In the vast majority of cases, however, brain dysfunction is due not to an acquired disorder but to a developmental one. A child with developmental brain dysfunction was born with inefficient brain functions. Genetic inheritance may be responsible in some cases.

Developmental brain dysfunction may also be due to nongenetic factors that affect brain development during gestation. A pregnant woman's use of nicotine, alcohol, and many drugs—over-the-counter or recreational—may hinder her baby's brain growth and introduce the risk of brain inefficiency. There is also a direct relationship between a woman's nutritional status and the brain growth of her unborn child. Cells can't grow without a plentiful supply of nutrients in general and an adequate supply of many specific ones. So both undernutrition and poor nutrition in the mother can result in permanent brain damage in the child.

Another possible cause of developmental brain dysfunction that may result in learning disabilities is maternal infection. For example, if a woman suffers from rubella (German measles) during her pregnancy, the chances are high that her child will be born with inefficient brain functions. Infections acquired from the birth canal during labor can also affect the baby's brain development. Brain dysfunction can also result from problems during delivery, such as a twisting of the umbilical cord that temporarily cuts off the baby's oxygen supply.

In summary, inefficient brain functioning may also be the result of genetic factors or of the health status of a woman during pregnancy or of injuries sustained during the delivery process. We also know that head injury, environmental pollutants, and viral or bacterial agents may be at the root of a child's inefficient brain functioning. There are undoubtedly a host of additional factors that we still do not know about. Full answers to the question of what *can* go wrong, in general, and what *did* go wrong, in the case of your child, are rarely easily obtained, if at all. You may never learn why your child's brain functions inefficiently, but you can learn how to get the help your child needs.

CHAPTER 3

Early Sensory-Perceptual, Motor, Linguistic, and Thinking Development

A child is born ready to adapt to the world. His ability to deal effectively with the world's demands, however, depends on his ability to learn. Broadly defined, learning is the ability to put skills and concepts into long-term storage in a form that allows us to use them later, as the situation requires.

People tend to think of learning as beginning when a child enters school, with the "three Rs"—reading, writing, and arithmetic. In fact, it begins at the moment of birth. It is then that a child begins to learn about his body and starts to develop abilities in areas that will profoundly affect all his subsequent learning. There are five major areas of development: sensory-perceptual, motor, language and speech, thinking, and psychological and social. (The first four will be discussed in this chapter, the last in Chapter 5.)

Starting at birth, a child's abilities in all five of these areas move through a fairly well established sequence, from one "milestone" to another. However, the timing varies: different children reach the various developmental milestones at different ages. What follows is a timetable of when these milestones will occur for most children.

If your child seems not to be developing at the expected rate and doesn't reach a particular milestone within the usual age-range, that's no immediate cause for alarm. But it should put you on the alert.

_____ SENSORY-PERCEPTUAL

Three of our senses, sight, hearing, and touch, are the most crucial to academic learning. A baby is not blind at birth, as doctors used to think. Newborns can determine the size of objects and some features of visual patterns, especially horizontal versus vertical. The ability to process more detailed and complex aspects of visual information develops quickly as the baby's brain develops. By six months, he can see colors as discrete categories—red, green, blue, and so on—just as adults do. Conjugate eye movement (coordinated movement of both eyes together) and binocular vision (the ability to see the same thing with both eyes, which is needed for depth perception) also develop in these early months. Research has established that an infant's visual experiences play an important role in the development of his visual abilities—that _what_ he sees affects _how well_ he sees. Toys are important here: their bright contrasting colors, their varied shapes, and their movement give vital lessons in visual perception.

The auditory system is also functioning at birth, with the inner ear, the auditory nerve, and the connections to the brain all in place. In his first few days, a newborn's hearing is muffled by amniotic fluid in the middle ear, but as this drains away there is a remarkable improvement in his hearing. Infants can discriminate the human voice from other sounds and seem to prefer the sound of a woman's voice to a man's. They are also attracted to sounds that change in rhythm, volume, or pitch. At present, the precise timetable of the further development of the auditory system is not really clear. We know, however, that a young child lacks an adult's ability to discriminate and interpret complex auditory stimuli and that sensitivity to sound reaches its fullest when a child is nine or ten years old.

The development of the sense of touch has not been well described, at least in humans. We do know that early in the development of the fetus, by around the ninth week of gestation, the sensory nerves make contact with the skin. There are conflicting views on whether touch receptors are present at this time. As a newborn, a baby responds reflexively to touch—he will turn his head to the left if his left cheek is touched. By the time he is six months old, he can distinguish between two different surfaces—such as a nubby pacifier and a smooth one—by touch alone, without looking.

As a child's sensory-perceptual abilities develop, his ability to integrate the information his senses provide develops, too. He begins to recognize sensory information and relate it to previous experiences. He comes to appreciate similarities and differences, categorize sensory experiences, and remember past experiences. The combined early growth of sensory-perceptual and integrative abilities is impressive indeed.

_____ MOTOR

A newborn's motor behavior consists primarily of reflexive responses to certain stimuli. When you put your finger in an infant's hand and press his palm, his fingers flex and he grasps. When he is startled, he will throw his arms and legs apart, cry, then bring his arms quickly together, as if trying to clasp something. This reflex may have evolved to safeguard an infant from falling, in the days when our remote ancestors lived in trees. A newborn also responds reflexively to particular body movements. For example, if you tilt his body forward, his arms will stretch out as if to break a fall. Even as a young infant, though, he gradually begins to acquire motor control. This happens in an invariable sequence: from the central part of the body to the outer parts; from head to foot; and from large muscles to small muscles. (The highlights of the expected sequence of motor development are given in Table 3-1.) Motor abilities are of three kinds: locomotor, nonlocomotor, and manipulative.

Locomotor abilities are those involved in moving the body from one place to another, using the large muscles of the arms, legs, and torso. Standing, crawling, and walking—the basic locomotor abilities—all develop during early childhood. The ability to walk is the basis of a number of other locomotor abilities—running and skipping, for example.

Usually, a child can stand with help at about eight months and

Table 3-1

Highlights of Motor Development	
Approximate Age	**Behavior**
newborn	primitive grasp
3 months	reaches for objects
	holds head upright when held in sitting position
4 months	deliberately reaches for and picks up object
	turns head to follow sound
5 months	sits with support
	holds back straight
7 months	sits unassisted
8 months	grasps objects with thumb and opposite finger
	stands with help
9 months	thumb-opposite finger grasp well developed
	bends forward without losing balance when sitting
	stands alone holding on to furniture
10 months	crawls
12 months	pulls self to standing position
15 months	walks alone
2 years	uses spoon to feed self
	holds crayon
3 years	turns pages of book 1 by 1
	scribbles with pencil
3 years and on	elaboration of previously mastered motor abilities

a month later can stand alone, holding on to a piece of furniture. At ten months he can usually crawl; at twelve months he can pull himself to a standing position; at fifteen months, he can walk. By the time he is two years old, he is walking well, and by age three, he can run, jump, and navigate stairs without a helping hand. Beyond the age of three, the development of locomotor skills is essentially an elaboration of basic motor abilities that have already been acquired. Hopping, for example, and walking backward, are elaborations of the ability to walk. The timetable for these elaborations depends on the interaction of two crucial factors: the amount of time a child spends practicing his motor abilities and the continuing development of his brain.

Nonlocomotor abilities also involve the large muscles, but in the service of more restricted movement—sitting, pushing and pulling, twisting, bending and stretching. A newborn is limp when he is held in a sitting position; he can't hold his head upright and needs constant support. At around three months this changes, and he can keep his head steady on his own. Between four and six months, you may notice him turning his head to follow sounds or movement. At around seven months, he can sit unassisted, and a couple of months later he can bend forward when sitting without losing his balance. By now he can also pull at things placed in front of him.

Manipulative abilities pertain to the ability to use the hands skillfully; they involve the small muscles of the hands and fingers. Skill in the use of hands and fingers enables a child to use the tools of childhood, such as toys, knives and forks, crayons and pencils.

Born with a primitive grasp reflex, an infant begins to reach toward objects that attract his attention at around three months. Between four and six months he will deliberately reach for an object and pick it up—if it is of a manageable size and weight. At around eight months, he can hold an object with his thumb and the opposite fingers; by nine months, he can pick up something as small as a pea with his thumb and *one* opposite finger. Sometime between ten months and two years, he can handle a spoon and feed himself, albeit messily. At this age, also, he can hold a crayon well enough to make marks on paper. By the time he is about three years old, he can turn the pages of a book one by one. He is now scribbling with a pencil. By the time he is a preschooler, his fine motor skills have developed so well that he can make a recognizable copy of several letters and numbers. Here again, practice goes hand in hand with the continued development of essential brain areas.

Motor ability involves more than the development of the motor system and increasing control over it. Other systems also come into play. Central to both locomotor and nonlocomotor skills is the sense of balance, which enables a child to sit without support, turn to watch his mother as she moves about the room, pull himself to a standing position, and take his first steps. The sense of balance improves dramatically between three and five years of age. Many motor abilities also require development of the ability to integrate visual information with the motor system. To hit a ball with a bat, for example, a child must be able to bring together visual information (the ball coming toward him) with a developed motor ability (a good swing). He will also need a sense of balance and an understanding of size, shape, time, and space. Seen in this light, a five-year-old's occasional success at hitting a ball with a bat is truly astonishing!

_____ LANGUAGE AND SPEECH

The development of language and speech abilities involves a child's growing mastery of the speech sounds, grammar, and vocabulary of his language community—that is, his family and friends and teachers. It also involves his ability to use those language skills appropriately, in everyday situations. (The usual course of language acquisition goes through a number of stages, which are summarized in Table 3-2.)

An infant begins to vocalize as he begins to breathe, with the drawn-out wail that is music to parents' ears. By the time he is about a month old, he is using different sounds for hunger and for pain. Cooing and babbling begin somewhere between one and six months. These sounds have no real meaning, as adults think of meaning, but they do have important learning and social functions. Through cooing and babbling a baby practices a wide range of sounds. He becomes even more vocal when he gets coos and babblings from the people around him. Other forms of prelinguistic communication also appear in the first six months. A baby begins to point at objects that interest him and make gestures to get his wishes known—he turns his head away from a spoonful of spinach or holds out his arms when he wants to be picked up. Through this kind of behavior, he starts to learn that language can be used to communicate thoughts and desires, and to refer to the important things and people in his world.

By the time he is about seven months old, a baby can usually imitate speech sounds. Doing this involves dividing the sound of a whole word into individual parts—*dad-dy, ba-by*. As the child starts to use the sounds that make up real, whole words, the babbling sounds that are not shared by his language community begin to drop out of his repertoire.

At about ten to twenty months—typically by twelve months —true speech begins to appear.

Most children have a vocabulary of about six simple words, like "mama" and "dada," by their first birthday. Some do not say their first words until later. The ability to use words rather than gestures to refer to things in the environment depends on the child's skill in associating speech sounds with the objects he sees around him.

Table 3-2

Highlights of Language Development

Approximate Age	Behavior
newborn	cries
1 month	uses different sounds for hunger and pain
1–6 months	coos and babbles
	uses gestures to communicate
	imitates speech sounds
7 months	babbling sounds that are not speech sounds disappear
10–20 months	true speech begins
	pronunciation improves
	vocabulary grows to about 50 words
	uses 2-word sentences
2–3 years	vocabulary grows to about 300 words
	uses 3–4 word sentences
3–4 years	vocabulary grows to about 1,000 words
	asks What, How, and Why questions
	uses grammatically correct sentences
5 years	adds prepositions and conjunctions to vocabulary
6 years	uses spoken vocabulary of about 2,600 words and can understand another 9,000 words
	uses opposites and irregular nouns and verbs
	uses articles correctly
	uses morphemes
7 years on	more language elaborations emerge and vocabulary expands

The first words are usually nouns, naming people and objects. A child will also learn words that refer to simple interactions—

"bye-bye," for example. There are demand words, too. "Up," for "Pick me up," and "Juice," for "Give me something to drink," are demand words that are often part of a young child's vocabulary.

A child just beginning to speak may have difficulty mastering all the sounds he hears. Vowel sounds are easiest and mastered first. (Highlights of the expected sequence of consonant articulation mastery are outlined in Table 3-3.) Among the easy consonant sounds, learned first after the sounds of the vowels, are consonants such as *h*, *m*, and *p*. Slightly more difficult sounds include those of the consonants *b*, *d*, and *g*. Harder for a child to master are the sounds of letters such as *f*, *l*, and *r*. The sounds of a few letters—*j* and *s*, for example—and certain consonant combinations, such as *ch* and *th*, are the last to be perfected.

Table 3-3

Highlights of Consonant Articulation Development	
Approximate Age	**Sound Mastery**
3 years	H, M, N, P, W
4 years	B, D, G, K
6 years	F, L, R, T, Y
7 years or beyond	J, S, V, Z, CH, SH, TH

At around eighteen months, there is a tremendous breakthrough. Pronunciation improves, vocabulary increases rapidly, and the toddler begins constructing two-word phrases and sentences. In these utterances, the basics of adult sentence structure—subject, verb, object—appear in various combinations and sequences, customary and not-so-customary.

At about two to three years of age, words expressing abstract concepts begin to be used—"tomorrow," "summer," "hungry," and so on. Nouns still outnumber all other classes of words, but more and more verbs are being used. Sentences consist of up to four words, sometimes in traditional subject-verb-object order. At this age, a child is polishing up his speaking skills. Striving for perfection, he may begin to stutter as he speaks. Lisping is another common characteristic of this age group, as children try to master tongue control and the correct formation of speech sounds.

The vocabulary of a typical three- to four-year-old is growing fast and may contain a number of multisyllabic words. This is the age of questions: "What?" "How?" "Why?"—*especially* "Why?"

By the age of four, a child is able to speak in sentences that conform to basic grammatical rules. The underlying basis of this aspect of language development is not well understood. Many argue that it is "prewired" or "in the genes"; others take the view that it is learned.

The five-year-old adds prepositions ("after," "under") to his growing vocabulary and uses conjunctions such as "and" and "but." A nonstop talker, he goes about his day chattering and singing to himself if a listener isn't available. He spins "tall tales" with clearly stated beginnings, middles, and endings. Some speech difficulty may still be present, with various consonants and consonant combinations being the usual problem areas.

By age six to seven, he has a spoken vocabulary of about 2,600 words and is able to understand another 9,000. He understands and uses irregular nouns ("goose" / "geese"), verbs ("I am" / "I was"), and articles. He begins to use morphemes, the inflectional forms that allow for more complex communication (for example, the endings "-ed" and "-ing," when attached to "work"). He can define words. He understands the concepts of duration, measurement, and time, and can answer questions about them.

By now, and without any formal instruction, the average child is a highly proficient speaker of his native language. In contrast, the acquisition of written language skills (reading, writing, and arithmetic) usually requires a great deal of specialized teaching. These skills depend on a number of important subskills that are not necessarily needed for language as such—for example, visual-spatial abilities and the understanding that three of something is more than one of something.

_____ THINKING

Of the theorists and scientists who have studied the process of a child's intellectual growth, one of the most influential has been the Swiss psychologist Jean Piaget. Our description of the mental growth of a child accords with his views and uses his terminology.

A young child's thinking processes are different from an adult's. An adult is able to handle more information more quickly and more efficiently than a child. An adult is able to think in concrete terms, dealing with the here and now, and also in symbols and in abstract terms. She can use both reason and intuition, and can deal with the hypothetical. Her learning may be through trial and error, planned experimentation, observation, or imitation. In contrast, a young child deals with his world exclusively in terms of the here and now, the immediate, concrete present. He does not reason or intuit; he reacts. And he learns through interaction with his environment.

According to Piaget's theory, a child's thinking develops in four distinct stages, from infancy through early adolescence. At each successive stage, the child's knowledge about the world grows and his thinking abilities expand. The stages are distinct but not set in stone. The age-range for each developmental period is approximate; each child develops at his own speed. Often a child who seems firmly "in" one particular developmental period may still think at times in ways that are characteristic of an earlier one.

The first main stage of thinking development, the period of "sensorimotor intelligence," spans the time from birth to about two years. It is called "sensorimotor" because motor responses to sensory stimuli form the connection between a baby and his environment. During this stage, the child arrives at a conception of his world as a stable, physical place that has an existence of its own, apart from his own sensory impressions and his own actions and movements. Starting life with nothing but his senses and his inborn primitive reflexes, a child reacts more than thinks. As he responds to his world, he begins to learn. Learning occurs through the direct physical process of trial and error. As he mouths and bangs and picks up and twists and turns and scrutinizes objects, he learns their properties. Hands-on manipulation and experimentation are vital to the learning process at this stage.

Toward the end of the sensorimotor period, the child begins to have a sense of time: he can think about the consequences of his actions and about things that happened in the past. He can also think about things that aren't actually present. These thoughts may take the form of words or they may be mental pictures of objects, people, or actions.

The second stage of thinking development, the "preoperational" stage (it precedes the "operational" stages), spans the years from about two to seven. During this stage, as the child acquires new words and makes his first attempts at drawing, his ability to represent things through symbols grows dramatically. This is the age of symbolic play, in which something is used to stand for something else. Parents of children in the preoperational stage of development are used to being set straight on this score: "Those aren't rocks," protests the child. "This is a *garage* and those are *cars.*"

During this stage, trial and error is still the primary mode of learning. Though he can think about objects and events that aren't physically present, a child does not yet have the ability to integrate different types of information about them. For now, he is limited to focusing on one aspect of a situation at a time. For example, if a child of three or four is shown two rows containing the same number of chocolate M&Ms—one arranged to spread out long, the other made short by spacing the candies more closely—he will likely say that there are more M&Ms in the first row. He is focusing only on the length of the rows and not on the number of M&Ms in each row. In the same way, he thinks a nickel is worth more than a dime because it is bigger.

A child at this stage of thinking development is also unable to consider another person's point of view, for the simple reason that he doesn't yet recognize that other points of view exist. Piaget called this "egocentrism," and it affects a child's perception of his physical environment. For example, in these years, a child can visualize an object only from his own perspective. Asked to describe his classroom, he will do so from the view of his own seat. His moral judgments are also egocentric: he understands the rules of a game, but changes them readily to suit himself. His ideas about the world are primitive. To a preoperational youngster, the clouds floating in the sky are following him.

The next stage, the period of "concrete operations," lasts from roughly age seven to age eleven. The child's thinking is still restricted to the here and now, and he still lacks the ability to make use of abstractions or imagery. However, during this stage a child develops a system of rules that allows him to "operate" on ideas about objects and events—that is, to manipulate them mentally. He is able to order objects according to a measurable dimension, such as height or circumference. Unlike the younger child, he knows that the two differently arranged rows of M&Ms contain the same number of candies. He can think about the relationships among objects—taller, darker, larger, and so on. Now he can "do in his head" what before he could only accomplish through action —he can "think about things." Playing checkers, he can plan a series of moves in his head and can mentally retrace his steps to the first one.

At this stage, also, a child can deal with the relations among classes of things. Up until now, classes of things—"boy" or "American," for example—have been thought of as particular instances. A preoperational child can't consider being a boy and an American at the same time. This is no problem for a child in the concrete operational period. Nevertheless, for all his ability to "operate" on objects and ideas, a child at this stage of his thinking development is unable to reason about abstractions and imaginary events, or to deal with hypothetical questions.

With the emergence at about twelve years of the final stage of thinking development—the period Piaget called "formal operations"—thinking processes change dramatically. The adolescent is able to consider theoretical propositions that do not relate to what is directly observable. He is no longer limited to the here, the now, and the actual but can theorize about possibilities and hypothetical situations. Ask a fifteen-year-old the question, "If there were no money, how would people buy what they need?"—and he will be able to use his reasoning powers to figure out the answer. A seven-year-old, who has difficulty reasoning about the improbable or impossible, is likely to answer, "But we have money."

At this stage, thought processes are characterized by the ability to seek solutions through systematic search. The adolescent possesses a broad underlying reasoning ability, which Piaget believed to be generally applied to all problem solving situations. In solving a problem, the adolescent is able to consider alternative approaches, judging the logic and effectiveness of each one. He also has the ability to organize his thinking so as to find a solution that can be applied to a whole class of problems—an overriding principle. This is in marked contrast to the approach of a younger child, who focuses on a particular instance.

The content of thought also changes markedly in adolescence. A broad range of issues—justice, the existence of God, morality—is now subject to examination. The adolescent also analyzes his own thoughts and feelings, his personality, and his appearance.

CHAPTER 4

Factors Affecting Development

The sequence of the development of sensory-perceptual abilities, motor abilities, linguistic abilities, and thinking processes is the same in all children, but the pace and the adequacy of the developmental process is different in each child. Pace and adequacy—the speed and soundness of a child's development—are dependent on three factors: the developing nervous system, personality, and experiences. These three factors always work together.

———— THE DEVELOPING NERVOUS SYSTEM

As we have seen, a child's nervous system begins developing very soon after conception. Development continues through infancy and childhood; in most cases the nervous system is fully functioning sometime between early adolescence and early adulthood. Thus, the biological building blocks of learning are in place from the earliest days, though the brain continues to mature and new abilities are developed as the child grows.

Although a child's personality and his experiences of the world play an important role in the timing and ease with which he passes through the developmental stages, researchers tend to agree that the neurological factor exerts the greatest influence, especially during a child's early years. The pattern of neurological development is the same from child to child. As a result, children typically have similar developmental patterns. A two-year-old, for example, can usually walk well, use a spoon to feed himself, talk in short sentences, and represent things through symbols.

_____ PERSONALITY

When we talk about a child's personality, we mean his characteristic way of perceiving, thinking about, and relating to the environment and himself. One of the earliest signs of personality is temperament. This is evident from birth and is widely believed to represent a child's basic personality structure. Temperament appears to be determined by genetic inheritance and by factors that affected the child while in the womb and during the birth process. Research suggests that infants fall into one of three categories, where temperament is concerned. "Difficult" babies tend to be active, easily distracted, and easily overstimulated. "Slow to warm up" babies tend to withdraw from anything new and are often fussy. Average or "easy" infants are adaptable, dealing comfortably with novel situations. Alert and happy, these infants move steadily and at a predictable rate from one developmental milestone to the next.

For the first few months of his life, it is an infant's temperament that determines his behavior. It affects his sleeping and eating patterns, his activity level and sensory threshold, his tolerance for frustration, and his willingness to be cuddled. Early on, though, the infant's inborn traits begin to interact both positively and negatively with his parents' style of child rearing and *their* personalities. This interaction affects the child's developing personality. The way that parents manage the critical events of infancy and early childhood—weaning, separation, toilet training, the birth of a sibling, for example—works in conjunction with the child's basic temperament to shape his personality.

Personality has a tremendous effect on the timing and ease with which a child achieves developmental milestones. A child's innate "stick-with-it-ness" affects the development of many motor abilities, since these evolve through the repetition of the same behavior over and over again. The development of language abilities is affected by a child's openness to the people in his environment—again a matter of personality. For example, a child must be open to interaction with others and listen to their verbal output in order to learn the speech sounds of his language community.

A child's personality has an effect on the development of his thinking. It also affects how he utilizes his thinking abilities. For example, a child who gets along well with his teachers and classmates, who feels good about himself and others, who is not caught up in his inner concerns, is able to focus on his schoolwork and make full use of his thinking abilities.

_____ EXPERIENCES

The drive of a normally developing child to master his body and interact effectively with his environment is nothing short of awesome. But without encouragement and stimulation—opportunities to practice, challenge, and refine his developing abilities—even a highly motivated child will be turned off. Thus, the development of sensory-perceptual, motor, and linguistic abilities, and thinking processes, is affected by his experiences.

An infant's communication skills develop through interaction with his parents, his siblings, and the other people who are close to him. A little later, playtime with his family and with children his own age fosters development of all the abilities we have been discussing. For example, the songs and stories of childhood foster language development; the games, development of motor abilities. Throughout infancy and early childhood, his environment—the people and the objects that surround him—encourages him to explore, to try, and to have fun.

As a child gets older, the effects of experiences outside the home become more significant. School and his peer group begin to exert their influence. These and other experiences, together with his personality and his maturing nervous system, affect his further development. Building on the groundwork laid in earlier years, sensory-perceptual and motor abilities are refined, speech and language skills become more sophisticated, and thinking processes approach more and more closely those of an adult.

———— THE IMPACT OF NEUROLOGICAL INEFFICIENCY ON DEVELOPMENT

The developing nervous system, personality and experience, all affect a child's development, as we have seen. But what if the nervous system isn't developing normally? People tend to focus on the impact of neurological inefficiency on a child's ability to learn in school. But, of course, it may also affect his development in a number of ways from infancy through childhood and on to adolescence.

Developmental Problems

Birth to Two Years

Infancy can be a very difficult time for a child with brain inefficiency. A baby is born with primitive motor reflexes and with the ability to attend to his environment by means of his built-in sensory-perceptual abilities. But compromised functioning in the brain regions that mediate reflexes and sensory-perceptual functions can jeopardize his ability to perform the most basic acts of receiving and responding to information from his inner and outer environments. To take only one example, a weak sucking reflex will interfere with the baby's ability to respond to the nipple when he is hungry.

As the baby's brain develops, he goes beyond simply reacting to his environment and displays more refined responses. For a child with an inefficiently functioning brain, however, this may be difficult. If regions of the posterior cerebral cortex are compromised, he may have difficulty making sensory discriminations—telling the difference between his caretaker's voice and someone else's, for example. If there is a disturbance in the motor centers of the brain, the child may be late in achieving the milestones of motor development—late in crawling, standing, walking; late in reaching for objects and picking them up.

Early language development may also be profoundly affected. Although a baby begins by babbling a wonderful collection of sounds, he eventually limits himself to the vowels and consonants he hears around him. If he doesn't hear those sounds accurately, babbling won't develop as it should. A child with compromised sensory-perceptual or motor functions may start to speak much later than is usual, or may speak in a way that no one—except perhaps his parents—can make out. If the temporal lobe of the dominant hemisphere (usually the left) isn't functioning efficiently, he may be unable to discriminate speech sounds, and so may be off the mark in his attempts to repeat words. Or he may have difficulty in distinguishing words that sound very much like one another—"bad" and "bed," for example—or in understanding what is said to him, and so will likely be late in attempting to speak. If there is inefficient functioning in the temporal and frontal regions, he may have difficulty expressing himself. If regions of the right temporal lobe are compromised, he may have difficulty understanding the significance of tone and rhythm in what is said to him. The raised voice at the end of a question and the firm tone that accompanies "Don't do that!" won't mean anything to such a child.

Inefficient brain workings, affecting sensory-perceptual and motor functions, also play a central role in a child's thinking development—especially in the sensorimotor stage of development, when his thinking processes are so closely linked to trial-and-error exploration of his environment. A child with compromised functioning in the somatosensory regions of the brain may be unsure of his sensory experiences. For example, a disturbance in the parietal lobes, the part of the brain that handles touch information, may make it difficult for the child to learn about his world by "feel." He may also have trouble manipulating objects. If there is inefficiency in the motor system, he may be poorly coordinated. Either way, he may lack the skills and the confidence he needs to investigate his environment.

Two to Seven Years

As his brain grows, the child who is developing normally makes significant strides in these five years. His motor and linguistic abilities are refined; his way of perceiving and thinking about his world reaches a new level of maturity. Because this growth is so dramatic, the signs that a child's brain functions aren't developing normally are often first noticed at this age.

Gross motor abilities build on the basic locomotor ability of walking—a child must be able to walk before he can run or hop or skip. Fine motor abilities, such as the child's ability to feed himself and do up buttons and laces, build on his ability to grasp and handle objects. A child with an inefficiency in the frontal lobe regions that mediate intentional motor functions may have difficulty with a whole range of motor activities, from handling a spoon to throwing a ball.

Motor activity requires more than the normal development of the motor region of the frontal lobe: other systems, mediated by other brain regions, are needed as well. A child may have an intact motor region, but if he has a weakness in a "support" system, the result may be a motor problem. For example, an inefficiency in the systems that control balance, located in the cerebellum and elsewhere, may result in the child's being poorly coordinated and having difficulty walking a straight line or hopping from foot to foot.

A wide range of problems comes from a compromised ability to integrate the motor systems with information from the eyes (processed in the occipital region of the posterior cerebral cortex). The child may have infinite difficulty learning to catch a ball. He may also have difficulty with fine motor tasks that involve handling crayons and pencils. This is first seen as a sloppy job of coloring within the lines, then as a poor ability to copy shapes, then as written work that is "every which way."

Language functions are subserved by the dominant temporal lobe (usually the left); by the association areas between the parietal, temporal, and occipital regions of the left hemisphere; by parts of the left frontal lobe; and by certain regions of the right hemisphere. Inefficient functioning in these areas or in the connections between them may hinder a child's ability to receive language as it comes in, or his ability to process or understand it, or his ability to express himself in words—or all of these. The type of language disability a child has depends on which part of the brain is not functioning as it should.

The child between the ages of two and seven is in the preoperational stage of thinking development. As in the previous stage, the development of his thinking processes is based on hands-on exploration of his world and the modification of earlier ideas about it. Neurological inefficiencies that compromise the quality of this exploration, or delay the development of such abilities as memory, will set him back.

Seven to Eleven Years

For the normally developing child, the span of the "middle years" is a time of striking development in motor and language abilities.

Thinking processes mature and new intellectual abilities come to the forefront. All this makes for tremendous strides in academic work. A child who comes to this stage with weaknesses in motor or language abilities, or with slowly maturing thinking processes, will be hard pressed to keep pace with children his own age. And he will almost certainly have difficulty in his efforts to make headway at school. For example, the development of skills in reading, written expression, and computation rests heavily on a child's ability to understand and use language. Inefficient functioning in the brain areas that mediate language may result in a child's not being able to understand the stories he reads. Or he may have difficulty formulating his thoughts correctly when he goes to write them down. Or he may not be able to grasp the "story" of arithmetic word problems and so not know what to do: should he add, subtract, multiply, or divide?

Twelve Years and Up

The brain is in its final stage of development by the time the average child is thirteen years old. Since educators are no strangers to the world of child development, there are matching changes in the academic curriculum and in school programs.

A brain inefficiency that interfered with or delayed a child's development does not disappear as he gets older. In fact, the effects of compromised sensory-perceptual, motor, or linguistic abilities, or slow-maturing thinking processes, may become more apparent in the face of the new demands of the junior and senior high school years.

It is not uncommon for a child's learning difficulty to go unnoticed until he reaches adolescence. He may, in fact, be an above average student until he gets to high school. In the lower grades, such a child gets around his areas of difficulty by using special study strategies and techniques of his own devising. But in high school more is asked of him, and his ability to compensate falters. Now the neurological inefficiency that has been subtly affecting his development all along comes to the forefront; it has a noticeable impact on his ability to deal effectively with the combined developmental, social, and academic demands of adolescence.

CHAPTER 5

Psychological and Social Development

Just as a child goes through stages in his sensory-perceptual, motor, linguistic, and thinking development, he goes through stages in his psychological and social growth. Here, though, instead of a progression from one "milestone" to the next, growth involves confronting and mastering a series of "tasks." Beginning in infancy and continuing through adolescence, a child deals with these tasks—often with more than one at a time—on his way to becoming a socially mature and psychologically healthy adult. Borrowing significantly from the work of Sigmund Freud and Erik Erikson, pioneers in this field, we can describe the major tasks as the development of basic trust, of autonomy, of self-definition, of competence, and, finally, of independence. As with the milestones that mark a child's sensory-perceptual, motor, and linguistic development, and the successive stages of mental development, there is a timetable here. But again, the age ranges are approximate. And again, there is overlap.

———— BASIC TRUST

As a newborn, a child experiences his body and his world as an onslaught of sensations, some pleasurable, some uncomfortable.

Gradually, though, greater rhythm in body functions is achieved. Regular eating and sleeping patterns emerge; the caretaker's job becomes less stressful. Gradually, too, as the child explores his world, he finds that things are becoming familiar to him—he has seen or heard or felt or tasted this before. He comes to recognize aspects of the external world. At around three months, the child smiles his first "social smile," in response to a familiar face.

By the time a child is about nine months old, certain people in his environment begin to take on special importance for him. These people—especially the main caretaker—come to be associated with pleasurable experiences and comfort, and the child feels that he is totally dependent on them. So he becomes fearful of being separated from these significant people, and fearful of strangers. A child of this age is not happy unless he can see his "special person" or hear her voice. By the time he is one and a half or two years old, the toddler begins to separate from her—at first for only a minute, but then for longer and longer periods of time. He will check frequently to see that she is still around, through, or return for a kiss or a hug. A "transitional object"—something that reminds him of his "special person" and the comfort she gives him—is often used by a child this age to bridge the times of contact: he carries that well-worn blanket or stuffed toy around with him wherever he goes. By the time he is three and a half, a child is usually able to let his main caretaker out of his sight without undue anxiety. He is able to separate from her because she has become an "inner certainty as well as an outer predictability."

The basic trust in another person that the child achieves in the early years is the basis of his later ability to form relationships with others.

_____ AUTONOMY

By the time he is two or three years old, a child's sensory-perceptual, motor, and linguistic skills have developed to the point that he is ready for the next major psychosocial task. Now he begins to gain a sense of autonomy, a sense of having control over himself and his environment.

Toilet training starts when a child is around two years old—perhaps a little later for boys. At this age, the child understands the relevant sensory signals; his muscular development is such that he can hold on to his bowels and bladder; he can respond to the societal demands being placed on him as to when and where he may relieve himself. And there's more to it than control over his own body: he also experiences himself as having a good deal of control over other people. He finds that he can please others by using the toilet or irritate them by wetting his pants.

At this age, a child's linguistic abilities also take a giant step forward. Articulation improves, vocabulary growth is dramatic, and the child can get his message across in two-word, telegraphic utterances. However, it often seems that "no" is the favorite word of a child in "the terrible twos." Though frustrating for parents, this negativism is part of the child's expression of his developing sense of autonomy and independence.

A youngster's sense that he is able to function independently, choose freely, stand up for himself and control himself is based on his experience of himself as an autonomous person—a person whose body and wishes are of value.

_____ SELF-DEFINITION

A child of three is full of exuberance. His thinking powers, and his sensory-perceptual, motor, and linguistic abilities reach new levels of development, and he revels in them. He reaches out eagerly to the world and relates everything around him to himself. His task in the next three years is to refine his sense of self and to take on the basic values of his family members—who, in turn, transmit the values of the community.

Part of the emerging self-concept is a child's gender identity— the sense of being male or female. Children develop a rudimentary gender identity sometime between eighteen months and three years of age, and usually adopt sex-type behavior by age two. Like his father, a boy will take on the heavy work of raking leaves or carrying out the trash; a girl will busy herself in the kitchen. And boys will play with guns and trucks, and girls will play with dolls, despite all the efforts of women's liberation. However, a preschooler's concept of gender is still pretty vague. A boy may think that he can grow up and have babies, just like Mommy; a girl may plan to be a daddy, just like her father.

Around the age of five, a child knows the occupational stereotypes for the sexes and the psychological stereotypes emerge: boys
are loud and aggressive, girls are quiet and gentle. Within a year or
two, a child has usually established a stable gender identity and
understands that it remains constant in spite of superficial physical
characteristics such as the length of a person's hair. Throughout the
middle years, a child's concept of the sexes continues to be modified.
His thinking becomes less stereotyped and he is better able to accept
divergences from traditional roles for men and women.

Another extremely important aspect of the child's self-definition
is the development of a conscience—the capacity for self-observa-
tion, self-guidance, and self-punishment. An infant has no sense of
right and wrong at all. As a toddler, a child gets some grasp of his
parents' standards about correct and incorrect behavior in specific
situations, but his understanding is limited, as is his capacity for
self-guidance or self-punishment. At around three years, however,
he begins to become his own authoritative parent. "Private speech"
plays a significant role in this process: a child, about to do something he is not supposed to, checks himself with a scolding. "No,
no," he says, "no cookie." By the time he is five or six, the rules
and guidelines about social relationships and moral behavior laid
down by the adults in his life have fused to form his conscience.
(For now, the child accepts these imperatives unquestioningly; in
his teens, he will reconsider them and develop his own value system.) Thus, at this stage, a youngster not only refines his sense of
self but takes major steps in becoming a full-fledged member of the
society into which he was born.

_____ COMPETENCE

From about age seven to about age eleven, a child's major task is to
develop a sense of being able to conduct himself well in his world.
He develops motivation to do, curiosity, and a desire to learn. This
period, often called the latency stage, is a time of relative tranquil-
lity: the emotional issues of the earlier years are behind him and
those of adolescence have yet to come. The child is free to pursue
competence, both social and academic.

The world outside the home now begins to play a major role in the child's development, and peer relationships take on a new importance and intensity. Boys and girls tend to move away from each other, and friends are usually of the same sex. Sex-typed after-school activities are dominant. Boys typically join sports groups and girls take dance classes. A new and often intense relationship is that of "best friends."

At the same time that they look for friends outside the family, children begin to learn how to interact with adults other than their relatives. Relationships with teachers often serve as the prototype experience—a child this age frequently develops a "crush" on his teacher.

The academic growth of the latency-age child is astonishing. New intellectual abilities, which allow him to deal with more information faster and more effectively, make it possible for the child to forge ahead in reading, written expression, and computation.

During this developmental stage, the child is mastering the social and academic skills that lay the groundwork for his participation in the "real world"—the world outside the home. He learns to navigate interpersonal relationships with his peers and with adults other than family members. And he gains recognition by producing in his workplace, the school.

_____ INDEPENDENCE

The body changes of puberty and the emergence of new thinking processes mark the end of childhood. The stage is set for the next developmental task: achieving independence.

A central aspect of an adolescent's establishing himself as an independent person is separation from his parents and their world. In his efforts to show that he has a mind of his own, the adolescent often becomes negative. Nothing that his parents do or say suits him. If they are Democrats, he argues the Republican platform; if they want him to go to college, he threatens to leave school as soon as he legally can. He may adopt all sorts of external trappings—the dances, the dress, the language of the day—to support him in his separation.

Independence also requires that the adolescent evolve a sense of identity based on an image of himself as a person with certain identifiable abilities, social characteristics, beliefs, thoughts, and feelings. He continually seeks to integrate various aspects of himself into one coherent, stable whole.

Initially, the adolescent's sense of self is dominated by the way he looks—or, rather, by the way he thinks he looks. Mainly concerned with physical changes, he is self-conscious and self-critical —or self-admiring. The boy standing in front of the mirror combing his hair may be thinking that he looks like Frankenstein's monster, so no wonder that special girl won't even say hello to him, or he may be imagining the compliments he will get from the rest of his crowd. He may also think of himself as unique, his experiences beyond the ken of others. "But you don't know how it is . . ." he says. Separating from parents, and not yet having a solid sense of self, young adolescents often seek refuge in the peer group. Many identify with "heroes"—rock musicians, sports superstars, movie actors or actresses—and almost all go through at least one consuming infatuation.

An adolescent's new thinking capacities enable him to think about his own thoughts. In conjunction with his struggle to separate from his parents, this new mode of thinking may lead him to question the values he learned as a child. His parents are no longer idealized: their values and their behavior are subject to his analysis and criticism. And not only parents—the existing political system, the social order of the times, and accepted religious doctrines all come under scrutiny. Often, attempts to create alternatives accompany this analysis. The adolescent may reject the values he grew up with and adopt new ones that are radically different.

Eventually, the adolescent begins to integrate the various identities he has tried on, and the social values he has been exposed to, with his basic picture of himself—his psychological characteristics, feelings, thoughts, and beliefs. The result is his own unique identity, which plays an essential role in his later life decision. His refined sense of self incorporates an ethical system that often replaces the morality learned in childhood. By the end of adolescence, he is ready for intimacy, able to commit himself to other people in close friendships or intimate relationships.

——————— THE IMPACT OF NEUROLOGICAL INEFFICIENCY ON PSYCHOLOGICAL AND SOCIAL DEVELOPMENT

For most children, psychological and social development goes smoothly, without serious problems. Even if they falter from time to time in dealing with the emotional and social demands placed on them, they can regroup and go on. But, psychological and social growth rely heavily on the timely development of sensory-perceptual, motor, and linguistic abilities. Thus, neurological inefficiency may affect a child's development in these areas. And, since a child's ability to deal effectively with each developmental task is based in part on his successful mastery of previous ones, the cumulative impact of neurological inefficiency on how a child perceives himself and his world can be significant.

A child whose brain is working inefficiently may have difficulty from the earliest days. He way be withdrawn, unresponsive, and generally lethargic—or overactive, easily distracted, and easily overstimulated. In either case, it will be difficult for him to establish regular sleeping and eating patterns, and his early interactions with the people who care for him will be fraught with problems.

A child's ability to establish basic trust and separate from his caretaker may be affected if his sensory abilities are compromised. If he doesn't experience his world as consistent, a sense of familiarity with it won't develop. He will have no reason to smile the "social smile" that says "I recognize you." The relationships that usually develop so easily between a young child and the significant people in his life will come only with difficulty. Further, a toddler who is unsure of his sensory-perceptual experiences or his skills may be utterly distraught when his caretaker is out of his sight. He doesn't have the motor skills to get back to her, or the language skills to express his need to return. All he can do is to try to prevent this ever happening again, by staying as close to her as her shadow.

Achieving autonomy depends to some degree on the status of a child's sensory-perceptual, motor, and linguistic systems. Motor difficulties may prevent him from readily gaining a sense of control over himself and his environment. Within the context of a shaky relationship with his main caretaker, dating back to problems in infancy, toilet training may be particularly difficult; the child may

be vulnerable to feelings of shame and guilt. If he has speech difficulties and can't easily make his needs and desires understood, his
sense of self-worth may be undermined and a perception of himself
as someone with free choice may not surface at all.

Establishing self-definition may be a frustrating task for a child
with compromised neurological function. A person's identity as
male or female is associated with a raft of behaviors that our culture
deems appropriate for each sex. Depending on the nature of the
child's problem, it may be difficult, or even impossible, for a child
to be "just like" the parent of the same sex. Take Trevor and his
father. Trevor's Dad was a star baseball player in high school. He
looked forward for years to the day his son would be old enough to
join the Little League and be a star in *his* turn. But now that Trevor
is six, it is painfully clear that he is not going to be an athlete at
all. He isn't well coordinated and, though he tries his very best, he
has yet to learn to throw a ball. Trevor's relationship with his father
has suffered, and so has his self-esteem. Trevor is left with little
sense of accomplishment and guilt for having tried and failed.

The development of the conscience as a moral arbiter may also
be jeopardized by a child's compromised neurological system. The
ability to internalize rules and guidelines rests in part on the ability
to grasp how they work—how social rules govern interpersonal
relationships, how rules organize a game, how a guideline is to be
understood. If a child's language abilities are compromised, or if
abilities such as memory are poorly developed, he may be hard
pressed to come to an understanding of what rules and guidelines
are all about.

School becomes a central focus in the life of a child between the
ages of seven and eleven—and a major problem area for a child
whose neurological system is not functioning efficiently. He may be
continuing an old struggle to keep up despite compromised skills.
Or he may be confronting learning difficulties that have surfaced as
academic demands have become more rigorous. If he is unable to
meet academic standards, the child may know the pain of feeling
inadequate and inferior and he may lose interest in academic pur-
suits. He may also fail to master the fundamentals of reading,
written expression, and computation that are required of someone
living in this society.

Peer relationships are another area of difficulty. Peer groups become important during the school years, a child's circle of friends broadens and friendships are more intense in the middle years. A child with an inefficiently functioning brain may have a great deal of trouble with friends and friendships, for two related reasons. One is the *direct* impact that his compromised abilities have on his relationships. For example, a boy with poor motor abilities, well aware that he's a klutz, may stay inside when all the rest of the neighborhood children are skateboarding in the street, rather than be embarrassed by his poor performance or teased by the others. The other reason is the *cumulative* impact of his neurological functions on his psychological and social development—for example, he may be markedly immature, or aggressive, or crippled by self-doubt.

Adolescence is extremely stressful for a youngster with an inefficient neurological system. His task is to establish himself as an independent person with his own unique identity and value system. Yet he comes to this with the baggage of unresolved issues from his infancy and childhood: insecurity, a sense of shame and doubt, guilt, and feelings of inferiority. His situation is made worse by the fact that his compromised neurological functions affect his ability to deal with the developmental demands he now faces.

Reluctance to venture out of the shelter of the family may frustrate his emotional separation from his parents. He may shy away from relationships with his peers, cutting himself off from opportunities to develop social skills and be exposed to new ways of thinking and behaving. And, if his thinking development has been affected, he may also have difficulty in establishing an ethical system by which to conduct his life.

CHAPTER 6

Learning in School

A child in school experiences many learning situations: the classroom, the playground, the halls, the lunchroom. He also has numerous teachers: his classroom instructors, his books, his fellow students, the cafeteria monitor, the bus driver. Only part of what is learned at school is in the form of academic knowledge and skills; learning includes experience with attitudes, emotions, and social interaction. Let's consider segments of a seventh-grader's school day, for what they show us about how a child learns.

_____ EDDIE'S SCHOOL DAY

It is the first period of the day and Eddie is in math class. The students are learning how to find the perimeter and area of geometric shapes. Toward the end of the period, the teacher, Mr. Flynn, asks if anyone can tell the class how to find the area of a shape that combines a triangle and half a circle. He draws the figure on the board—it looks rather like an ice cream cone—and tells them that they should be able to figure out the solution because the answer lies in something they've learned already. Eddie, like the rest of the class, studies the shape for a few minutes. He can't think of anything they've been taught that would give the answer, nor can anyone else. Mr. Flynn tells the class that their homework assignment is to figure out how to solve the problem.

The next period is study hall, and Eddie and a couple of his friends begin to work together on the math problem. For the first five minutes, they don't make any headway at all. Then Eddie suddenly has an idea: first find the area of the triangle, then add to it one-half the area of the circle. They work this out and check the answer in the back of the book. He was right! They try another similar problem. Again, they get the right answer. They can hardly wait for tomorrow's class to tell Mr. Flynn. Eddie basks in his success and his friends' admiration. He thinks to himself, I love math.

The class moves on to Ms. Palmeri's room. She is the history teacher and they are studying the American Revolution. A unit test is scheduled for next week. Ms. Palmeri distributes an outline of the test to help them focus their studying. She tells the class that the test will include identification questions ("Explain in two sentences the importance of the following person or concept"), a map they will have to fill in, and a section where they will be asked to match the names and the dates of battles. They have the rest of the period for study time and are free to come to her with any last-minute questions.

Eddie figures that the identifications will be easy and that he will have the greatest difficulty with the map and the battles. He decides to focus on the map first, takes out his textbook and studies it for a while. Then he closes the book, draws a rough outline of the East Coast, and starts filling in the names of the thirteen original states, the major rivers, and the principal cities. This presents no difficulty, because he has a clear mental picture of the map in the textbook. He is unsure of some of the spellings, but when he checks he finds that he has spelled everything correctly except Massachusetts and Philadelphia. He knows from experience that Ms. Palmeri takes points off for spelling errors, so he closes his eyes and tries to spell the words. They are both tricky, and he can't think of any spelling rule that would help. He stares at "Massachusetts" and "Philadelphia," trying to fix them in his memory, and reviews the map a couple more times.

He turns to the list of battles in his notebook. He knows that this is going to be difficult: there are so many names, so many dates. He copies out the list of battles and starts adding the dates from memory. Lexington: April 1775. Bunker Hill: June 1775. Long Island: . . . Eddie can't remember. He tries skipping around, putting in what dates he can, but this doesn't get him very far. Just then, two of his classmates begin fooling around in the back of the room. Eddie watches them and strains to hear what Ms. Palmeri is saying to them. Back with the list, he decides he can't do any more. By now, he is beginning to feel bored. He looks around the room and begins to signal to his best friend, Billy. Ms. Palmeri calls out, "Eddie, this is quiet study time, remember." Somewhat embarrassed, Eddie returns to his work, discouraged by his slow progress.

The last period of the day is gym. It is basketball season and Eddie has worked hard after school and on the weekends with Billy at improving his shooting and passing skills. The coach, Mr. Robertson, has told him that he is impressed with his progress.

For the first half, Eddie plays perhaps his best game ever. He is able to move with his man and makes three intercepts. Each time, he reaches up at just the right moment, preventing the opposing player from catching the ball. He also makes a difficult basket. Hearing his teammates cheer, he beams with pride. Mr. Robertson tells Eddie he did a fine job and takes him out of the game, giving Billy a chance to play. Eddie compliments his teammates on the bench on their playing.

Back in the game at the beginning of the second half, Eddie misjudges a jump and collides with another player. But a few plays later, he gets in stride. When he has a chance to shoot, he hits the backstop on the first try but is able to recover the ball and make the basket. Eddie is disappointed when Mr. Robertson takes him out of the game. Sitting on the bench, he watches the game intently, hoping to pick up some new techniques. Afterward, his teammates tell him what a great game he played, and Mr. Robertson makes a special point of coming over to him to praise his performance.

Throughout Eddie's day, he has been learning: skills and concepts have been put into long-term storage in a form that allows them to be used later. Though we do not see Eddie over a long-enough period of time to observe all the effects of learning on his behavior, we can note a number of instances when he's learning and identify the mechanisms by which learning occurs. We can also identify some of the factors that affect the learning process.

_____ WAYS OF LEARNING

There are at least three different ways in which learning—broadly defined as the ability to put skills and concepts into long-term storage in a form that allows us to use them later, as a situation requires—can occur: through reinforcement, through the formation of associations, and through insight.

Reinforcement may be direct or indirect. Eddie's correct spelling of the names on the map is directly reinforced when he checks his textbook and finds that he is right. His willingness to try to solve the math problem, and his understanding of the solution itself, are directly reinforced by his friends' praise. And his performance on the basketball court in the first half of the game is directly reinforced by the coach's approval and the cheers of his teammates. All these behaviors are followed by desirable results, and so the frequency of these behaviors will increase. On each occasion the reinforcement was rapid—Eddie self-corrects his map immediately, is immediately praised by his friends in study hall, and is immediately cheered by his teammates. The fact that the reinforcement is not delayed probably increases his learning. In contrast, the techniques that resulted in a poor performance on the basketball court are not reinforced—so presumably their frequency will diminish.

Reinforcement may also be indirect. This type of learning is often called observational learning. The child observes another person and then imitates or does not imitate his behavior, depending on whether reinforcement is received or not. Listening to Ms. Palmeri's reprimand of his classmates, Eddie is reminded of the consequences of fooling around in class. When he watches the game during the second half, he is learning from the successes and failures of other players' techniques.

A second way in which learning occurs is when a situation becomes associated with a new response—usually, when a previously neutral situation takes on an emotional flavor. When Eddie fails in his efforts to complete the list of battle dates, he is frustrated and discouraged. He is embarrassed when reprimanded for signaling to Billy during study time. Though he says nothing, Eddie has perhaps come to associate history with negative feelings and, as a result, dislikes the topic. Learning has taken place. In contrast, the pleasure he feels when he is able to solve the math problem results in a positive attitude. The learning of attitudes and feelings toward people, objects, and situations is based on this mechanism.

When Eddie "gets the point" of the math problem, a third type of learning process is in action. Eddie has attained some insight into the relationship between the triangle and the circle, put together to make a new shape; he understands the organizing principle that forms the basis for solving the problem. This insightful learning comes quite suddenly, after a pause in which he studies the figure. Eddie is also able to transfer his new knowledge to the next problem. His correct answer shows that he has achieved a real insight. This learning is in marked contrast to his struggles with the history list.

FACTORS AFFECTING LEARNING

The Learner

A child learns best if he is taught in a way that takes into consideration his developing sensory-perceptual, motor, and linguistic abilities, his evolving thinking processes, and his developing academic skills. As we saw in earlier chapters, development proceeds in a well-established sequence, though with some variations in timing. Educators use their knowledge of children's developing physical and mental capacities when they design academic curricula and establish academic standards.

Eddie's ability to memorize information for the history test, "see" the point of Mr. Flynn's geometry lesson, and perfect his basketball game are very much dependent on his current level of development. Earlier, he would have had trouble. The history test requirements are far beyond the capabilities of a third-grader, who is just beginning to develop skills in written expression and whose memory simply isn't ready for such work. A younger child also requires more structure, a greater focusing of his study efforts, than a seventh-grader such as Eddie, who can be expected to take on more responsibility for his schoolwork. And, try as he might, Eddie could not have reached his present level of athletic ability at a younger age.

A child's personality—how he perceives, thinks about, and relates to his environment and himself—has a profound effect on learning. Eddie, who feels good about himself and enjoys his interaction with others, is open to learning. He is not preoccupied with private concerns, nor do his private concerns distort his perception of his experiences. His mind is free to focus on the tasks at hand: the history test, the geometry problem, the basketball game. He experiences frustration and disappointment but is able to go on to the next challenge.

The Situation

Features of the learning situation also affect a child's learning. The physical environment must be conducive to the learning process. We can assume that Eddie's school is appropriately designed, with adequate space for each child, well maintained, properly equipped with teaching materials, and that there is a reasonable degree of order in the building. The proper learning environment must be established in the individual classroom as well. We can see how Eddie is distracted by the disruptive activity of other students during what is supposed to be study time.

The impact of the people in the learning environment is enormous. Of them, the most important are a child's teachers and his peers. Why does a child learn better from one teacher than he does from another, equally experienced, just as well qualified? It has been found that certain specific characteristics in a teacher interact with the child's personality to affect learning. One such characteristic is sex: most children learn better from a teacher of the same sex. Eddie's preference for math and sports over history may be due in part to the fact that his geometry teacher and his basketball coach are both men, while his history teacher is a woman. Another important characteristic is the teacher's pattern of praising and criticizing. Although we don't know how Eddie usually feels about studying history, we have seen that his discouragement on this particular day probably has at least something to do with the reprimand he receives from Ms. Palmeri. On the other hand, praise from Mr. Robertson and anticipated praise from Mr. Flynn reinforce his positive attitude about basketball and math.

A teacher's expectations of a child are also crucial in his learning. They affect his motivation, his self-esteem, and his own expectations of himself. So a teacher's belief that a child will learn well may, in fact, result in better learning. Unfortunately, the reverse is also true: a teacher's low expectations of a child may be a self-fulfilling prophecy.

Teaching style is another important consideration. Eddie does better when the teaching style is "alive," actively engaging the students and presenting them with a challenge. He also appears to flourish when learning is a cooperative venture—he is totally engaged in the group effort to come up with the area of the figure, and with the team effort to win the game.

The other extremely influential people in a child's learning environment are his peers. A child's peer group also teaches him social skills that he cannot learn from the adults in his life: how to get along with others his own age, how to share, how to negotiate and reach a compromise with his equals. The peer group is a primary source of learning because the group's response serves to reinforce behavior—or not to reinforce it. Eddie is proud of his classmates' reaction to his math solution and his teammates' reaction to his performance on the court. This suggests that he will make similar efforts in the future.

The Information

A child's ability to learn well is further affected by features of the information itself. Among the features that play a significant role in how well material is learned are repetition, relevance, and salience.

How frequent the exposure to information is—or, in the case of motor learning, how much an activity is practiced—has a great deal to do with how well it is mastered. Ms. Palmeri gives the class time to study before the test. Eddie knows that repetition works for him, so he keeps going over the map, to be sure he has learned it. And his performance on the basketball court is, in large measure, the result of his hours of practice in and out of school.

Learning is also affected by the relevance that the information or the skill has for the learner (or, at least, by the relevance the learner judges it to have). Eddie probably sees little point in learning about the American Revolution. On the other hand, it is very important to him to do well on the basketball court—and be admired by his friends. This gives him the motivation to practice and perfect his playing technique.

The third factor that affects how well information is learned is its salience—how well it stands out. Eddie has difficulty with the list of battle dates, each one much like the next, but no trouble with the identification questions because the individuals and concepts stand out in his mind.

Eddie's school day provides us with a wealth of information on how a seventh-grader learns. But learning in school begins the moment a child enters his first classroom. What follows are some highlights of the average child's development from nursery school through the beginning of adolescence.

_____ DEVELOPMENTAL ACHIEVEMENTS AND ACADEMIC DEMANDS IN THE PRESCHOOL AND SCHOOL YEARS

Nursery school: three and four years. A child becomes increasingly independent. Motor skills continue to develop: he is running, jumping, and riding a tricycle. Fine motor skills improve and he is more proficient in cutting, block building, and coloring. Though his listening span is still relatively short, he is beginning to tell somewhat involved stories and enjoys word-play, such as rhymes. He learns best by interacting with others and with materials. He seeks out the company of his peers, and there is an increase in joint efforts involving role taking (for example, playing house) and problem solving (for example, figuring out how to fix the collapsed roof of a building in the block corner). By the end of this period, he knows the names of colors and shapes, and understands size—big, small, long, short.

Kindergarten: five years. Large muscles develop further, and a child acquires an improved sense of balance. Language and speech abilities continue to evolve. He is increasingly interested in activities and people outside his home. Sensitivity to the needs and interests of others increases; the ability to compromise emerges. Learning may occur through listening and watching, but he does better through interaction with others and through real, hands-on experiences. The basic skills needed to start learning to read, write, and do arithmetic are in place. Among his accomplishments are recognizing a few written words, writing his name and counting objects.

First grade: six years. Motor abilities, especially fine motor skills, continue to be refined. Language and speech abilities are well developed. By now, he is in every way an effective communicator: he speaks grammatically and has an extensive vocabulary. Social skills continue to evolve. He still learns best by doing, and learn he does. At school, his reading and writing skills are a primary focus. His arithmetic skills develop further, and he learns beginning computation.

Second and third grades: seven and eight years. The rate of his sensory-perceptual, motor, and language development has leveled off, though, of course, further refinement is occurring. He can learn by listening better than he could, but still does best by doing. He is beginning to solve problems in his head. Socially, he joins informal groups that come together and quickly dissolve. By the end of the primary grades, he is reading smoothly. Script takes the place of print, and he can write clearly and neatly. He can add and subtract and is beginning to do multiplication and division.

Fourth to sixth grades: nine to eleven years. Sensory-perceptual, motor, and language abilities are in place; thinking processes continue to evolve. The peer group takes on increased importance, both in terms of friendship groups and formal organizations such as the Scouts. During the middle grades, academic demands change dramatically, reflecting the dramatic changes in his capacities. In reading, it is assumed that he can read the material; comprehension of what is read now becomes the main focus. He can express his thoughts in writing and formulate essay answers. The basic arithmetic computation skills are reviewed and more advanced topics, such as positive and negative numbers, are introduced. Now able to be self-directed and more responsible for his work, he is beginning to develop good study skills. Increasingly, he is expected to be able to learn by listening, and to sit still for longer periods of time.

Seventh grade and on: twelve years and older. All the neurological building blocks of learning abilities are in place and thinking processes are at a new high level, allowing him to deal with more information more quickly and efficiently. Socially, he may be spending more time with his peer group than with adults. During the junior and senior high school years, academic demands again take a giant leap forward. Demands on reading comprehension are greater than ever, both in terms of the nature of the material itself and in the sheer amount of reading that is expected. Writing skills are also expected to reach a new high. The ability to formulate essay answers continues to be important, and there is a greater emphasis on creative writing. The groundwork of math topics such as algebra is elaborated upon. Some youngsters go on to study more advanced topics, such as trigonometry; instruction here assumes mastery of previously taught arithmetic skills. With the possible exception of the sciences, instruction is on a lecture basis, and the youngster is expected to maintain focused attention for long periods of time. It is assumed that by now he has good study skills, both in and out of the classroom, and can take total responsibility for his schoolwork.

Your
Action
Program

INTRODUCTION

In the earlier chapters of this book, we discussed the roles that the central nervous system and development play in learning. We outlined the neurological underpinnings of learning, emphasizing that a very subtle inefficiency in a particular brain region or pathway can interfere severely with early learning. Now, in Part Two, we'll provide you with an action program that will help you feel more confident—and be more effective—in helping your child learn.

The first step in that action program is to learn to recognize the signs that your child might have a learning problem, so that you can respond to these symptoms with support rather than punishment, with concern about how to help your child rather than anger or disappointment. We all have our own individual learning styles, our own strengths and weaknesses. Nevertheless, you can zero in on some everyday signs of a learning problem if you know what to look for. Some questions you might have are: What signs might you notice at home? What might you expect to hear about your child when you meet with his teacher? How do you integrate the information given by the school with the things you have noticed at home?

The second step in your action program, if you and your child's teacher agree that he may have a learning problem, is to find the right person to evaluate your child. This is not the time to leaf through your phone book: you need an informed referral network. We will tell you how to find the appropriate professional and setting, what questions to ask, and what answers to look for. We'll describe the evaluation process that can identify a learning disability, and give you some guidance about gauging the thoroughness of the evaluation process. We will also discuss the very important issue of confidentiality—something you must consider carefully as you enlist a professional's help.

The third part of your action program is tackling the problem: making a wise decision about treatment, if treatment is recommended. You'll need to decide what kind of treatment is appropriate and what it might entail, as well as how to explain your child's disability to him and prepare him for what's ahead.

The fourth and final step of the action program is, in fact, not so much final as ongoing. It accompanies all the others. Coping at home, day to day, when a family includes a child with a learning disability, is no simple undertaking. There are your special child's special needs, your own needs, and the needs of all the others (family and nonfamily) who are close to you. There is the emotional fallout from learning that your child has a disability, which may include feelings of disappointment, anger, failure, even guilt. There is the problem of accommodating one child without making him feel "different," or making his siblings resentful. There is the delicate balance that must be struck between providing supervision and encouraging self-reliance. How do you cope, day to day? Here, as well, we can help you to help your child.

CHAPTER 7

How to Recognize the Signs of Difficulty in Learning

Again and again, parents of children with learning disabilities tell us that their first inkling of the problem came when they noticed that something just wasn't right with the way that things were going for their child in school. And teachers, having a hard time putting a finger on any specific sign that a child is struggling with learning, often sum up their concern the same way: "Something just isn't right." Perhaps a child is behind his siblings or classmates in the mastery of one or more basic skills, such as doing puzzles or reciting the alphabet at about age five, picking up the basics of reading and writing at age six or seven. Maybe a twelve-year-old who was always a crackerjack at written computation and solving number story problems is now struggling with geometry, a math topic that depends heavily upon additional brain functions. In a case like this, it is pretty obvious that something just isn't right—that something is interfering with the child's ability to learn.

In other cases, the signs that a child has a learning problem are more subtle, even insidious. His early development or later performance may be marked by unevenness. Perhaps a three-year-old, a great rememberer of songs, can't remember the words for the things he uses every day or the names of familiar people. Or a ten-year-old, one of the smartest kids in her class, is having tantrums about her homework and taking forever to get it done. Sometimes a child with a learning problem achieves up to grade level in all his subjects but behaves disruptively. He is sent out of class most days for verbally or physically attacking someone. Another child may be getting average grades but is obviously not interested in school. He finds one excuse after another for not doing his homework and complains of stomachaches or tiredness every morning, trying to get out of going to school. Here again, something just isn't right.

_____ LEARNING STYLES, STRENGTHS, AND WEAKNESSES

We all have our own learning styles, strengths, and weaknesses. One person may best grasp difficult new information by first reading, then writing notes, then rereading the notes. Another may do best by studying graphs or diagrams that present the new information pictorially. We also all have some areas in which learning is, and always has been, "a piece of cake"—picking up new melodies, perhaps, or assembling anything that comes in kit form. At the other extreme, we all have areas in which learning seems close to hopeless, or at least very slow going. For some people, the hardest thing may be learning a foreign language; for others, it might be figuring out how to use a word processor.

It is the same, of course, with all children—both with those who *do not* have a learning problem and with those who *do*. They all have individual learning styles with areas of relative strength, areas of weakness, and areas where their ability is average. But in children with learning problems, the particular combination of weaknesses and strengths is disruptive to learning. This is true even though the weaknesses may be—and, in fact, often are—quite subtle. And, unlike youngsters who do not have learning problems, these children typically do not discover on their own how most effectively to use their strengths to compensate for their weaknesses. They usually need help in developing learning strategies that are the best ones for them.

——————— **BECOMING AN EDUCATED OBSERVER**

Sometimes a child's individual learning style masks the signs that a learning problem exists. But sometimes these signs are hard to miss —if parents know what to look for. So the first step in learning how to help your child is to become an educated observer.

The signs that a child has a learning problem may be primarily "academic" or "nonacademic." "Academic" signs revolve around the quality of schoolwork: what it looks like, how it is done, as well as what he says about school. Or the signs may be "nonacademic" having to do with the child's overall behavior: his interests, his feelings, his rhythms, his willingness or unwillingness to try new things, his ability to tolerate the frustrations that accompany new challenges, how he goes about his daily activities. With these basic distinctions in mind, let's begin by observing together some children who are likely to look familiar to you in some important ways.

——————— *Donald.* This very attractive twelve-year-old was a straight-A math student (math was far and away his favorite subject) and had been in the honors group in his class for years. But at the end of the year he not only failed his math final but scored in the eighth percentile across the board on standardized tests. Neither his parents nor his school could figure out what was wrong. Donald seemed to them a hard worker, a bright child. Donald himself was understandably at least as upset as were his parents and teachers.

——————— *Edward.* Edward was the middle child in a family of three boys. He had been a calm preschooler who enjoyed playing by himself more than with his brothers or their friends or neighbors. In fact, he was able to occupy himself quietly and happily for hours on end. But everything about first grade was a disaster. Edward hated his teacher and took to ignoring her, sometimes even threatening her when she asked him to do something he didn't feel like doing. He became the class bully early on and often got into fights. Despite his attitude that school was a bore, and despite the fact that he had been sent out of the classroom over and over again, by the end of the school year Edward was reading and spelling at third-grade level. His math, though, was at kindergarten level.

_____ *Michael.* Michael, age seven, was an early walker and talker, an outgoing, well-coordinated child with a special talent for creating the most wonderful buildings out of blocks. He impressed his nursery school teacher as a budding mathematician. By age four he could reel off the numbers up to a hundred; he could count objects; he seemed to understand the concept of addition. His vocabulary and his ability to express his very imaginative ideas were also outstanding. So midyear reports from his first-grade teacher couldn't have come as more of a surprise to his parents. Michael was struggling to learn the sounds of letters and was forgetting the names of written numbers. Consequently he was in the slowest reading group and looking shaky in math. His teacher saw many signs of Michael's keen intellect, especially in his ability to understand quite complicated ideas (presented orally) and in his creative projects. But she commented that he often talked around an idea instead of making his point succinctly, and that he seemed frustrated with some basic academic skills. She was also concerned about the way he was adjusting to his difficulties, either trying hard to "wing it" or adopting an obnoxious know-it-all, tough-guy approach.

_____ *Ann.* Even before she entered first grade, Ann knew the letter sounds and the names of written numbers. She went through the first, second, and third grades with no difficulty. Things changed in fourth grade; she no longer participated actively in class discussions, had difficulty expressing herself well on paper, and could not do quite complicated mental arithmetic. Her oral book reports were inadequate. It was evident that Ann was having a hard time remembering from day to day what her teacher had talked about in class. She frequently misremembered her assignment (announced by the teacher at the end of each class), misunderstood new concepts, and even responded inappropriately to spoken questions. Although Ann's teacher felt that the girl was interested in her schoolwork and paid attention in class, she was at a loss as to how to help her. She tried the usual remedy for inattentiveness and had Ann sit at the front of the classroom. This did not help.

_____ *Steven.* Steven's kindergarten teacher had described him as bright, very cautious, tending to avoid many new activities, quite forgetful, and generally immature. Now eight years old and in the second grade, he was falling behind. His main stumbling block was arithmetic: he just didn't seem able to learn the basic math "facts," such as simple addition and subtraction. Also, he had difficulty remembering how to spell irregular words (those that don't come out right if you rely totally on letter-sound rules). His parents wondered whether Steven just wasn't applying himself well enough to these rote tasks. Maybe Nintendo and karate practice were taking too much of his time and energy.

_____ *William.* Twelve-year-old William was getting poor grades largely due to "careless" work. His teachers maintained that this was merely a sign of William's laziness, his not taking school seriously enough, and his lack of desire to succeed. But his parents knew that William spent hours on the simplest homework assignment. He impressed them as a child trying very hard to do his best —often, even, as absurdly perfectionistic—and they marveled at his willingness to keep going when he had such disappointing results from all his efforts.

_____ *Elizabeth.* An only child, Elizabeth was eleven years old. She was described by her parents as demanding, stubborn, and very smart. She had always been able to occupy herself and early on had taken quite an interest in her father's work, computer programming. (By age nine, she could explain, much better than her teacher could, how and why computer programs work.) Elizabeth's progress in school had always been apparently quite effortless. But in the fifth grade, she started saying that school was dumb and boring and that homework was a waste of time. Her teacher was concerned about this attitude and also about Elizabeth's frequent lack of attention in class. When her teacher and her parents compared notes about her, they agreed that writing seemed to be the thing Elizabeth objected to the most.

_____ *Rebecca.* Six-year-old Rebecca had seemed to be the brightest of the three children in her family, a verbal, keenly curious, and creative girl. She thoroughly enjoyed nursery school and kindergarten, but when she entered first grade there was a new and obvious lack of enthusiasm about school that was heartbreaking to her parents. She was keeping up with her classmates, but she was not the academic star that her parents and her teacher thought she would be. Her teacher reported that Rebecca was the last one in her class to be disruptive but that she seemed moody and had become rather withdrawn. At home, she spent hours daydreaming. When her parents asked her what had gone on in school that day, Rebecca usually answered, "I don't remember."

_____ *Eric.* Eric, age nine, was in the slowest group in both reading and math in his class. His parents characterized him as a child who was "just all over the place." Sitting still was torture for him, and he had a hard time keeping his hands off things he wasn't supposed to touch. He shared a room with his brother and was constantly ruining his brother's buildings and playing with his toys without permission. Dinner was a battleground. Since Eric was in so much trouble at home, it didn't surprise his parents that he wasn't doing well at school.

_____ *Ellen.* Beginning in the first grade, Ellen had spent much of the school day in the resource room for children with special learning needs. Her progress there had been slow and steady. Now that she was nine and in the third grade, the school felt that Ellen no longer needed special help. But her parents, though pleased with the progress in her academic work, remained concerned about the child they saw at home. Ellen rarely asked classmates over to her house, saying that she preferred to play with her Barbie dolls. When she was invited to a birthday party, she often tried to get out of going. She seemed to be searching out the younger children in the neighborhood and sometimes even talked baby talk, something her parents hadn't heard for years. Recently, she had complained about not being able to get to sleep at night and had begun to insist that one of her parents stay in her room until she dropped off.

_____ **EVERYDAY SIGNS OF A LEARNING PROBLEM**

With our observations of Donald, Edward, and the others as background, we'll spell out some common signs of a learning problem.

These can alert you to the fact that there is a problem. Parents can easily observe these signs in the work that a child brings home from school, in the information he shares about his schoolwork, and in the way he does his homework:

- Overall disorganization. Papers are crumpled, homework is sloppy, library books are lost, class notes are all over the place.
- "Careless" errors. There are misspelled words, misread instructions and computation signs, misheard directions.
- A know-it-all facade. When asked how today's test went, the child's usual answer is "It was easy." A new book is generally "boring." Homework is usually "all done" in what seems to be too short a time.
- Underachievement. There are clear signs of good intelligence coupled with equally clear signs of serious difficulty in some—or several—academic areas. The child is struggling with at least one area. There may be a change from a "good" to a "bad" student in one area or in several areas.
- Forgetfulness. "I forget" is his favorite phrase. When asked about his history test or science assignment, or what his teacher said about some particular topic, he says, "I forget."
- Refusal to do schoolwork. The child's learning difficulty may result in his refusal to perform in school or to do his homework. He may also grudgingly carry out an assignment or study for a test. He may hand in half-done work or study only part of the test material.
- Slow performance. The child takes an excessive amount of time to complete homework and rarely finishes in-school work. Sometimes this is due to laborious efforts; other times it is due to procrastination.

Other signs that indicate that a child has a learning problem are seen not only as he does his schoolwork and talks about school, but also as he goes about his daily life. These include:

- Inattentiveness. The child does not seem to pay attention to directions or to what he is supposed to be doing.
- Anger or sadness. When asked to do something, he becomes irritable and may even "blow up." He seems to lack interest in things he used to love. He complains about stomachaches on school mornings. He complains about his teachers as unfair or mean or boring. He says he has no friends.
- Impulsiveness. The child often does not use his verbal skills to

express himself but just bursts into action and as a result, his performance often suffers.

- Daydreaming. The child often seems to be off in his own world. He is "tuned out," preoccupied.
- Restlessness. He fidgets, has a hard time sitting still, and is always dropping things. He often talks too much, almost compulsively.
- Poor ability to tolerate frustration. He has difficulty sticking to and working through hard tasks. He tries to avoid things that are difficult for him, loses his temper, and may become aggressive when he is unable to accomplish something. He cries.
- Regression to earlier interests and routines. He returns to playing games he gave up several years ago. He reverts to baby talk.
- Need to be his own boss. He tried to set the rules and to make decisions about what he does and when he does it. He tries to decide his bedtime, his dinner menu, and whether or not he will go to visit his grandparents.
- Poor self-esteem. The child is full of self-doubt, as if he knows that something is not quite right.

_____ THE PARENT-TEACHER CONFERENCE

If your child exhibits any of the signs listed above, you should ask yourself, "Might he be struggling with learning?" And if your child's teacher has not contacted you, you should request a conference. Do not assume that because the teacher has not voiced a concern there is no problem.

The Teacher's Observations

At this conference you may hear the teacher describe what he or she has observed about your child on both the academic and behavioral fronts. In later chapters (Chapters 17 through 19), we will discuss what the teacher may have noticed about your child's schoolwork. At this point, we'll focus on behavior. You may be told that your child

- is sloppy and scatterbrained. His desk is always a mess, his assignment book is never to be found, he takes the wrong books home.
- seems withdrawn. He doesn't participate much in class and seems isolated from the other children.

- is very bossy. He seems to need to be in charge, is a poor sport, and has difficulty playing and working with other children because he insists on having his own way.
- has difficulty working independently. He needs more attention and guidance than his classmates.
- has trouble paying attention in class. His mind wanders and unless he is seated at the front of the classroom the teacher loses him altogether.
- has trouble switching from one activity to another—from math to English, for example, or from lunch to gym.
- seems to march to a different drummer. He doesn't seem to give much thought to other people's feelings or ideas. He is on a different wavelength.

What You Should Ask

There are several questions that you should ask the teacher at this conference. These points may be covered by the teacher's initial comments, but if they are not, ask them one by one. Bring a pad and pencil and write down the answers.

1. How does the child's performance on tests compare with his everyday use of certain skills? For example, how do his arithmetic test results compare with his use of numbers in handling lunch money?
2. How does his performance in class with the teacher's supervision compare with his performance in independent work? Is he well organized?
3. How does the teacher rate the child's connectedness to adults and to other children?
4. Is there a noticeable difficulty switching between activities?
5. Does the child avoid certain activities, such as gym or written work or oral reports?
6. Does he daydream in class? Is he a loner?
7. Does he seem less mature than his classmates?
8. Does he seem resigned to failure? Has he given up? Is he an underachiever?

Answers to these key questions will be very useful, maybe critical, in defining the source of your child's difficulties.

CHAPTER 8

How to Seek Professional Help

FINDING THE RIGHT PROFESSIONAL AND FOLLOWING UP ON A RECOMMENDATION

When you have very good reason to believe that something just isn't right and that your child may be suffering from a learning problem, you need to take the second step in your action program: to seek professional help. The professional must be someone who can establish whether or not your child does in fact have a learning problem. He (or she) must be able to identify significant difficulties with learning and also the source of those difficulties—whether they have an emotional source, or an environmental one, or are based on inefficient workings of the brain (a learning disability).

It is not an easy task to find the right professional to evaluate your child. Unfortunately, it too often happens that evaluations are incomplete, or that the findings are inadequately interpreted. Joe's mother, for example, was told that her son had an arithmetic disability. The basis for this statement was that Joe couldn't answer some simple orally presented number story problems. But his difficulty dealing with these was a reflection of his problem remembering what he had heard, not of an arithmetic disability (and, in fact, he had no trouble with written computations or number story problems). So it was no wonder that, after two years of twice-a-week remediation, he still couldn't respond to math problems posed by his teacher in classroom discussions. Another instance: Samuel was said to have a reading disability. This was based on his poor answers to some questions about an article in a children's magazine. Here the "reading disability" was in the reading material itself: the magazine article was meant for a much older child. Samuel also was referred to twice-a-week remediation. In his case, skills improved greatly—but at the cost of much time and money wasted. He would have made good progress without the extra help.

Another story that is very fresh in our minds is that of ten-year-old Sally. Sally was referred to us because she was daydreaming in school and refusing to do her homework in the evenings. A month before we met her, an evaluation had been done and Sally's parents had been reassured that she had no learning problems. Tests had pointed to superior intelligence and revealed across-the-board grade-level skills. Sally's parents were told that her school and homework problems were rooted in her "attitude." The recommendation was that they impress on Sally that good grades are important and that hard work is what is needed to get them. But a bad "attitude" wasn't the problem at all. Rather, Sally was struggling with severe fearfulness about school performance. Without help to overcome it, this fearfulness would interfere with her progress more and more in the years ahead. On the basis of her intelligence and educational opportunity, Sally should have been performing well *above* grade level and outstripping her classmates. Her unrealistic fear of failure was preventing her from moving ahead more quickly.

We know of children who have been identified as having reading disorders when in fact their difficulty in reading was a reflection of a serious difficulty in understanding complex sentence structure, or a problem in paying attention. We have known numerous children with learning disabilities who were seen as having no problem at all, because an evaluator was unfamiliar with age-expected development or unfamiliar with signs of inefficiency in brain functioning. And we know too many parents who have been reassured that their child was just a little young for his age and would certainly catch up, when in fact his development was not only slow but not normal as well.

The Right Professional

A capable professional should be able to identify a learning problem and its source. If treatment is necessary, the professional should be able to make the appropriate referrals, most often to a remediator (to treat a learning disability) or to a psychotherapist (to treat an emotional problem). He or she should be able to recommend a new school, if necessary, to correct a mismatch between a child and his educational setting. And if further special evaluation is needed, the professional should be able to put you in touch with the right specialist.

How do you find this capable professional? Phone numbers off a grocery-store bulletin board won't do. You should rely on a carefully thought-out referral network, people you know and respect who have had experience with this kind of problem—say, your pediatrician, your child's teacher, or a colleague whose child was recently evaluated. You will probably be given three or four different names of individuals or settings that offer evaluations. How you decide among them is perhaps the most crucial step in your action program. The expenditure of time and effort here are guaranteed to serve you well as you set out on the long and often bumpy road that lies ahead.

Let's examine the credentials of the professionals likely to be recommended to you to evaluate your child.

• Learning specialists or special educators are trained to assess academic skill achievement and to teach academic skills. Their degrees are in education; for example, they have a Master of Arts (M.A.) or Doctor of Education (Ed.D.). They also have specialty licenses.

• Medical doctors have degrees in medicine—M.D., with both general and specialty licenses: general practitioners are trained to assess general medical health; psychiatrists are trained to assess emotional well-being; pediatricians are trained to assess the medical health of children; neurologists are trained to assess the overall health of the child's nervous system.

• Psychologists are trained to study human behavior in a variety of contexts—the home, the school, the work place and so on. They hold Doctor of Philosophy (Ph.D.) degrees, with a license to practice. Within the field, there are several different specialties. Some psychologists specialize in the learning process; their training includes work in the assessment of the intellectual, educational, and emotional factors that affect learning and the identification of brain inefficiencies that underlie learning difficulty.

From our perspective, a psychologist with specialized training in the learning process is uniquely qualified to identify a learning problem and distinguish a problem with an emotional basis from one due to inefficient workings of the brain (that is, a learning disability). He or she will be able to tell when a learning problem has both neurological and emotional sources, and will also be able to define the role of the child's environment—home and school—in his learning difficulties. Further, if a learning disability does exist, a psychologist with this kind of special training will be able to tell what aspects of a particular task are affected. Take a child whose handwriting is every which way on the page, with the letters distorted almost beyond recognition. Does the child's brain "take a poor picture" of the written letters, so that he doesn't, in fact, see the letters accurately? Or does the brain "take a good picture" but then send confused commands to the muscles in the fingers, so that the child's writing is deformed? Clearly, this knowledge is crucial to the remedial treatment of a child who is struggling with writing. And the same holds true across the board for all learning disabilities.

Here are some of the options you are likely to have regarding the setting in which a professional can evaluate your child:
• Public school
• Community mental health center
• Outpatient clinic in a hospital
• Clinic associated with a Department of Education or Psychology in a university
• Private office of an independent mental health or learning center, group practice, or individual professional

Following Up on a Recommendation

Let's assume that you have been given the names of facilities or individuals to do the evaluation. When following up on a recommendation, you must be prepared to ask some pointed questions. We can tell you from our own experience that, rather than offending, questions like these will enhance respect for parents both as educated consumers and as strong advocates for their children. Here are the things you need to know *before* you make an appointment to begin the evaluation process. By asking these questions when you make the initial phone call, you can save yourself time, energy, and possibly money, too.

What are the evaluator's credentials? Does he or she hold an advanced degree and a license to practice in your state? Does he or she have specialty training? In what area? If appropriate, what about hospital or university affiliation? (Affiliation requires rigorous review of credentials and ongoing peer review of professional competence.) How long has he or she been doing evaluations to identify learning problems and their primary source (emotional, environmental, or neurological)? What about publications—are these accessible to a nonspecialist?

What about cost? An evaluation done under the auspices of a public school is free. The cost of an evaluation in a clinic is typically based on family income. It is free for some. For those who pay, the cost is usually, but not always, lower than in the private sector. As a consumer, you should know what the fee, if any, covers. Does it include the initial session with the parent, in which background information is gathered? Does it include a written report of the findings and a follow-up session with the parents (and possibly with the child as well, in the case of older children)? If you want a second follow-up session to go over the results or discuss the recommendations, is there an additional fee for this? Is the fee reimbursable by medical insurance? An evaluation, whether done in a public or private setting, may or may not be covered by your medical insurance policy. If it is, there may be limitations in your coverage; for example, the maximum reimbursable amount for this service. When is payment expected—at the outset of each session, or at the follow-up session?

How long will the evaluation take? An evaluation of a child thought to have a learning problem can range from a quick screening to a lengthy comprehensive examination. The quick exam might involve tests of reading, spelling, and arithmetic skills, a partial IQ test, and a clinical interview. This type of exam is often attractive to parents. It take less time. And you may be told that your child's problems seem so well defined and so minor that a limited confirmatory examination will suffice. But in our view, such a mini-evaluation is very dangerous, since it is based on incomplete information. (Would you be satisfied if your doctor identified a breast lump as benign on the basis of a physical examination alone? Wouldn't you want him to schedule more extensive tests—say, a mammogram and a biopsy?) So, if the answer to the question here is "An hour or so, not more," then we would advise you to go no further with this professional.

On the other hand, if it is clear that the examination will be a comprehensive one, there are a number of important questions that you should ask about the time frame. How many office visits are required? How long will each visit take? Can two sessions be scheduled on one day?

In general, it is our view that the required testing takes four to eight hours, depending on such things as a child's age and skill level, and that it should never be done in one long session—even with a number of breaks. Children under the age of six should not be examined in sessions of more than forty-five minutes each, and not at the end of a long day in school. Multiple office visits may be trying for the parent or the child or both, but don't shortchange your child by arranging a testing schedule that is dictated by convenience. What is important is getting the information that is needed.

What about referrals for treatment? If treatment is necessary, the evaluator should be able to refer your child to an appropriate setting or professional. The settings in which appropriate treatment may be found include the public school, clinic, and private office. You should ask at the outset whether the evaluator has good working relationships with remediators and psychotherapists in private practice and in various public facilities. And you should ask about how he or she determines which facility or individual to refer a given child to. A good answer here would be: "On the basis of a particular area of needed expertise." This might mean, for example, that the evaluator would refer a child with an arithmetic disability to a remediator with special expertise in math. Or that that evaluator would pick a facility with a psychotherapist who he or she knows has had successful experience with children similar to your child in age, sex, and temperament. In every case, the professional who evaluates your child should be willing to talk, with your permission, to the person who sees him for treatment, when the time comes.

Because the appropriate intervention may be a change of school, you should also ask about whether the evaluator is knowledgeable about the schools in your area. Can he or she recommend private or public school settings? Will he or she be available to discuss your child with the schools, given your permission?

And what about referrals for further testing? One outcome of an evaluation may be a referral for further testing. You should be prepared for the possibility that even the most finely hewn evaluation may require the input of another specialist. For example, the primary evaluator may identify a speech problem. However, he or she may not be trained as a speech pathologist and may be unable to tell exactly how the speech process is impaired or come up with the remedial strategy of choice. In this case, he or she should refer you to a speech specialist.

You should also ask about the primary evaluator's working relationships with appropriate specialists, in case a further referral is needed. He or she should be able to refer you to the best person available, whether this is a neurologist, a psychiatrist, an audiologist, an ophthalmologist, a speech and language pathologist, or some other specialist.

What about confidentiality? You should ask about issues related to confidentiality. With whom will information about the test results be shared? Who will make this decision? It must be made clear that you consider the professional / client relationship a private one. If ideas about confidentiality differ from yours, you will have to continue your search for the professional or setting that is right for you and your child.

_____ THE EVALUATION PROCESS

Successful treatment of your child's learning problem—treatment that has long-term benefits—depends first on a comprehensive evaluation. This evaluation should identify a learning problem and its source. Is it primarily environmental, emotional, or biological? Without this information, the learning problem will be treated by hit-or-miss methods or by methods that "usually work." It is even possible that, in the absence of a proper evaluation, the symptoms (for example, in the case of a learning disability, the emotional fallout) and not the disability itself will be treated.

Ideally, a comprehensive evaluation has several stages. The first is a background stage, an initial meeting with at least one parent, preferably both. The second stage is the testing of your child, the comprehensive psychological examination. The third is a follow-up or feedback meeting—with both parents whenever possible and perhaps with the child as well, depending on his age and his particular problem. At this meeting, the nature of your child's problem will be discussed and recommendations for treatment, if any, will be made.

The Background Meeting

What should you expect when you first go to meet the professional who is to evaluate your child? What is the purpose of this meeting? One important purpose of this first office visit is for you to meet the person who will be playing such a crucial role in your child's life, and for that person to meet you. You will have a chance to reconsider your decision to move forward with this person, having met her (let's assume, for the purposes of our discussion, that the evaluator is a woman).

At the beginning of the meeting, the evaluator is likely to ask, "Why are you here?" or "What are your concerns?" In answer, you might perhaps describe your child's grades this year: A's and B-pluses in the midterms, a C-minus and two F's in the finals. Or you might express your concern more generally: a fear that your child is sliding into failure at school. Or, perhaps, that he seems withdrawn and easily frustrated.

Another question you may be asked is "What are *your* goals in having your child evaluated? What questions do *you* want answered by this examination?" Even if you are not asked this question directly, you should make clear what your goals are. In our view, you should have a minimum of four goals or expectations. First, you should expect that the testing will either reveal a learning problem or rule it out. Second, if a learning problem is uncovered, you should expect that the testing will explore the relationship between that problem and your child's emotional state, his environment, and his brain functions. Thus, it will establish whether or not the learning problem is in fact a learning disability (based on weak or inefficient brain functions). Third, you should expect the evaluation to provide an assessment of your child's emotional and intellectual strengths and weaknesses. Finally, you should expect it to result in clear recommendations about where to go from here.

These are things that every parent should expect from the evaluation. You may have more specific goals as well. You might want to know, for example, whether you should encourage your child to learn how to play a musical instrument or to try out for the soccer team. You should make all your expectations clear to the evaluator.

Background Information

As she gathers background information, you will be asked about your child's developmental and medical history. You should be prepared to describe your pregnancy, your child's birth, and his place in the family—whether he is a first child or a middle child, for example, and how old his siblings are. You will be asked about when your child first sat, walked, and said his first words. Another question concerns your child's health: has he had any significant illnesses or medical problems?

School will probably be another topic. The evaluator will want to know about your child's academic, nonacademic, and social experiences there. You should be prepared to review your child's progress—or lack of it—since his earliest school days. When and where was his first school experience? Were there any problems in first grade, in second grade? What about his teachers' comments over the years? How about nonacademic areas such as art and gym —any problems there? What kind of relationships has he had with teachers and classmates? Was he ever given extra help in his schoolwork, in speech, in motor coordination? If so, on whose recommendation and by whom? Was he ever tested before? If so, why and by whom? (If your child was tested previously, and you have the test results, bring them with you to this meeting.)

You will be asked about your child's school reports. If you can, bring them with you. If you can't, make a summary. Note your child's standardized test scores and his classroom grades; describe his study skills, his relationships with others, and his behavior at school as far as you can. Bring some samples of recent schoolwork. Bring also any notes you have from parent-teacher conferences over the years.

In terms of family history, you will be asked to describe your child's relationships with other members of your family and the interrelationships and conflicts among family members. Be sure to mention any significant family events, such as death, illness, or divorce. You will be asked about your family living arrangements and what support systems you have available to you. The evaluator will want to know if there is any family history of medical disease or psychiatric disturbance, or dependence on drugs or alcohol. She will also want to know whether learning problems, or developmental or emotional ones, have affected other family members— siblings, parents, grandparents, aunts, or uncles. If the answer is yes, she will want you to describe the problem as best you can. If you have the answers to questions of this kind ready at your fingertips, it will save time.

Another set of questions is designed to get a full description of your child and his problem as you see it. What kind of temperament does your child have? How does he handle frustration and disappointment? What makes him angry and how does he show and control his anger? How does he spend his time at home? What are his main interests? How has he adjusted to important events in his life—a divorce, a new school, a new caretaker, a new brother, a new home? You will be asked when you first became concerned about a problem. What academic difficulties were apparent at the beginning? What emotional and behavioral changes have you noticed? What precipitates the problem or makes it worse? What makes things better?

The more background information you can provide, the more finely tuned the outcome of the evaluation will be. We have provided a checklist on preparing for this part of the evaluation at the back of the book (Appendix 1). This should help you organize ahead of time the materials you need.

Testing

After the initial meeting, it is time for your child to be tested. Don't feel anxious, or worried that your child will never forgive you for this—he may even end up enjoying it. And don't feel guilty. If your child complained that his ear hurt, you wouldn't think twice about taking him to the doctor, even if he did protest. You shouldn't think twice about the testing either, especially now that you are aware that his problems will not simply go away on their own. To help your child, you need to know exactly what is wrong

—and also what is *not* wrong. You cannot know this without a thorough evaluation.

A comprehensive psychological examination has three parts: psychological, educational, and neuropsychological. All three parts of the examination yield both quantitative and qualitative information about a child's functioning in relation to that of others his age. The integration of quantitative information is central to the evaluation process. Quantitative information is numerical. It is supplied in the form of scores. Qualitative information, which is just as important, is descriptive. It includes the evaluator's notes describing the nature of a child's behavior during the evaluation process. This involves such things as his spontaneous comments and his approach to different tasks. It also includes descriptive information about a child's background and present behavior, obtained during the background meeting. The names of some of the tests commonly used are listed in Appendix 2.

Comprehensive Evaluation

Psychological testing to assess:
   intelligence
   emotional well-being
Educational testing to assess:
   basic academic skills
Neuropsychological testing to assess:
   strengths and inefficiencies in brain functions

Psychological Testing

The psychological assessment measures intellectual functioning and emotional well-being. Let's discuss intelligence testing first.

Intelligence can be defined as the overall ability to meet the educational and cultural demands of one's society, using both verbal and nonverbal abilities. Research has repeatedly shown that a child's level of intelligence is associated with his ability to learn: the higher the intelligence, the great the learning ability. On the tests of intelligence, called IQ (intelligence quotient) tests, your child will be asked questions and presented with tasks that tap a broad range of functions. For example, he will be required to draw on his fund of general knowledge to explain the meaning of words. He will also be asked to put puzzles together and copy arrangements of blocks.

A child's emotional state clearly has a profound impact on his learning. To take just one example, not an uncommon one: a child who is extremely upset by the birth of a sibling will be spending a great deal of energy worrying about his place in the family, and so will have less of it to spend on learning.

The tests that are used to evaluate a child's emotional state are called projectives. These tests may involve your child looking at pictures and telling a story about them, or looking at ambiguous inkblots and telling what they remind him of. Other projective tests require your child to draw pictures or complete sentences that have been left unfinished.

Educational Testing

The educational evaluation concentrates on academic skills. The tests focus on the basic areas (reading, writing, and arithmetic), not on special topic areas such as science or social studies. The evaluation also explores certain subskills—for example, the mastery of letter-sound associations and the ability to identify written numbers.

Neuropsychological Testing

The neuropsychological part of the comprehensive examination focuses on how well the brain goes about its business. The aim of this part of the evaluation is to identify strengths and inefficiencies in brain functions that affect learning. This information is key to understanding whether a learning problem is in fact a learning disability.

The information used in the evaluation process comes from three sources. First is the understanding of how the workings of the brain are involved in tests of intellect, emotional state, and academic functioning. Second are tests of neuropsychological functions. Third is the observation of the quality of a child's behavior and his performance on all kinds of tasks during the examination.

Among the neuropsychological functions that are commonly assessed are: perception, motor skills, memory, and language.

Preparing Your Child for Testing

When you do a good job of preparing your child for testing— explaining to him why this is happening, as well as what will happen and how it will happen—he will start off on the right foot. It is important to be honest with him: don't trick him into going to his appointments. Make it clear to him that you are on his side. Above all, impress on him that you have arranged for the testing because you want to help him, and the first step is to find out what's going on and what his learning strengths and weaknesses are. Or, perhaps, you could tell him that everyone learns differently and by finding out about how he learns it may be possible to make school more fun and easier.

You will want your child to know a little bit about the person he is going to see and what will happen in the office. Tell him about the kinds of things he will be doing during testing. Drawing pictures and doing puzzles won't seem so daunting. Tell him that the person he's going to see is a specialist—a doctor—and that she will want to talk to him and get to know him better; she'll want to hear how he feels about school—what are the best and the worst things about it. Also tell him that she will really appreciate his special interests and talents, and that you are sure that he will find the visit fun. You can reassure him that most kids do. (You can also reassure him that there's no possibility that *this* doctor will give him a shot!)

It is important that, from the outset, your child know that the decision about testing is not a negotiable one. All too often, we get calls from parents saying that their children refuse to come in for an evaluation. If you have decided that your concerns about your child warrant an evaluation, make it clear that this is what is going to happen. Don't present it as a question: "How would you like to visit a doctor who knows all about children?" Present it as a fact: "Tomorrow after school we have an appointment to see a doctor who can help us both make school go a little better for you." The more confident and comfortable *you* are about the evaluation, the more confident and comfortable your child will be.

The Follow-up Session

The first focus of the all-important follow-up session is the possible existence of a learning problem. If there *is* a learning problem, what is its source? Is it in fact a learning disability? The evaluator should review all the test scores and give you her interpretation of their overall pattern. She should provide an explanation of her findings in terms that you can understand (don't settle for a sentence loaded with incomprehensible polysyllables). The explanation of the findings should be more than a restatement of the problem that brought you and your child to the doctor's office in the first place. For example, if your original concern was your child's slow progress in reading, the evaluator should do more at the follow-up session than announce that your child is reading two grades below expected grade level.

For your part, you should make sure that the evaluation has provided you with what you expected of it—that the goals we outlined earlier have been met and that all your more specific questions have been answered.

There is also the question of how the findings are to be communicated to your child. Should the evaluator tell him? Should you? How much detail should you go into? The answer here depends on you, your child, and the nature of his problem. There is no one right way. You should discuss this with the evaluator. Another question concerns what you should tell your other children. The answer to this one isn't difficult: you should tell them the truth and help them to understand it.

The second main focus of the follow-up session is the immediate future. Where do you go from here? Is your child in the right class? Is he in the right school? If the answer to either question is no, the evaluator should recommend appropriate alternatives. She might recommend, for example, special class placement or placement in a different school, in the public or private sector, that better matches your child's needs. Or she may recommend no changes in school routine but, rather, other types of intervention. In making recommendations for any type of intervention the evaluator often has to set priorities. It is important to discern where the child is in the most need and take care of that area first. The evaluator should weigh carefully all the factors that have been unearthed and set a plan of action accordingly. She should also take into consideration your family's schedule and overall resources. Before you leave the office at the end of the follow-up session, you need to know what the goals of follow-up intervention are; who the evaluator would recommend to treat your child—a remediator or a psychotherapist, or both; whether a school change would make sense; whether the evaluator, with your permission, will communicate her findings to the appropriate professionals; and whether any other tests need to be done.

Further Testing

As we mentioned previously, one possible outcome of a comprehensive psychological examination is a referral to a specialist for further testing. The results of these tests will be reported to the primary evaluator, who will review her findings in light of the new information. The most likely referrals are to a neurologist, a psychiatrist, an ophthalmologist, an audiologist, or a language and speech pathologist. We'll list here the usual reasons for each of these referrals and mention the diagnostic tools and tests used by each specialist (these tools and tests are described in the Glossary). This should help you to better understand the recommendations made to you. It should also help you prepare your child for a visit to yet another specialist.

Neurologist. Among the most common reasons for a referral to a neurologist following a comprehensive psychological evaluation are: behavior or reports that point to a possible seizure disorder; the parent's or child's report of certain headache patterns or marked changes in headache patterns; signs of other possible neurological disturbance. The neurologist will do a thorough neurological examination and, in addition, may recommend an electroencephalogram (EEG), computerized tomography (CT scan), or magnetic resonance imaging (MRI).

Psychiatrist. Significant emotional disturbance, hyperactivity, and the possible need for drug therapy as part of follow-up treatment are the most common reasons for a referral to a psychiatrist after the evaluation. The psychiatrist meets with the parent to learn about the results of the comprehensive psychological evaluation. Then he or she meets with the child and interviews him.

Ophthalmologist. If it seems that a child may have a vision problem and might need glasses, a referral to an ophthalmologist will be made. The exam will include such tests as identifying letters —or, in the case of a very young child, pictures—of varying sizes.

Audiologist. Often, what seems to be poor language ability or slow speech development is in fact a hearing problem—or vice versa. A referral to an audiologist may be necessary if there has been a delay in your child's speech development or understanding of spoken language. "Negative" behavior may simply be a manifestation of a hearing problem. If your child is persistently uncooperative (always doing something other than what he has been told to do) or persistently forgetful (never doing what he was told to do), an audiologist may be asked to test him. Among the tools that an audiologist uses are the audiometer (an instrument to measure the degree of sharpness of hearing) and a technique called brain stem auditory evoked potential (BAEP). With BAEP, no child is too young or too impaired to be evaluated for a problem in his auditory system.

Language and speech pathologist. Whenever a child's history, his behavior including his verbalizations during testing, or his performance on specific tests suggests a significant language or speech problem, a referral is made to a language and speech pathologist. This individual examines in detail the full range of your child's language abilities—the quality of his spontaneous speech, his comprehension of spoken words, his ability to name things, and so on. The specialist also notes specific aspects of your child's speech, such as the way he articulates and the rhythm and fluency of his speech. In addition, the mobility of your child's lips, mouth, and tongue are examined.

Are You Satisfied?

The final question you have to ask yourself, when the comprehensive evaluation is over, is whether you have confidence in the findings and recommendations. What if you have received answers to all your questions, but somehow they just don't hang together? What if you see downright contradictions between the reported test scores and the interpretation of the results? What if the evaluator's recommendations don't fit with her interpretations—for example, suppose she tells you that your child has a learning disability but recommends no follow-up treatment?

The evaluation is only the beginning of the process of helping your child. To go forward effectively, you must have confidence in what you have learned about your child and how best to help him. Do you have lingering doubts? Doubts are a common initial reaction when parents are first told about the presence of a true problem, but if yours persist, you should get a second opinion. Once again, use your referral network to identify another qualified professional, in the public or private sector, who can review and interpret the results of your child's evaluation, or perhaps reevaluate him, if necessary.

CHAPTER 9

Treatment–What Kind? How Long?

L et's assume that your child has gone through the evaluation process outlined in Chapter 9, that the main issues of concern to you have been untangled, and that it has been determined that a learning disability does exist. Let's also assume that the evaluation, provided as it should, information about your child's emotional strengths and weaknesses as well as his strengths and weaknesses in learning. We know that emotional well-being is crucial to learning—a child cannot learn if he is distressed, full of self-doubt and misgivings. What kind of treatment might be recommended, and how long will it take?

_____ WHAT KIND OF TREATMENT?

The forms of treatment most likely to be recommended on the basis of a comprehensive psychological examination are remediation, for treatment of a learning disability, and psychotherapy, the usual treatment for emotional problems. The recommendation may be for remediation only, for psychotherapy first and then remediation, or for both psychotherapy and remediation at the same time. Sometimes it is suggested that psychotherapy is all the treatment that a child with a learning disability needs. We strongly disagree with this position, for reasons that we'll explain as we briefly discuss the different treatment options. In any case, given a recommendation about treatment from a professional, you, the parent, must decide about what kind of treatment, if any at all, your child is going to have.

Remediation alone. All children who are struggling with learning show some degree of emotional distress—it is one of the hallmarks of a learning disability. Nevertheless, in a good number of cases, and especially when the evaluation is done early, children with learning disabilities can be successfully treated with remediation alone. They can make significant strides forward, both in learning and in the emotional domain, without psychotherapy.

A recommendation that a child with a learning disability be treated with remediation alone should not be seen as a downplaying of his emotional shakiness. Rather, it is a testimony to the power of positive feedback, coming from the child's new experience of learning successfully, and to the effect of a positive relationship with a skilled remediator. When remediation helps a child succeed in school, he will begin to believe in himself again. His ego will get an enormous and much-needed boost, and his emotional state will improve immensely—particularly if he is young and doesn't carry scars from years and years of school failure. This is not to say that the feelings of self-doubt and the fears of failure are forgotten but, rather, that the child can now move on in a productive and relatively healthy way.

Psychotherapy followed by remediation. Sometimes psychotherapy is needed before a child's learning disability can be directly treated through remediation. This may be the case, for example, when a child is feeling so bad about himself, so full of doubt and uncertainty, that he is in no state to undertake the hard work of remediation. Psychotherapy will help him feel better about himself. He will become more open to new experiences and better able to profit from the relationship with the remediator when the time comes. He will be better able to handle his frustrations as he confronts learning.

But psychotherapy alone is typically not enough. There is a limit to the extent to which improved emotional well-being translates into an improved ability to learn when particular academic areas are compromised by a learning disability. Specialized teaching strategies are essential. Without them, he will continue to falter in his schoolwork and will experience the same old frustration and shame. And this, in turn, may undermine the gains he has made in psychotherapy.

How much psychotherapy is needed before remediation can begin? There is no cut-and-dried answer to this. If remediation is started too soon, the psychotherapeutic process of rebuilding the child's self-confidence may be affected. If remediation is delayed too long, and school continues to be a negative experience for the child, much of the good work done in therapy will be lost. Remediation should begin when a child is ready emotionally—and this may happen quickly or may take some time. Once he is emotionally on an even keel—but not before—remedial treatment will help him learn. Once again a professional can make recommendations about whether your child is ready for remediation. As a parent, you must make the final decision.

Remediation and psychotherapy together. Sometimes, it makes good sense to provide psychotherapy and remediation at the same time. The benefits of remediation will be greater and will come faster when concurrent therapy reinforces the child's growing sense of well-being. In other cases, the best treatment may be to combine remediation with counseling about college plans or vocational goals. Or remediation might go hand in hand with family counseling to deal with problematic relationships among family members.

———— REMEDIATION

Remediation is the treatment of choice for a learning disability. It follows a comprehensive evaluation that has identified areas of intellectual strength and weakness and the role neurological functions play in a child's academic difficulty. The treatment utilizes a variety of teaching strategies including techniques that recruit adequately developed or strong functions to do the work that less developed or weak ones can't manage so well. To the extent that it's possible, a child learns to capitalize on his strengths. His treatment is designed on an individual basis to meet his specific learning needs.

The brain can go about its work in many different ways. Remediation focuses on the best way to bypass a subtle neurological problem that interferes with the learning of some basic skill. The neurological problem that causes a learning disability does not "disappear" through remediation, and at present we do not know how to "fix" it. We do know, though, that it is often possible to defuse it through alternative teaching strategies. No one can ever guarantee the success of remediation, or a child's ability to apply the gains made in his remediation sessions to daily work in the classroom. But with this kind of treatment, there is a greater possibility that a child's learning and his sense of himself as a student will improve.

There are as many ways to get around a learning disability as there are types of disability. Yet, by and large, appropriate remediation should include certain techniques and exclude others. A parent can assess at the outset whether a professional is using a remedial strategy that has a good chance of succeeding. Here are some guidelines:

- The remediation should build from a level where the child is competent. Using the child's strengths, it should proceed in tiny steps to the challenge of more difficult tasks.
- The remediator should start out by teaching the child a new and special way to master something that he has been struggling with in school—for example, a kind of "trick."
- If your child remains disillusioned and frustrated over many months, the remediator should continue to search for better strategies and techniques.
- The remediator should always be in close contact with the parent and also with the child's school, if appropriate.
- As the remediation begins to work, your child will, it is hoped, begin to show a new confidence and interest in school subjects he used to avoid.

Treatment that begins with rote drills or the repetitive copying of words or the recitation of multiplication tables is *not* remediation. It is tutoring, and this is neither individualized treatment nor adequate treatment for a child with a learning disability. This is such a key point that we'll repeat it: tutoring is not remediation.

Tutoring involves the repeated review and practice of poorly understood material. But practice does not make perfect with a child who has a learning disability. If it did, he would be at the top of his class, in command of all the skills he has tried so hard and so often to master. Tutoring such a child simply doesn't help. Tantrums and tears are more likely to be the result than a significant improvement in skills when a tutor—or for that matter, a parent —tries to help a child by using repetition and drills. It is impossible to overemphasize how important it is that a child's treatment program be fashioned specifically to address the core problem found in his comprehensive evaluation.

Consider Susie's story—and pat yourself on the back, knowing that you would have handled the situation differently.

_____ *Susie.* This very verbal eight-year-old impressed adults as a bright child. Her problem first became apparent at the end of second grade, when her marks dropped. Scores on standardized tests revealed that her skills were below grade level, especially in reading comprehension and arithmetic number story problems. She also began to have behavior problems at home, arguing with her siblings, even sometimes disobeying her parents.

Susie's parents thought her problems at home were a passing phase. They would help her with her school work during the summer. This was a total disaster. The more they insisted on a study time each day, the more she rebelled. By the time Susie returned to school in the fall, she was refusing even to mention reading or arithmetic. This continued into the term: her parents rarely saw her doing homework, and she wouldn't show them her books or talk to her parents about school. In the first marking period of third grade, Susie did very poorly in all her subjects except art and music.

In despair, Susie's parent's told some neighbors how badly their daughter was doing in school. These neighbors recommended that they get in touch with Joanna, a high school girl who baby-sat for them and also did some tutoring to earn money for college. Susie's parents contacted Joanna and told her they wanted to have their daughter tutored. By the time they went for their next parent-teacher conference, everything was in place and Susie's teacher applauded their quick attention to the problem.

For the rest of the school year, Susie worked with Joanna three afternoons a week, going over homework and studying for tests. But the gap between her performance and that of her classmates widened. And she began to complain about her teachers and about having to go to school at all. As if that were not enough, her behavior at home worsened. As things escalated, her parents became increasingly angry—with the school, the tutor, and their daughter herself.

At the final parent-teacher conference that year, Susie's parents were told that the current school placement was not meeting their daughter's needs and that she should be evaluated for possible special class placement. In their eagerness to help right away, and in their ignorance about learning disabilities, Susie's parents had just barged ahead. The underlying disability had never been identified or addressed.

The Remediator

The evaluator should be able to give you the name of a good setting, public or private, or a particular remediator, with experience in teaching children new ways to learn particular academic skills while bypassing the specific underlying disability.

In our view, those best suited to the task are educators who are experienced in the normal learning process, who have an understanding of how specific brain inefficiencies affect certain aspects of learning, and who appreciate the impact of emotional and environmental factors on learning. Educators with this kind of background can address the numerous problems that a child with a learning disability so often has. They have the training and experience to grasp the findings of a comprehensive evaluation and to design and implement a remedial program based on its results. They can also tailor the remedial procedures to the learning needs of a particular child, gauging a child's responses to the learning task and the remedial techniques, and then modifying those techniques as needed.

Let's illustrate. Suppose a child has been evaluated and has been found to have a learning disability rooted in inefficient visual memory functions. He has great difficulty remembering information that is presented visually and has a somewhat easier time remembering information he hears. A remediator with the kind of specialized training and experience we have described will understand the implications of the evaluation. He or she will be able to develop and carry out remedial techniques that minimize the need for the child to hold a "picture" of new information in his mind. If, for example, he has to learn the relative locations of the thirteen original states (something that children usually learn by memorizing what they see on a map), he or she will teach him to say them in order, in a north-to-south sequence. This "trick" makes use of the child's auditory memory functions (a relative strength) and bypasses his weak visual memory functions.

As we mentioned earlier, a factor in the choice of a remediator is his or her particular area of expertise. We can illustrate the importance of this by looking at Paul's case.

_____ *Paul.* Ten-year-old Paul had been struggling with his schoolwork, especially math, all year. Finally, his parents decided to take him for a comprehensive psychological evaluation. The results suggested that Paul had a number of underlying weaknesses that were affecting his ability to learn through traditional approaches. Because math was especially difficult for him, the evaluator recommended a remediator who was skilled in working with children with arithmetic disabilities. Though Paul needed work in other areas, too, the remediator initially focused on computation. In written computations, Paul always had trouble knowing where to begin. Somehow he had managed in the earlier grades to do multicolumn addition and subtraction, but faced with multiplying two digits by two digits, he was at a loss. The remediator taught Paul a special trick for doing double-digit multiplication: drawing a bow tie on top of the four numbers (Figure 9-1). First, Paul was taught to join four dots in a special sequence. He practiced this until the sequence was well known or automatic. The process of drawing resulted in the learning of a motor pattern. Next, he was taught to superimpose the automatic motor act on a 2 digit by 2 digit multiplication problem. This provided a fail-safe work pattern for double-digit multiplication. All the tutoring in the world would not have achieved this. Paul's remediator worked with him through the rest of the year, taking one stumbling block at a time and designing a new approach—perhaps, a new gimmick—whenever Paul faltered in his learning.

_____ **PSYCHOTHERAPY**

Psychotherapy, sometimes in conjunction with medication, is the treatment most often used for emotional and behavioral problems in

FIGURE 9-1

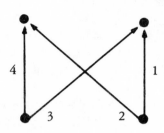

The child is taught to join the dots in the sequence illustrated above. He practices this until the sequence is very well known, or automatic.

Next he is taught to superimpose the "automatic" motor act on a two-digit by two-digit multiplication problem. This provides a fail-safe trick for remembering the order in which these numbers are multiplied.

children. Nor surprisingly, children with learning disabilities often have a variety of such problems, which affect their sense of self and their interpersonal relations.

Emotional and Behavioral Problems

The psychological development of a child whose brain is working inefficiently is hindered on two levels. First, his ability to deal with the "tasks" he faces in infancy, childhood, and adolescence is jeopardized. Second, he feels emotional distress, in reaction to his difficulties in the social and academic areas of his life. And so, in response to the consequences of his neurological inefficiency, he experiences a range of uncomfortable feelings: frustration, anger, embarrassment, confusion, sadness, fear.

This emotional distress may not always be easily recognizable, but it is always there. Signs of even slight emotional stress may be very noticeable in one child, and much greater emotional distress not noticeable at all in another. One child may deal with his confusion by withdrawing. He may seem to be content with going to his room and occupying himself. His parents will probably see him as happy, independent, and "good"—a child they need have no concerns about. Another child may express his frustration by acting out, flying all over the place like a windup toy let loose, and being uncooperative. His parents will likely see him as a "difficult" child who is angry and upset about something but will get over it soon. These two children are both at risk for not attracting the kind of attention and support they need.

The emotional and behavioral problems associated with learning disabilities may have a number of effects. One effect is that the emotional and behavioral problems aggravate an existing learning disability. Phil is an example of this. He is in the third grade and having enormous difficulty learning to read. His anger, frustration, and sense of self-doubt are intense—so intense that he can seldom read the shortest passage without crying, or throwing his book on the floor, or actually bolting from the classroom. It's the same at home, when his parents try to help. Socially Phil is isolated; his peers and his siblings find him angry and aggressive. Because of his emotional state, and the resulting behavior, it is hard to make sustained attempts to work on his reading. Hence, Phil's reading difficulty is not abating, and the emotional and behavioral consequences of his disability are getting worse and worse.

Emotional and behavioral problems may also undermine an ability that had developed adequately. This is the case with Leslie. She has terrible difficulty remembering material for tests at school. In truth, her memory abilities are fine, but they are undermined by self-doubt that sweeps over her whenever she is confronted with any schoolwork. This self-doubt started in reaction to difficulties with reading early on. Although she now reads well, through intensive remediation, a vicious circle has set in: her self-doubt, originally triggered by her reading disability, has created a situation in which she can't make use of her memory abilities.

In the long term, the emotional and behavioral problems associated with learning disabilities may eventually become more than a reaction to the learning difficulties; they become part of the way a child experiences his world and part of his behavior pattern. The uncomfortable feelings and the behavior they produce come to permeate all aspects of the child's life, not just his life at school. This is how it is with Tom, a tenth-grader. His learning difficulties are extremely subtle and he has been able to compensate for them with long hours of study. But the price he has paid emotionally and behaviorally is high. Tom feels that he is "damaged" and "not quite right." He avoids close relationships for fear that, when people really get to know him, they will realize his weakness. A relationship with a girl is out of the question. Overcompensating for his feelings of inferiority, Tom comes across as an intellectual snob. He has a know-it-all facade.

The Therapeutic Approach

There are different therapeutic approaches to the treatment of emotional and behavioral problems. The therapeutic approach may be psychoanalytic (or a modification of this) or behavioral. Psychoanalytic theory holds that emotional problems stem from unconscious conflicts—an individual's attempts to defend himself against unacceptable feelings and impulses that are a product of his early experiences. The modified psychoanalytic approach also holds that emotional problems result from unconscious conflicts, but rather than focusing on an individual's past history, it emphasizes the role of interpersonal relationships and cultural factors. Behavioral theory holds that emotional and behavioral disturbances are the consequence of maladaptive learning.

Although these three therapeutic approaches differ in their theories about the source of emotional and behavioral disturbance, they share a number of common goals and practices. They all aim to educate or reeducate an individual regarding his emotions and his behavior, to help him reach a better understanding of the basis of his feelings and actions, and to develop new and better ways of interacting with other people. It is important to remember that, whatever the particular approach, psychotherapy is a gradual, step-by-step process. Only rarely does an individual have sudden flashes of total understanding or make sudden and dramatic behavioral changes. But over time he may come to apply in his daily life what he has learned in his therapist's office.

The Psychotherapist

A child with emotional and behavioral problems may be treated in a public or private setting by a psychiatrist, a psychologist, a psychiatric social worker, or a psychiatric nurse. These mental health professionals differ in their educational background (for example, a psychiatrist has an M.D. degree; a psychologist has a Ph.D.) and the scope of their practice (for example, a psychiatrist is licensed to prescribe medication; a psychologist administers and interprets psychological tests).

Whatever his or her formal qualifications, the psychotherapist working with a child who has a learning disability must be someone who appreciates both the impact of a learning disability on a child's emotional state and the impact of emotional and environmental factors on his learning. An understanding of brain-behavior relationships is also important, because this will enable the psychotherapist to tailor the approach to a child's strengths and weaknesses.

_____ FOLLOWING UP ON A RECOMMENDATION

Let's assume that you have been given the name of a remediator, a psychotherapist, or both, in a particular setting, public or private, such as a public school, clinic, or private office. When following up on the recommendation you should be prepared to ask some pointed questions. There are things you should know at the outset, before you make a commitment to go forward. Ask these questions when you make the initial telephone call.

Credentials. In the case of a remediator, you should ask whether he or she has a degree in education and is licensed in your state. Does he or she have specialty certification? If so, in what area? Has he or she received other types of special training, done extra course work, or attended specialty workshops? If appropriate, is he or she affiliated with a hospital, clinic, or university? How long has he or she been working in this area? How much experience does he or she have in working with the particular learning disability at hand?

In the case of a mental health professional, you should ask

similar questions. You need to know about educational background, licensing, and additional training. Affiliation with a hospital, clinic, or university is also important, since this involves ongoing review of credentials and professional work. (Remember, though, that there are some fine professionals who are not affiliated with any institution.) Experience is again the key factor. You should ask how long this professional has been working with children and how many children he or she has seen with specific needs similar to those of your child.

Cost. Remediation and psychotherapy provided in a public school setting are free, regardless of family income. In clinics, fees are based on family income. They range from no charge on up. Fees for remediation and psychotherapy in the private sector are usually, but not always, higher than the maximum clinic fee. You should ask what the fee, if any, covers. How long is a session? Is there a charge for phone conferences? You should also establish at the outset when the payment, if any, is due.

Under most conditions, remediation is not covered by medical insurance. Psychotherapy, whether in a public or private setting, may or may not be covered by your insurance policy. If it is, you should check to see whether there are limitations in your coverage. The policy may stipulate who can provide the service, how many sessions a year are covered, and the maximum amount that is reimbursable per year (or per lifetime).

_____ PREPARING YOUR CHILD FOR TREATMENT

Many young children have the clear sense that remediation is for "dummies" and that psychotherapy is for "crazies"—they have heard all about it from their classmates. They announce to their parents in no uncertain terms that they will not be tutored, that they don't want or need any help at all. What can you do to help your child get ready for treatment?

• Be sure that you yourself really appreciate the importance of this treatment for your child. If you feel ambivalent about your child's need for treatment, or angry at the evaluator about her recommendation for it, your child will pick up on your negative feelings.

• Tell your child that you have arranged for treatment because you know that he wants to do well in school, get along better with his friends, and have things be easier at home. In the case of remediation, tell him that he needs to learn some special ways to do his schoolwork. His work will look the same as his classmates' but he may get it done in a different way: perhaps, he'll use a tailor-made, streamlined "trick" that the remediator will teach him. If psychotherapy has been recommended, tell him that by seeing the therapist he will feel better inside. By feeling better, he may be better able to do his schoolwork and may find that things are easier for him with his friends and at home.

• Rest assured that, with good individualized teaching, your child has a better shot at learning and that with psychotherapy his overall well-being is likely to improve. Tell him that you know he feels frustrated by how things are going now, or that you know that with help he may be able to do his work more easily and enjoy it more, too.

• Don't broach the subject with an apology: "I know you won't like what I'm going to tell you, and I promise it won't go on very long, but . . ." If you begin by apologizing or by offering bribes to get your child to his sessions, he is certain to start off on the wrong foot. Reassure your child that he will probably like the remediator —or the psychotherapist—very much, and that this person is really looking forward to meeting him and working with him.

• Don't give him a choice as to whether or not he'll have treatment. You have decided, on the basis of the comprehensive psychological evaluation, that treatment is a must. Arrange for it and tell your child about the plan you have made. As in the case of going for the evaluation, this is not negotiable. If your child needed physical therapy after breaking a leg, you would be sure he got to his appointment every week, even if he did complain about it.

———— LENGTH OF TREATMENT

One question parents almost always have about their child's treatment, whether it is remediation or some combination of remediation and psychotherapy, is how long it will take. And we have to answer that we don't know—there are simply too many factors to be considered. These include the state of the child's emotional well-being; the type of learning disability he has and how severe it is;

the strengths and weaknesses he has; his motivation; the size of the gap between his current performance and the performance expected of him; the amount of support his family and his school give him; and the caliber of the treatment he is receiving or will receive. With so many crucial variables, it is impossible to say that the needed work will take a certain, definite number of months or years. Parents should be wary of any professional who promises a "quick fix" or who says confidently at the outset that treatment won't take longer than, say, six months or even one year.

CHAPTER 10

Coping

What about *you?* What have you been feeling since the early days when you began to suspect that something about your child just wasn't right? His development and behavior must have been cause for concern. What were your reactions when you were told that he did indeed have a learning disability? Has this brought back all your worst memories of how you yourself suffered in school? Does knowing that the problem can be treated bring some relief, along with the pain and worry? The more in touch with your own feelings you are, the more comfortable you are likely to be with your child's learning disability and the better you'll be able to help him deal with it, in all its aspects—academic, emotional, and social.

THE EMOTIONAL FALLOUT

The presence of a child with a learning disability affects parents' feelings about themselves, their relationships with their other children, their jobs, their friendships, and their marriage. Again and again, parents have described the same range of feelings to us. You may have experienced some of these emotions in the past; you may be experiencing some of them now. They are what most parents cannot help but feel in response to a child's learning disability and its consequences.

Sadness. The sorrowful feeling that your child is not the perfect being you expected and wanted; deep distress about the "loss" of that perfect child. The reliving of past losses.

Frustration. The sense of being worn down, at your wits' end. You have tried everything to help your child learn better, feel better, and behave better. Nothing has worked.

Ambivalence. The feeling of vacillating back and forth—on the one hand wishing that your child's problem had never existed and, on the other, being certain that there is no single problem in the world that you are more ready and willing to tackle.

Shame. The embarrassment you feel when your child performs so badly or behaves so inappropriately, in school or out.

Pain. The feeling you have as you see your child's frustration, confusion, and distress in the face of his social and academic failures. No matter how hard he tries, it is never enough.

Deprivation. The feelings accompanying the giving up of the short- and long-term plans you had for this child; the sense that some of your goals and hopes have been taken away from you.

Disappointment. The sense of being thwarted in your desire for a "normal" child whose development and performance are just as expected.

Envy. The wish that your child was like your friend's child, who is just sailing right along. Sometimes envy takes the form of resentment toward another person whose child seems problem-free.

Inadequacy. Feelings of not being up to par, of not having enough of what an individual needs to be a competent person or parent. These feelings may occur when a parent experiences a child's disability as a measure of his or her own shortcomings.

Fear. The feeling of dread about all the unknowns that lie ahead. Who is going to help? Will these problems ever go away? Will *you* survive? Will *he* make out all right? Also the sense of overwhelming apprehension about the well-being of your child today.

Having lived for many years with a flood of feelings about this special child, you may think that you have run the emotional gamut as far as he is concerned. But when you are told that he does indeed have a learning disability, you can expect to experience a number of emotions that may be new to you. These emotions are in many ways similar to those experienced by anyone confronting a significant loss.

One reaction is typically that of denial. You ask yourself, "Can this be true?" and quickly answer, "No, of course not." The competence of the professional who evaluated your child is questioned. The competence of the child's school is questioned. The child's significant difficulties in school or at home (or both) are denied—even though they triggered the decision to get an evaluation in the first place.

In addition, parents commonly experience feelings of anger. The anger may be directed inward, or toward the other parent, or both. Anger may also be directed toward the child's teacher, or the evaluator, or the child himself. Often a parent's anger is spread around and everyone gets a taste of it.

There are attempts to assign responsibility for the child's learning disability. If you turned your anger about the situation inward, against yourself, you may also put the blame for your child's disability on yourself. You may find yourself thinking, If only I had been home more . . . not taken that job . . . been more observant. A history of learning disabilities in your family will heighten your tendency to blame yourself. On the other hand, if you directed your anger outward, a pattern of placing responsibility for the disability on others will develop. You see the child's difficulty as the fault of the *other* parent and the history of learning problems in *that* family, or as the school's fault, or the teacher's.

There is acceptance. Feelings of denial, anger, and blame are part of the emotional process through which parents come to accept the fact that their child has a learning disability. In time, most parents work through them, resolve them, and reach a state of acceptance. They recognize that a problem exists and something must be done about it. Occasionally, however, resolution is not obtained and the feelings linger, becoming destructive not only to the parents and their relationship but also to the child who needs help and to the family as a whole.

Parents can also expect to experience a feeling of relief. It springs from having charted an action plan and being on the way to getting the child the help he needs. For some, it comes early, when they are first told that a learning disability exists. For others, it comes only when acceptance is in place. Either way, acceptance and relief are not usually lasting feelings; they will come and go in the months and years ahead.

When the child faces a new difficulty, when a parent's own emotional energy is on the ebb, all of the old feelings of denial, anger, and blame are likely to resurface. If these feelings are long-lasting, or interfere unduly with daily living, get back to the professional who evaluated your child, for guidance about where to go for help.

COPING, DAY TO DAY

So many aspects of day-to-day family life are problematic for parents of a child with a learning disability. There are the other children in the family. What are they feeling and how do their feelings translate into behavior? What can you do to help them? What about daily routines? How can they be adjusted to accommodate one child without upsetting everybody else's family life? Another area of difficulty is homework. Should you be actively involved or not? And what about all the extra social support that your child needs to get through the day fairly smoothly? What should you do to help him? And at the same time, how do you encourage him to be more independent?

Every child needs his parents' support and the structure they give to his life. A child with a learning disability often needs more support, more structure. It's no easy task to balance a child's special difficulties with his need to learn age-appropriate behavior (saying "please" and "thank you") and skills (taking messages). But it is important to begin this learning early so that your child's self-care and social skills keep pace with those of children his own age. Flexibility, creativity, and understanding are a parent's best allies.

Siblings

The impact of a child with a learning disability on the relationship among siblings can be profound. *All* the children are affected, and the special bond that parents want their children to feel toward one another may be threatened.

Siblings usually feel shortchanged when parents seem to devote a disproportionate amount of time and energy to one child. They feel jealous of their sibling and unimportant in their parents' eyes. They resent what they see as their parents' favoritism, overindulgence, or permissiveness. They begrudge their sibling the time he takes away from their own story time or playtime or special outing time with their parents. They feel angry about a perceived double standard: one set of rules and expectations for them, another for him. They may start to imitate their sibling as a way of getting attention or become guilt-ridden because they themselves don't have a learning disability.

In school, siblings often pay a price for their brother's or sister's disability. Their friends call them part of the "dumbo family" and are always making fun of their sibling. There are times when they find him an embarrassment—and other times when they feel guilty about their embarrassment or their resentment or anger. They may be concerned that they, too, might have a learning disability or will "catch" one. One child we know insisted on having an evaluation, even though she was a good student at a highly competitive school. Her sister had been diagnosed as having a learning disability and in need of special education. She wanted to be sure that she was "all right." She also wanted equal treatment.

The child with the disability often experiences the same feelings of jealousy, anger, guilt, embarrassment, and concern as his siblings —but on different grounds. He may be jealous of his siblings' superior abilities, angry that things are so hard for him, guilty about the sacrifices the family is making on his behalf, embarrassed by his failures, concerned about day-to-day existence in school and about the future.

The best way to help all your children feel better about the situation is to have a frank discussion with them. Everyone should be included. You might start the discussion off with something like this: "John has a learning disability, as you perhaps guessed. That means that he learns differently from the way the rest of you do. It's not his fault or anyone's fault. And it doesn't mean that he's sick or anything—in fact, he's as healthy as you are. What it *does* means is that he needs help in learning some things in special ways. He'll be going to a remediator for help, so that he can learn to do many things quicker and better. His work will look just the same as yours, but sometimes he'll be using some tailor-made 'tricks' to get there. Maybe he'll even want to share some of those tricks with you." If your child will be seeing a psychotherapist, you will want to discuss this in the same frank manner.

Such a family discussion may have to be repeated from time to time. Watch for signs that trouble is brewing—more squabbles than usual, more tattling—and call a family conference before things get out of hand.

You don't have to deal by yourself with the impact of your child's learning disability on the rest of the family. There are support groups for the parents of children with learning disabilities, and we have been told time and again how helpful they are. Some of the national organizations that provide information for parents about learning disabilities, listed in Appendix 3, can provide names and addresses of support groups. Family therapy and counseling can also be extremely useful in helping all of you deal with your painful feelings and with the demands of daily living, as these are affected by the needs of a child with a learning disability.

Daily Routines

When one family member's special problem renders some aspect of a daily routine particularly cumbersome or difficult, the regular beat of day-to-day living for an entire family loses its rhythm. A child with a learning disability often can't pull his full weight. He needs more supervision and more time to do his share at home. The more structure you provide and the more guidance you give him in developing adequate skills, the easier he will find the routines of daily living—and the sooner he will become more independent.

We'll mention some of the situations that parents describe as being especially problematic and give you some suggestions about ways in which things can go more smoothly. Many of these practical ideas come from parents we have worked with.

Getting ready to leave for school. Because a child with a learning disability often needs more time than others to get washed and dressed, eat breakfast, gather his papers, and leave for school, he should get up earlier. He will also probably need many reminders about what he has to do. It will be helpful to pin up a chart with pictures (for younger children) or a list of what is to be done and in what order. He'll also need help in organizing what he has to bring to school and what he is going to wear. It is a good idea to get this done before he goes to bed, rather than in the morning.

Mealtimes. Family chores such as setting the table and clearing the dishes may be especially difficult for a child with a learning disability. He can learn to do his share, but standards may have to be adjusted a little for him. If he has trouble remembering how to set the table, it is helpful to give him a paper mat with the correct place setting drawn on it. He will also benefit from your help in organizing the job. Tell him to go first to the kitchen and count out four forks, spoons, knives, and glasses. Then spell out a strategy for the next step—for example, tell him to put a knife next to each glass. If counting to four is a problem for your child, adjust the first step by giving him the right number of things or by having him put one of everything in front of each chair (you then arrange the flatware and glasses for him).

Table manners may also be a problem area. If your child's motor coordination makes cutting difficult, you should cut for him, but at the same time insist on appropriate eating behavior. If table conversation is difficult for your child—because he has a language problem, or a memory problem, or is just so self-conscious about his poor ability to express himself that he has nothing to say—be sure to make every effort to include him. Give him opportunities to contribute at his own level. Try to avoid making him feel "different," because this usually results in the acting-out behavior that gets him into trouble. In the mind of a child with a learning disability, negative attention is often preferable to no attention at all, and he knows just how to get it at home.

Bedtime. A major area of difficulty for a child with a learning disability is organizing what he has to do and when. Transitional times are also difficult. So bedtime often presents problems. Your child will probably need help structuring his bedtime activities—bathing, brushing his teeth, saying good-night, and so on. Again, a set of pictures or a list may help him remember what he has to do. Getting clothes ready for the next day can be made easier for him if spaces in his drawers and closets are marked with bright signs or appropriate pictures. Reading to your child, after all bedtime preparations are completed, helps make this transitional time smooth and pleasant.

Household chores. Children need to learn to be responsible, and having a share of the household chores is the usual starting point. A child with a learning disability typically has difficulty doing his full share. This often creates conflicts with his siblings as well as frustration in his parents. But it is very important that you expect this child to be a contributing member of the family and that you act on this expectation. Your ten-year-old may not be like other ten-year-olds who can be expected to run an errand to a neighbor. But rather than avoid asking him to do such an age-appropriate chore, you may be able to get around his anticipated difficulties. You could write out simple instructions for him, for example, or give him a written message to deliver. His ability to remember telephone messages may be poor, but a pad and pencil readily available by the phone should help him. And a reminder list, using pictures or words, of the household chores he is expected to do should be pinned to the bulletin board in his room.

Homework. Homework is often a battleground for a child with a learning disability. Bad enough to have to go to school, but to have to do school work at home is too much altogether!

To what extent should a parent be involved? Every case is different. Help with homework may range from directly working with a child on his assignments to establishing a good environment for study. In some cases it helps to have a parent very much involved. In others, a hands-off policy works best. Your child's teacher, remediator, and psychotherapist should be able to help you to decide how much help, and what kind of help, you should give him. It is important to find the style of helping that best matches your child's needs, his temperament, and the overall demands on his time—and *your* needs, temperament, and schedule as well. Your first role is that of parent, not educator.

Whatever your child's specific disability, and whatever your style of helping, homework will go more smoothly when you give your child guidance with organization and when you provide him with structure and extra time.

A child with a learning disability usually has special difficulty organizing his things. He may need help getting his books and papers together and organizing what he has to do. Notes and tests can be kept in order by putting each subject in a separate, colored folder; books can be carried in a knapsack, keeping everything in its proper place. It may be necessary to work out a system with his teacher to ensure that all assignments are correctly noted and that all needed books find their way home. One parent of a fourth grader we know established a "homework buddy system" at the start of each school year. This enabled her to get hold of notes and assignments from her child's individual classroom "buddy" whenever her child missed a class.

Establishing a set time and place for doing homework provides structure. Homework requires quiet and freedom from distraction, so settle your child somewhere out of the household hurly-burly. Whether the work is done immediately after he comes home from school or after a short break, the time should be the same every day, overall schedule permitting.

Extra time for certain kinds of assignments—perhaps a book report or an oral report—is usually a must for children with learning disabilities. Your child may have to stay up later than his siblings or start his work earlier than they do; he may have to do more homework on weekends. If you feel that he is spending too much time getting his homework done, you should let his teacher know. Accommodation may be possible. For example, a child with a writing problem might be excused from copying a spelling list or might be allowed to turn in a book report that he has dictated to you.

Social Problems

A child with a learning disability often becomes withdrawn, avoiding contact with his classmates and with neighborhood children. When he does venture out, he may look for children younger than himself as playmates. Or he may want to play with children his own age but be rejected by them because he is aggressive, bossy, or immature. Often unable to accurately read social clues, he may have difficulty getting on with other children. Many children with learning disabilities also have difficulty learning the subtleties of social interaction with adults. They may tend to gravitate toward adults, however, because adults are generally more accepting than are their peers. At family gatherings, they talk to the aunts and uncles, not to the cousins.

There are at least three different ways in which you can smooth your child's path while at the same time helping him develop good social skills. You can make good judgments about what social behavior should be expected of him and teach him the necessary skills —for example, shaking hands. You can anticipate areas of difficulty and promote his opportunities for successful social interaction—for example, a summer job as a camp counselor, rather than as a clerk in the local deli, for a youngster who has difficulty with arithmetic. And you can monitor his social activities. Remember that the approach you use should match your child's age and his social development.

Never allow your child to behave at home in a way that is unacceptable or inappropriate outside the home. There should be no forgetting to say "please" and "thank you" and no eating with fingers for a five-year-old. All children need to learn the rules of social behavior, and the learning starts at home.

It is important to encourage social activities that don't set this child apart from other children. For a child with a reading problem and great athletic ability, you should encourage all kinds of sports activities. For a child with a reading problem and poor sports skills, activities such as moviegoing or hobby clubs should be fostered.

As the parent of a child with a learning disability, you must monitor closely his interaction with other children. Knowing that this is almost certainly an area of difficulty for him, you should pay close attention and be ready to help him. While he is a preschooler, you can intercede on his behalf, teaching him appropriate behavior on the spot. By the time he is in fourth grade, such intercession is more problematic—if it is possible at all. Suggestions about better ways of handling social problems usually have to wait until later.

Your youngster should not be allowed to retreat or withdraw, but he shouldn't be pressured into social interactions that are beyond him; he should enjoy his social life. His social activities may require more than the usual amount of supervision on your part, but his participation in these activities is essential if he is to develop social skills, become confident and self-reliant, and establish his own identity.

In your concern about your child's social life, don't forget to make sure that he also has time to himself. All children need time to think, to develop interests and pursue hobbies, to be alone. This child of yours is no different.

THE SCHOOL

You should be aware of an important legal fact that applies to every child with a learning disability, whatever the particular circumstances. The letter of the law is this: your child has a *legal right* to a free and appropriate education in a setting that meets his needs. In 1976, the federal government passed a law—Public Law (PL) 94-142, the Education of all Handicapped Children Act—which gives children with specific learning disabilities, as well as children with a wide range of other handicaps, both protection and certain rights. The law stipulates that education is a fundamental right of all handicapped children and that every child has a right to an appropriate education. You should be familiar with the provisions of this law, which applies to children age three through twenty-one years. You should also be familiar with PL 99-457, passed in 1986. It extends the protection and the rights defined in PL 94-142 to children with handicaps who are two years old and younger. The major advocacy groups that provide information about learning disabilities to parents (see Appendix 3) can send you summaries of the laws and can answer your questions about the laws and what they mean in terms of seeing that your child gets the help he needs.

In addition to the extremely important legal question hinging on PL 94-142, you should bear in mind a number of vital issues regarding your child's schooling. The first is communication. Communication between you and your child's school can take very different forms, depending on everyone's style and schedule. In some schools, it may be best to deal with the child's teacher. In others, it is better to be in close communication with the head of the school or the head of the division (lower, middle, or upper school) as well as with the teacher. Sometimes school specialists—the reading specialist, the resource room teacher—are the best source for up-to-date communication about your child's progress or lack of it. In any case, regular meetings between you and school personnel are essential. Some parents find face-to-face meetings most productive; for others, regular telephone conferences are satisfactory.

Good communication between you and your child's remediator or therapist is also very important. In turn, with your permission and when appropriate, they can be in touch with the school. The better those educating your child understand his learning disability and his strengths and weaknesses, the more accurate their perceptions of him will be. And the more accurate their perceptions, the more realistic their expectations.

The need for close communication raises the issue of confidentiality. You must balance your feelings about your family's and your child's right to privacy against your wish to give the school relevant information about your child. This is never easy, and it is a question that deserves a great deal of attention. Discuss the confidentiality issue with all the professionals involved and draw up a plan for protecting your child's private relationship with each of them.

One important aspect of your child's experience in school is not mentioned anywhere in the curriculum: he must learn to ask for what he needs and deserves. This might be extra time on a math test, or permission to hand in a taped history report rather than a written one, or a change in class assignments, or ongoing extra review sessions with his teacher. He must learn to see his teachers as his helpers, people who are "on his side." Your child will take his cues here from you. The younger he is, the more you should do for him. But as he moves through his teens, his own relationships with his teachers will gradually allow him to take over. By the time he is well into high school, he will have become his own best advocate.

Working with your child's school is an ongoing process that does not end until your child actually leaves the school. The education plan that works wonders for him today may not work so well tomorrow. As he moves through the school years, he will meet new teachers and face new demands and expectations. Old problems may abate and new ones surface. Thus, your child's optimal education program is an evolving rather than a static one. And your role vis-à-vis his school is to be sure that school personnel always respect both your child and the spirit and letter of the law that guarantees him the education he deserves, today and tomorrow.

PART THREE

Learning: "Core" Abilities and Common Disabilities

INTRODUCTION

As we go about our lives, we tend to focus on the impact that our environment and our emotional state have on our daily activities, often forgetting the role of the brain. The brain, however, is the biological basis for our experience of our worlds, both inner and outer, and for all our behavior. Inefficiency in the brain's workings may profoundly affect our ability to function.

Consider the brain's involvement in something as routine as our evening meal. The brain is central to our ability to decide the menu, write out a shopping list, get to the food store, pick out what we'll need, handle the purchase, cook the food, set the table, and—finally—eat. Each of these activities involves a series of steps not unlike the sequential steps in the manufacture of an automobile. During each step a brain area (or, more often, areas) carries out some special job.

Some of the things we do are relatively simple and involve relatively few steps and the workings of relatively few brain areas. For example, hearing the teakettle whistling involves only the processing of simple auditory information. But other actions involve a great many steps and a correspondingly large number of brain areas. To write out a shopping list, we have to remember what we need and how much of it, to translate that knowledge into words, and to get those words down on paper. All this involves the workings of a multitude of brain areas. The same is true for the "three R's."

The three R's—reading, writing, and arithmetic—are the basic building blocks of all academic learning. At first glance they appear quite simple: what, you might ask, could be simpler than reading "cat," writing one's name, or adding 1 + 3? But the three R's are, in fact, extremely complicated endeavors, and if you break them down into their component steps, they make manufacturing a car look like child's play.

There are several central or "core" abilities, associated with the workings of particular brain areas, that are important to the three R's—indeed, to all learning, academic and nonacademic. We will focus on five of the most important ones.

• *Sensory-perceptual abilities* interpret the sensory information that impinges on us from the external world and from the inner workings of our own bodies. Perceiving this information accurately —especially visual, auditory, and tactile information—is a prerequisite for learning.

• *Motor abilities*—the ability to move and control the body— are crucial to a child's ability to master academic skills. He must, for example, be able to control his arm and fingers in order to write legibly; his eyes must move down the page as he reads.

• *Memory* enables a child to retain his teacher's lessons and the information in the books he reads, and to retrieve them when required. He memorizes his addition "facts," his list of spelling words, and the names and dates in his history book, and calls on this information when he needs it.

• *Language abilities* involve the reception, interpretation, and expression of ideas, information, and feelings in spoken and written words. They enable a child to understand what his teacher is saying and demonstrate that understanding in a written test.

• *Attention to the task at hand* is also an important "core" ability. Given good sensory-perceptual, motor, and language abilities, and a memory that is functioning as it should, learning also requires that a child pay attention to what he is doing.

Because "core" abilities are important to all learning, impairment in any one of them typically affects a child's ability to learn in several academic areas. Thus, a disorder or disability in one academic area is often accompanied by a disability in another. Suppose a child has a problem in the workings of the brain areas that subserve language, a "core" ability. With this impairment, the child is likely to have trouble with all three R's. How much trouble he has will depend not only on the nature and severity of the language disability but also on the language demands of the tasks in each academic area at any given time. For example, the language demands in reading, writing, and arithmetic are much greater in fourth grade than in the first. In the first grade, reading consists mostly of decoding simple words, writing involves mastering individual letters and short words, and arithmetic is basic addition and subtraction. In fourth grade, reading with good comprehension, writing compositions, and solving complicated number story problems are among the skills emphasized. A child's language disability may not interfere greatly with his academic work in the first grade, but may have a considerable impact on the reading, writing, and arithmetic demands in fourth grade.

And remember a point we made much earlier. When a child's difficulties with his academic subjects stem from a particular disability, this disability and *not* its symptoms must be addressed. Teaching him to read more slowly won't help his reading comprehension. Working on arithmetic computation skills won't help him tackle tricky number story problems. Only when his language difficulty is dealt with may his abilities in reading and arithmetic improve, too.

In addition to "core" abilities, there are other abilities that are crucial to more than one basic academic area, but not to all three. Reading and writing both require the brain to form associations between the picture of a written letter and the sound of that letter. So a child with a problem based on the brain's difficulties forming picture-sound associations is likely to have both a reading disability and a writing disability—even when his "core" abilities are intact.

Other abilities are essential only to one basic academic area. Only reading requires the ability to blend the sounds of individual letters to create a word. Only writing requires a child to convert the sounds he hears in a word to graphic form. Only arithmetic requires an understanding of numbers.

Figure P3-1 illustrates the interrelationships of the abilities required for various aspects of the basic academic skills. In the center of the overlapping circles are five "core" abilities that are basic to all the three R's. Moving outward, the next region repre-

FIGURE P3-1

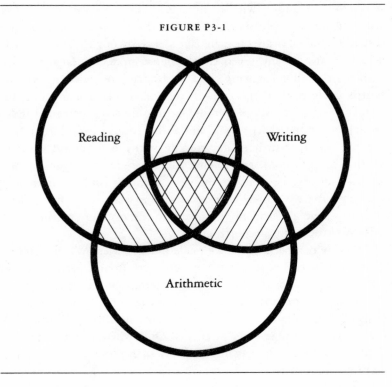

sents those abilities that are shared by two of the basic academic areas but not by all three. The outermost region of the figure contains those abilities peculiar to one academic area only.

To understand learning in the basic academic areas, it is necessary first to understand the five "core" abilities. Having this broad knowledge base is essential to appreciating what may not be working quite right in the brain of a child struggling with his schoolwork. We'll begin with this. Then we'll describe the three R's, and the common learning disabilities: dyslexia (developmental reading disability), dysgraphia (developmental writing disability) and dyscalculia (developmental arithmetic disability). The word "developmental" in these definitions signifies that the brain inefficiencies involved are due to a child's neurological makeup. They have not been "acquired" as the result of a head injury, for example, or a viral infection of the brain, or a brain tumor.

CHAPTER 11

The Senses: Receiving and Interpreting Information

L earning begins with the accurate reception of information, which is the job of the senses. A child's senses keep him informed about what is going on in him and around him. All the senses influence a child's learning, but three play an especially important role: sight, hearing, and the perception of body sensations.

Generally speaking, learning problems that involve the sensory systems fall into two categories. First are difficulties children experience because of disturbances in the sense organs themselves, such as a child's difficulty following spoken directions because his hearing is impaired. Second are those difficulties in which the sense organs register incoming information accurately, but there is a problem in the transmission of the information along central nervous system pathways or in the brain. A child may hear a spoken word perfectly well but be unable to learn its meaning because his brain cannot process the word effectively.

_____ SIGHT

The Neurological Basis of Vision

Visual stimuli enter the eye through the cornea and lens, falling on the retina at the back of the eye. The retina contains the receptor cells of the visual system: rods and cones. The outer part of the retina consists mostly of rods, and is responsible for peripheral vision—the visual area that lies just outside the line of sight—and for registering light, dark, and movement. The central part of the retina is predominantly cones and is responsible for detailed visual perception and color vision.

Rods and cones convert light into electric impulses that the optic nerves carry to the thalamus, the major subcortical relay station for all sensory information (except smell). From the thalamus, the visual information travels to the reflex centers that control eye movement and to the cortex. In the cortex, the optic nerves terminate in the occipital lobes, where the electric impulses are interpreted to create a visual image.

Visual Disorders

Sometimes signs of visual disorders are very plain. A four-year-old scrunches up her eyes as she looks at her new picture book. A seven-year-old skips words and lines when he reads. A twelve-year-old's handwriting is barely legible. But sometimes signs are ambiguous and easy to miss. A child may misread words that look very much the same, like "then" and "than," or "play" and "ploy." Or he may be late for class because he "got lost" on the way.

Visual Acuity Disorders

A child with a visual acuity (keenness or sharpness of vision) disorder does not see clearly. This diminished sensitivity to visual stimuli can range from very slight nearsightedness (myopia) or farsightedness (hyperopia) to blindness. Depending on the problem, the cause may be in the eyes themselves or lie somewhere in the visual system between the eyes and the occipital lobes of the brain.

_____ *Matthew.* This articulate seven-year-old was struggling with reading. His parents noticed that when he read he held his book inches from his face. When writing he bent so closely over the paper he seemed to be writing with his nose. His eyes were tired, he complained, and he rubbed them often.

Eye Movement Disorders

The muscles attached to the eyeballs move the eyes constantly, without any conscious effort, to focus on objects in the environment. This is called involuntary (or reflexive) movement. The other kind of eye movement is voluntary movement, the deliberate and conscious movement of the eyes in order to look *at* something.

An involuntary eye movement disorder that sometimes occurs in children with learning disabilities is nystagmus. The eyes roll rhythmically or unrhythmically up and down or from side to side, or they continually drift away from the direction of gaze and then jerk back again. A more common disorder is strabismus—cross-eye —in which one eye fixes on a visual target while the other wanders off elsewhere. All newborns have some degree of strabismus, but they usually outgrow it by about six months of age. If it persists, it needs medical treatment and possibly surgery—otherwise the sight in the wandering eye will be lost. Because the cranial nerves mediate involuntary eye movement, both nystagmus and strabismus are associated with cranial nerve problems. Nystagmus may also be due to a problem in the inner ear, or to problems in the cerebellum or the brain stem.

Voluntary eye movement is the responsibility of the motor regions of the frontal lobes, and dysfunction here may result in a condition known as ocular dysmetria (Greek *dys*, "bad," + *metron*, "measure"), an inability to track a moving object or rapidly change focus from one object to another.

_____ *Jonathan.* Jonathan's teacher sometimes doubted that he made any effort at all with his reading. When she questioned the class about what they had read, Jonathan never volunteered an answer. When she questioned him directly, he usually said, "I didn't get it." Yet Jonathan was a bright boy and an enthusiastic participant in class discussions. It turned out that reading lines of written material was very hard for him. He couldn't read across one line from left to right, across the next in the same fashion, and so on down the printed page. Instead, he "jumped around" as he read, skipping over groups of words, sometimes over whole lines. With things scrambled like this, what he read hardly made any sense at all, and it was no wonder that he "didn't get it."

Visual Information-Processing Disorders

Processing visual information may include, depending on the task, three different steps: analysis, integration of visual and spatial information, and construction. Visual analysis involves critically examining patterns to ascertain their details and the way their different parts relate to one another. Visual-spatial functions have to do with processing the layout of the visual information, such as the way letters are arranged on a page. In visual construction, visual-spatial information combines with the fine motor functions needed to put parts together and form a whole—for example, constructing an open circle and a short vertical line to form the letter "b." Disorders of visual information processing may appear as visual analysis disorders, visual-spatial disorders, or visual construction disorders.

A child with a visual analysis disorder has difficulty appreciating differences between different visual stimuli. He may not be able to tell a circle from an oval or an "F" from a "P." He may have difficulty coming up with a mental picture of what a whole object looks like when only part of it is visible—he may not be able to "see" the whole horse when all he has in front of him is its tail. He may also have difficulty figuring out what the main subject of a picture is and what is just background. Visual analysis disorders are associated with problems in the right hemisphere of the brain.

Visual-spatial disorders, usually associated with unilateral (usually right-sided) parietal lobe problems, involve a failure to appreciate the spatial characteristics of visual information. A child whose printing is characterized by uneven spacing between letters and between words may have a visual-spatial disorder. So may a child who cannot write on the ruled lines of his workbook.

In another type of visual-spatial disorder, a child may have marked difficulty orienting himself in familiar space, or on a map. He may panic when he goes to a new school because he's afraid that he won't be able to get around to the different classrooms. For the same reason, he may be reluctant to travel to and from school by himself. At home, on his way to the bathroom, he may open the door to a closet instead.

Visual construction disorders fall into two groups: assembly disorders and graphomotor disorders. Assembly disorders involve difficulty putting pieces together to make a whole object. A child with this kind of disorder may have difficulty with puzzles and construction toys. Graphomotor disorders involve difficulty in drawing or writing. A child with this type of disorder may have trouble coloring neatly, getting two lines to join, putting the nose between the eyes when drawing a face. Learning to print or write script is, typically, very hard for him. When he *has* learned, his handwriting may be legible only when he takes tremendous pains to make it so. This type of disorder is a form of dysgraphia, or developmental writing disorder, a term that covers a broad range of writing difficulties.

Visual construction disorders are typically associated with a disturbance in the brain processes that integrate information from the language, visual-perceptual, visual-spatial, and motor areas. The dominant temporal lobe, the occipital and parietal lobes, and the frontal lobe are all involved here.

——————— *Tracy.* Tracy was doing so poorly in school that her parents received a warning letter indicating she might have to repeat third grade. Although her reading skills were at grade level, she often failed to complete her reading workbook assignments on time and had difficulty answering questions based on the material she had read. The same pattern cropped up in science and social studies as well. The culprit was Tracy's writing.

Tracy took longer than the other children in her class to master printing and had trouble with the switch to script at the beginning of third grade. After nearly a year her writing was still poor, her letters wobbly and undecided. When she made an extra effort and took extra time, things improved, but sometimes her work was completely illegible. As a result, she lost credit for sloppy penmanship. She also tended to write as little as possible, so she lost more credit—for poorly developed answers. Tracy was clearly losing confidence in herself and increasingly showed signs that she wasn't interested in school.

At home, there were behavior problems, mostly centering around homework. Instead of getting on with her work, Tracy procrastinated, finding a thousand other things to do. Often she denied having any homework at all, which was far from the truth. She also began to talk baby talk, like her little brother.

Associated Emotional and Behavioral Problems

A disorder that affects a child's ability to see or to process visual information will clearly affect his ability to perform in school. It will also affect his emotions and his behavior at home as well as at school. In fact, when the visual disorder is a subtle one, behavioral problems may provide the first clues that a problem exists.

As a toddler, he may grimace, squinch up his eyes, or turn his head to the side to look at what is in front of him. When looking at something small—a picture in a book, for example—he may hold it right up to his face or bring his head down so as to get close to it. He is likely to display no interest in tasks that tap his area of difficulty.

Common Warning Signs of a Visual Disorder

Slow development of skills such as writing or playing ball that require intact functioning of the visual system

Difficulty finding the way around a familiar place

Avoidance of tasks using visual material

Excessive time and effort expended on writing tasks

Skipping words or lines when reading

Difficulty with even spaces between letters and words when writing

Signs of emotional distress and behavioral problems

As he gets older and starts school he is likely to avoid activities that tax his abilities—reading and writing, for example—or when he does try his hand at them, his efforts may seem careless, with misread words or sentences all over the place. Or his frustration may show itself in bursts of anger and ripped pages, in sadness, or in irritability. Such a child may also show embarrassment as he compares the quality of his work with that of his siblings and classmates, and will often procrastinate as long as he can before attempting the kind of task that he finds so difficult. He may daydream in class.

A child's emotional and behavioral reactions to his visual difficulties may also influence his relationships with other people. His restlessness, disorganization, regression to earlier interests, or need to be in control all make for difficult relationships with his classmates, siblings, and parents.

_____ HEARING

The Neurological Basis of Hearing

Hearing depends on the ear and its connections to the brain. Sounds —which are in effect vibrations—are funneled through the outer ear, magnified in the middle ear, and transferred to the fluid that fills the shell-shaped cochlea in the inner ear. Vibrations stimulate the tiny hairs that line the cochlea, and they transmit these stimuli to the brain stem and the thalamus. When the neural pathways from each ear reach the thalamus, the first relay station on the way to the cerebral cortex, they divide. At this point, some of the fibers from each ear continue upward on the same side of the brain, while the majority cross to the other side of the brain and travel upward on that side. In this way, sets of fibers from each ear ascend to the temporal lobes, the primary auditory receiving areas of the brain. Information from each ear is processed in both temporal lobes.

Auditory Disorders

The presence of certain auditory disorders is fairly obvious. You would certainly notice if your young child didn't look at you or turn his head when you called his name, or if an older child consistently failed to respond to the ringing of the telephone, a fire engine's siren, or music. But many signs of auditory problems are much more subtle and may not be readily recognized by parents. Perhaps your child sometimes fails to distinguish the sound of the telephone from the sound of the doorbell. Or when you tell him to do something, he makes a muddle of your instructions—gets his sweater, for instance, when you told him to get his sneakers. Or maybe he continually asks, "What did you say?" Sometimes a child's parents don't notice any problem, but his teachers comment that he seems inattentive and "tuned out" much of the time.

An inefficient auditory system can result in many different types of disorders, which divide into two groups: hearing disorders (deafness to greater or lesser degree) and discrimination disorders (difficulty in distinguishing sounds from one another).

Hearing Disorders

Nerve deafness is impairment in the sensitivity to sound frequency (pitch). The range of sound frequencies involved may be very small (equivalent to less than a whole step on the diatonic scale) or quite wide (equivalent to an octave or more). Sometimes the symptoms of nerve deafness are obvious: a child clearly doesn't hear sounds in the range that is affected—perhaps the chime of a clock or the ring of a telephone. In other cases, when the disorder is mild, the symptoms may be easy to miss. A child may have difficulty hearing what other people are saying to him when the background level of noise is high, as in the school cafeteria, but he can follow a conversation perfectly if it takes place in quiet surroundings.

Nerve deafness is caused by a disturbance in the auditory nerve, or a disturbance in the brain-stem pathways. Damage or dysfunction in the auditory nerve itself usually results only in reduced sensitivity to a limited range of sound frequencies. A common cause of damage to the auditory nerve is sustained exposure to excessively loud noise: the sound of airplanes taking off, of heavy machinery, or overamplified music. Inefficient functioning in the brain-stem pathways produces a more severe and generalized deafness.

_____ *Laura.* When Laura was an infant, she didn't respond to sounds like other babies. Often, she didn't turn her head when her parents spoke to her, show an interest in her music box, or seem to notice the clamor of traffic. She was very late starting to speak, and when she did start, at age two and a half, her speech was strange, more like random pieces of sound than real words. Over and over again, Laura's parents would tell her the names of things, trying to get her to imitate them, to no avail. Finally, they admitted that their daughter's speech development was more than just slow, it was not normal, and they took her to a specialist.

Conductive deafness is due to an interference with the conduction of sound from the air to the fluid in the inner ear. It might be due to earwax or a ruptured eardrum. Or a there might be a problem with one of the bones of the middle ear, preventing the vibration that is needed to conduct sound to the inner ear. Whatever the cause, the result is a compromised ability to hear sounds. However, when sounds are presented in such a way that the bones of the skull vibrate, they can be heard. Someone with conduction deafness can often hear a voice on the telephone, for example, when the same voice, speaking face to face, would be inaudible. Conductive deafness can often be cured surgically. The same is not true, unfortunately, with nerve deafness.

Auditory Discrimination Disorders

A child with an auditory discrimination disorder has difficulty distinguishing one sound from another. If the disorder is severe, all spoken words sound more or less the same to him, so his response to "Go" is no different from his response to "Come." All nonspeech sounds may seem much the same, too: the telephone, the car horn, music, a dog barking. If the disorder is mild, however, he will only have difficulty discriminating sounds that are quite similar, such as the words "go" and "show," or the ring of one doorbell and the ring of another.

Auditory discrimination disorders may be caused by problems at many different sites within the auditory system. The auditory nerve may be implicated, or the brain pathways, or the temporal lobe itself.

—————— *Geoff.* Geoff had been a cheerful infant. As a toddler, he was into everything. His preschool years were uneventful. But now, as he started first grade, he seemed like a different person. He was having trouble with reading and was angry and sad much of the time. His teacher noted that, though Geoff could recite the alphabet and arrange a set of letter-cards in the proper alphabetical order, he couldn't consistently come up with the sounds of some of the letters. The vowel sounds were especially difficult for him. This, of course, made reading extremely difficult. Sometimes, also, Geoff had difficulty following spoken instructions—once he got his boots out of his cubby instead of his books. Mostly, though, he managed to figure out what he was supposed to do, by watching others.

Associated Emotional and Behavioral Problems

Because developing skills that depend on intact processing of auditory information are key, a child with an auditory disorder is likely to have social difficulties and problems with family relationships from the start. While he is still very young, he may show little interest in the world of sound and frequently confuse familiar sounds in his environment, such as the telephone ring and the doorbell. He may lack interest in his music box, the radio, and the stories you read to him. If you try to teach him a song, he may do everything he can to avoid learning it.

As he gets older he may misunderstand your instructions and then be distraught when you scold him for not doing what you asked him to do. If his auditory disturbance has resulted in speech difficulties, he is likely to become very frustrated when trying to answer a question or tell you what he is thinking and feeling, and he may give up on using words. Once in school, he may not follow directions very well, and he may not respond appropriately to the questions and statements posed by his teachers and classmates. As the lecture style of teaching takes over in the years ahead, a child's auditory difficulties are likely to become more and more interfering in terms of his school performance. Such behaviors as regression to earlier interests, daydreaming, restlessness, or bossiness in response to frustration with his difficulties are likely to become more and more prominent.

Common Warning Signs of an Auditory Disorder

Lack of response to sound cues
Incorrect response to sound cues
Incorrect response to verbal directions
Slow or deviant development of language or speech
Difficulty learning academic skills
Reliance on action, where words would be more appropriate
Misinterpretations of sounds or spoken words
Signs of emotional distress and behavioral problems

A child with an auditory disorder is also likely to withdraw from his peers. His difficulty processing auditory information makes it hard for him to follow his friends' lively conversations, and hard for him to join in, too. He doesn't fully appreciate the movies they talk about, the songs they sing, the jokes they tell. His slowness in picking up academic skills puts him still further out of step with them. So he may become a loner, actively avoiding social activities because of the shame that often accompanies them.

He does not pay attention to his family's dinner table conversations. He may sit quietly thinking about something else, or he may act out impulsively and get himself sent from the room—and so avoid the pain. When his siblings get mad at him because of the mistakes he makes, he will either fight back or go to his room and do something by himself, feigning indifference to whatever it is *they* are doing.

_____ SOMATOSENSORY SYSTEM

The somatosensory system (from the Greek *soma,* "body") keeps us informed about sensations that originate on the surface of the body (the skin) and inside the body. It tells a child about what is touching his body, about possible pain and temperature damage to his skin, and about the general state of his muscles—tense or relaxed, working smoothly or aching with fatigue. It is also crucial to a child's posture—the position and carriage of his body—and to his motor responses to gravitational influences. A child's ability to land on his feet when he jumps off a chair is due in part to his well-functioning somatosensory system.

A child's ability to process somatosensory information, especially touch, is crucial to his early development. His sense of touch affects his ability to hold a spoon, learn to dress himself, and arrive at an understanding of what numbers are all about. Somatosensory ability is basic to academic learning.

The Neurological Basis of Somatosensory Functions

The somatosensory system is complex. It is made up of large numbers of sense organs (receptors) located throughout the surface and the interior of the body, as well as the central nervous system pathways that transmit information from each of the receptors to the brain.

Two different systems are involved in transmitting somatosensory information. One, the lemniscal system, is concerned with light touch and pressure. The other, the spinothalamic system, deals with body sensations such as temperature and pain. In both systems, information enters the receptors in the skin and body and travels via the spinal cord to the thalamus and then to the parietal lobes, which are the primary somatosensory receiving areas of the brain. Most of the information—but not all—ends up on the side of the brain opposite the body side where it originated. Thus, most touch signals originating on the right side of the body are processed in the left parietal lobe, and vice versa.

Somatosensory Disorders

Somatosensory disorders differ according to the nature of the sensory information involved. Thus, a child with a somatosensory disorder affecting information about temperature may have difficulty telling hot from cold. Another child might not notice a light touch on his upper arm. Another might have trouble recognizing a familiar object by "feel" alone, when it is placed in the palm of his hand.

_____ *Courtney.* At five years old, Courtney was still not able to button her own buttons or tie the ribbons in her doll's hair. At school, she was one of the best at hopscotch and other games that call on gross motor skills but was far behind her classmates in everything that required use of the hands. She had to struggle to hold a crayon properly, and her attempts to write her name usually ended in failure, despite the fact that she had no difficulty moving her fingers in a coordinated fashion.

Common Warning Signs of a Somatosensory Disorder

Slow development of any skill that requires holding pencils or utensils

Extra time and effort expended on learning to tie laces, button buttons

Avoidance of opportunities to manipulate small objects

Clumsy handling of small objects

Signs of emotional distress and behavioral problems

Body Schema Disorders

Body schema disorders are disturbances of an individual's mental image of the spatial layout of his own body. They are often discussed in the context of somatosensory disorders because of the major role that the somatosensory system plays in an individual's sense of how his own body exists in space. These disorders are associated with inefficiency in the parietal lobes.

The body schema disorder most readily recognizable by parents and teachers is known as left-right disorientation. Usually, a child of six can identify his own right and left sides; a twelve-year-old can also identify the right and left sides of his environment—the right-hand door, left field, and so on. A child with right-left disorientation can't do this. He may not be able to write his name on the right side of the page and the date on the left, when he is told by his teacher to do so. In adding columns of numbers, he is hard pressed to follow instructions to start with the right-hand column. He has trouble following right-left directions in gym.

Another disorder involving body schema, occasionally seen in children with learning disabilities, is finger agnosia. This is an inability to tell, when not looking, which of one's fingers is being touched by another person. (A psychologist tests for this disorder by asking a child to close his eyes and give the name of the finger —pointer, or pinky, for example—that she is touching, or say how many fingers she is touching.) A child who does not have an internalized picture of his fingers is very likely to have difficulty mastering such skills as buttoning buttons, tying laces, holding his silverware, and counting on his fingers. Identifying one's fingers depends on the interaction of several skills—visual-spatial, language, and tactile—which develop gradually throughout childhood.

———————— *Shauna,* a first-grader, still has difficulty getting dressed by herself. At home, her mother automatically does the corrective touches for her, though her father thinks this is pampering her. At school, however, Shauna's teacher does not help her. As a result, Shauna often looks disheveled and is frequently teased by her classmates.

Associated Emotional and Behavioral Problems

A child with a somatosensory disorder involving touch is likely, early on, to show a lack of interest in activities that involve a good grasp and control of objects held in the hand. As a young child, he may resist learning to hold his own bottle or use a spoon. As a toddler, he is likely to avoid activities such as coloring and doing puzzles. Manipulating the crayons and the little pieces of the puzzle is just too frustrating for him, and he will become very upset if such activities are forced on him. His struggles with learning to tie his shoes, zip his coat, and button his buttons are so great that he may end up in tears. Alternatively, he may refuse even to try and may demand that others do these things for him. As he gets older, he may develop ways of avoiding activities that depend on intact touch perception. Making models from kits, for example, is not for him. Sometimes not participating in such activities isolates him from his friends. Continued participation may expose him to teasing and frustration.

Emotional and behavioral problems associated with body schema disorders may be apparent early on in a toddler's confusion and frustration with his early efforts to dress himself or to hold his spoon or crayon. By the time he is four or five, he still may not be able to get his shoes on the correct feet or to manipulate puzzle pieces. He is likely to be a child full of self-doubt.

As he gets older, a child with a body schema disorder is likely to have a hard time following right-left and left-right directions. This is certain to get him into trouble with his teachers. Given his mistakes, he may be described as inattentive, impulsive, or day-dreaming. It will also make for difficulties with his friends; he may react to their teasing and impatience by avoiding group games, or even board games played with just one other person. He may develop a pattern of choosing to play mostly by himself, both at school and at home. Or he may adopt a know-it-all facade and boss his friends.

He also has problems at home. When it is his turn to set the table, everything ends up in the wrong place—the fork is on the right side of the plate; the knife on the left. When it is his turn to take out the trash, it ends up in the wrong pail. If he does a favor for one of his siblings or for a friend, he makes similar mistakes, fetching a book from the wrong end of the bookshelf, for example, or putting a pair of gloves in the wrong cubby. All these failures feed his frustration with activities that require an adequate body schema. In turn, his upset can result in behavior such as withdrawal or aggression.

As a child with a body schema disorder reaches his early teens, independent travel may become a major issue and a source of further shame and frustration. Following left-right directions in order to get around and go to new places has always been a problem for him, and when he was younger someone usually escorted him. Now, however, he is likely to refuse this kind of embarrassing help, or sidestep the difficulty by making no social plans at all. He may appear restless or lethargic as he spends more and more time at home alone instead of out with his friends.

Common Warning Signs of a Body Schema Disorder

Difficulties with orientation in surroundings, with consequent distress

Difficulty following left-right directions in schoolwork, in organized games, and at home

Avoidance of group activities or games in which directional discriminations are involved

Reliance on others for help getting dressed or refusal of such help

Reliance on others for help with following left-right directions to "get around," or refusal of such help

Difficulty learning to correctly hold flatware and pencils

Signs of emotional distress and behavioral problems

CHAPTER 12

Motor Functions

A three-year-old child seems to stumble over his own feet. A five-year-old has trouble holding a pencil or keeping within the lines in his coloring book. A six-year-old can't begin to put pegs in a pegboard with the same ease and speed as his sister, who is only four. A nine-year-old makes peculiar repetitive grimaces. Difficulties like these reflect some problem in the development of the nervous system. The problem may involve the motor system itself, or the muscles, or both. A moderately severe motor problem is usually quite easy to recognize: a child's motor development lags behind that of other children his age. A severe problem is impossible to miss: the child's development is so compromised as to be a problem for a child of *any* age. But very subtle dysfunctions are hard to identify.

_____ *Robbie.* Age eight and a third grader, Robbie was a superathlete. He was the star soccer player of his grade, a first-rate swimmer, and a great runner. But when it came to quickly zipping his jacket or completing his written homework, it was slow going. Robbie's parents were convinced he was basically "lazy" about everything other than sports.

———— THE NEUROLOGICAL BASIS OF MOTOR FUNCTIONS

As we mentioned in an earlier chapter, movement is either reflexive or nonreflexive (intentional). In this chapter, we'll focus on intentional movement, the movement or movements that we make deliberately.

A child's ability to move and control his body depends upon the interplay of two motor subsystems, the pyramidal and extrapyramical systems. These are made up of the motor nerve pathways of the central nervous system and the major peripheral nerves, most of which have sensory as well as motor fibers. The sensory fibers are important in keeping the muscles in a state of "readiness to respond" and also in regulating movements once initiated. In addition to the cortex, certain brain structures such as the cerebellum and the basal ganglia are also key in motor ability: they are essential to the control and timing of intentional movements.

The pyramidal system, named for the shape of its cortical neurons, is responsible for initiating and controlling intentional motor movements, like picking up a cup and holding it, or swimming laps. Some of the neurons of this system originate in the motor area of the cortex (located in the frontal lobe) and terminate in the spinal cord. Others originate below the level of the cortex, either in the brain stem or in the spinal cord. Motor impulses begin in the motor area of the cortex and descend via the pyramidal fibers through the brain, the brain stem, and the spinal cord to the muscles. In the brain stem, 80 percent of the fibers cross over to the other side, so motor control of each side of the body is largely controlled by the opposite side of the brain.

The extrapyramidal system (the system that is outside of, or not part of, the pyramidal system) is involved in coordinating the movements initiated by the pyramidal system and maintaining the carriage and position of the limbs and the body as a whole. Like the pyramidal system, the extrapyramidal system is made up of some motor neurons that originate in the cortex and others that originate at lower levels of the brain. The latter directly activate the muscles. But, unlike the pyramidal system, the extrapyramidal system includes other brain structures—parts of the cerebellum and the basal ganglia.

_____ MOTOR DISORDERS

Many different kinds of motor disorders result from dysfunction in the nervous system. A child's pediatrician is often the first to pick them up; a referral to a neurologist for further examination often follows.

Muscle Disorders

Good muscle tone and adequate muscle strength are needed for all motor activities. Signs that a child may have inadequate muscle tone or muscle strength include difficulty picking up things, holding them, or manipulating them.

Muscle Tone Disorders

Muscle tone is gauged by the resistance of the muscles when an individual's arm or leg is moved through its normal range of motion by another person. In muscle tone disorders, the degree of resistance in the muscles may be either too great (hypertonia) or too small (hypotonia). Hypertonia is associated with dysfunction of the basal ganglia or the frontal lobes, hypotonia with dysfunction of the basal ganglia or the cerebellum.

_____ *Jennifer.* Four-year-old Jennifer was in nursery school, where her teachers were concerned because she seemed to have enormous difficulty holding on to small objects. Pencils and crayons often slipped out of her grasp; cutting with scissors was just about impossible. Jennifer's parents were also well aware of her problems with keeping things in her grasp, making the hand movements for pat-a-cake, wiggling her fingers independently, and buttoning her buttons. Jennifer's parents assumed she would outgrow these problems, sooner or later.

Muscle Strength Disorders

Lack of muscle strength is a clear sign of a dysfunction in the nervous system. The lack of muscle strength may be total (paralysis) or partial (paresis). The problem in the nervous system is always *above* the level of the body at which muscle strength is compromised. For example, injury at the bottom of the spinal cord affects muscle strength in the legs; injury at the top of the spinal cord, near the neck, affects the muscles of the arms and chest as well as the legs. If the dysfunction site is in the brain stem or the frontal lobes, muscle strength usually decreases on only one side of the body; when the dysfunction is in the spinal cord, both sides are generally affected. A seemingly clumsy child who has great difficulty grasping and handling a pencil may be suffering from inadequate muscle strength.

Movement Disorders

Involuntary Movement Disorders

An involuntary movement is a spontaneous or an unintentional one. Some such movements, such as blinking when a bright light shines in one's eyes, are perfectly normal. Others are not.

One of the most common involuntary movement disorders in children—and in adults as well—is the rhythmical shaking of the limbs called a tremor. For example, a child's hands may shake slightly as he tries to carry out a delicate act, such as building a tower of blocks. Tremors always disappear during sleep and tend to increase during periods of stress, reflecting changes in mental state and brain activity. Sometimes they are associated with problems in the basal ganglia or the cerebellum; sometimes they reflect chemical changes in the brain.

──────── *Katie.* Seven-year-old Katie was having difficulty learning to write the letters of the alphabet, cut with scissors, and color neatly inside the outlines of shapes. Her teachers had noticed that there was a slight shaking of her hands during activities like these and that the end products—the written or cutout work—often had wobbly lines or perimeters. Slight tremors were, in fact, apparent every time she attempted any task involving fine motor skills.

The other common involuntary movement disorder in children is a tic. Tics are repetitive movements of single muscles or groups of muscles, usually in the face or neck but sometimes in other parts of the body as well. If a child blinks rapidly, or grimaces, or has a persistent repetitive cough, he may have a tic.

Tics typically start at about age six and may disappear as a child gets older. They vanish during sleep and often get worse in times of stress. According to some experts, tics are associated with widespread brain dysfunction or with imbalance of certain chemicals of the brain. Others, however, believe that they are symptoms of emotional distress.

_____ *Charlie.* Charlie had a very visible rapid and repeated grimacing of one side of his face. Sometimes Charlie could control this, but only for a minute or two. After that, he was helpless to do anything about it. From time to time, the tic would disappear, perhaps for a month or more. But it always returned, usually unpredictably and with a vengeance. Over the last few months, the grimacing had been getting worse and had been happening more often. At the same time, Charlie's schoolwork had gone downhill. He also seemed to have lost interest in his previously active social life.

Associated Movement Disorders

An associated movement is movement that accompanies another movement. Some of these movements, such as the swinging of the arms while walking or the general body movements that accompany a sneeze, are normal. Others, however, are not. Associated movement disorders usually reflect a disturbance in the pyramidal motor system.

The most common type of associated movement disorder in children is mirror movement, sometimes called overflow. In this disorder, intentional movement on one side of the body is mirrored on the opposite side of the body, or in movements of the mouth. Hand and finger movements are the ones most often mirrored in this way. A child makes grasping movements with his right hand as he reaches for something—and also makes grasping movements with his left hand. Or a child draws a circle—and also makes circular movements with his tongue. A tendency toward mirror movement is normal in children under the age of five. But in a child nine years old or older, mirror movement that the child himself cannot stop is cause for concern.

Coordination Disorders

There are two types: gross and fine motor disorders. Gross motor disorders affect coordination of the movements of the large muscles. A child who runs awkwardly, or has a stiff walking gait, or has trouble jumping or hopping, may have a gross motor disorder. Fine motor disorders affect movement of the fingers. A child's ability to manipulate small objects such as blocks, buttons, or pencils is based on his fine motor coordination. His ability to write also depends in part on it.

Gross and fine motor coordination disorders are sometimes found together, but more often not. For example, a child may trip over his feet and fall when climbing but have beautiful penmanship and be a skillful block builder. Or he may be a fantastic skier but have enormous difficulty writing neatly. Gross motor disorders are associated with dysfunction of the basal ganglia or the cerebellum. Disorders of fine motor coordination are associated with dysfunction of the motor regions of the frontal lobes.

_____ *Abigail.* At six years old, Abigail was already an exceptional gymnast: no exercise on the rings or the parallel bars seemed to faze her. However, learning to write her ABCs and numbers was another story. She seemed unable to master the lowercase letters, and her written numbers were wobbly and badly proportioned. Knowing how enthusiastic Abigail was about sports, her parents were both surprised and concerned when she got a C for effort in gym. They arranged to speak to the gym teacher, who told them that Abigail's grade reflected the fact that she seldom "remembered" to bring her sneakers to class, or, if she did bring them, tripped constantly over untied laces. When she was told to tie her sneakers, she would do so, but the loosely looped bows always seemed to come untied of their own accord.

_____ *Joel.* Unlike Abigail, nine-year-old Joel had not been especially slow in learning to write the letters and he didn't have trouble with the act of writing itself. However, his teachers in the early grades had described his work as sloppy and careless. Now that he was in fourth grade, the quality of his written work was well below that expected of children his age, although his reading was above grade level. He lost points on math tests because he misread the numbers he had written on his work sheet. This wasn't surprising, because the numbers were hardly recognizable. His written assignments were often unfinished when handed in, or else were much too short—a four-line book report, for example. Also, his teachers said, Joel was very restless and inattentive in class. His parents had noticed that Joel had become moody and generally uncooperative at home, too. He complained about school being boring.

_____ **Peter.** Peter's parents were enthusiastic about sports and naturally hoped that their son, now twelve years old, would be athletic, too. But despite many weekends devoted to sports activities, Peter continued to have a lot of difficulty throwing and catching. When he ran, he was all elbows and knees; in gym class he was always "last pick" for teams. Recently, he had started going to the nurse's office before gym, trying to get excused. Peter was an excellent student, the class whiz in computer games. Peter's parents noticed that computer games were taking up more and more of his after-school and weekend time and that Peter was spending less time with friends.

Disorders of Learned Skilled Motor Activities

Disorders of this kind are often called dyspraxias (Greek *dyspragia,* "ill success"). A child with a dyspraxia has no trouble learning motor skills, such as zipping up his jacket or handling his knife or fork, and can perform these skills perfectly adequately whenever he wishes to. The problem is that he is unable to perform certain skilled motor activities when someone else asks him to do so. Joshua, aged five, for example, could tie his shoes when he put them on by himself each morning, but not when his parents or his teacher told him to. Of course, a disorder of skilled motor activities mustn't be mistaken for a child's difficulty understanding a verbal request, or for his occasional unwillingness to do what he is told to do.

Dyspraxias are associated with poor communication between distinct regions of the cortex. The language region of the temporal lobe, the left parietal lobe, and the motor region of the frontal lobe are involved.

Perseveration

Perseveration can be defined as the repetition of a motor activity, such as waving good-bye, when it is no longer appropriate. Inappropriately repeating a spoken or written word, or parts of a written word, may also be perseveration. This disorder is often associated with dysfunction of the frontal lobes.

_____ *Lloyd.* This nine-year-old was not doing at all well in school. His teachers had noticed that he kept "getting stuck on" words when he was speaking or reading aloud, and that he repeated individual words and letters when writing. He wrote, for example, "The boy in the the the red jacket said 'Helllo.' " It was easy to see how these difficulties would interfere with the work he was expected to do in fourth grade.

Associated Emotional and Behavioral Problems

Not surprisingly, a child with a motor disorder often goes out of his way to avoid activities that depend on motor abilities. During preschool years, he may seldom play on the jungle gym or in the block corner. At home, he may ignore puzzles or seem clumsy when he runs. In first grade, he may openly express his lack of interest in learning to write the letters and numbers. At home, his frustration with these tasks may show itself in irritability or tears.

Common Warning Signs of a Motor Disorder

Marked lateness in reaching motor milestones
Poor-quality coloring or cutting
Extreme slowness and exceptional effort in writing tasks
Inconsistency in performing motor tasks
Lack of interest in sports or writing activities
Presence of unusual motor behavior, such as sudden jerking
    or inappropriate repetition of response
Signs of emotional distress

As he gets older, his teachers may complain about his apparent lack of effort in sports or in written work. Since sports ability and writing skills become even more important over the years as social tools and academic ones, respectively, his teachers in the middle school and junior high are likely to describe him using words such as "sad," "angry," or "inattentive." They may describe him as an uninterested student who barely completes assignments or frequently fails to hand in his work. What he does complete is often messy, full of erasures and crossouts.

At home, his pain from his lack of social and academic success may result in a grandiose facade, withdrawal, or a short fuse. Such responses to a motor disorder make for difficult relationships with all family members.

CHAPTER 13

Memory

Achild taking a spelling test, learning his multi-plication tables, or answering essay questions in an exam is using his memory abilities. So, perhaps less obviously, is a child playing stickball or a board game with his friends (he is remembering the rules), a child getting himself dressed (he is remembering that his shirt buttons left over right, that each foot has its own shoe), or a child calling home when he reaches his friend's house safely (he remembers that he promised to do this).

Memory is crucial to a child's social and emotional growth. It guides his performance of motor and mental acts, his interactions with other people, and the way he conducts his life. It is also crucial to his progress in school. Many subjects—arithmetic, science, social studies, and foreign languages, among others—are typically taught with a heavy reliance on memory abilities.

Although memory disorders are frequently a factor in a child's learning difficulties, they often go unrecognized. In part, this is because memory functions are only one component of a task and the other components often seem to predominate. For example, memory functions are involved in taking a science test, but a child's study habits—good or bad—may seem to have more to do with the grade he gets. Or, to take another example, it may seem that a child has failed to do his chore of the week because he would rather be out playing, or because he resents having to do the work whereas, in fact, he has forgotten all about it. In addition, memory disorders are often unrecognized because they are typically subtle or they affect only specific types of information. For example, a child might have no difficulty remembering words to songs or the plot of a movie but cannot remember the facts for his history test or the definitions for his new vocabulary words.

MEMORY PROCESSES

There are at least two stages to memory: the storage and retention of information; and the retrieval and remembrance of information.

Information is derived from an individual's experiences. Every day brings a host of experiences: a classroom lecture on how rocks are formed, the pleasant taste of a new food, the feeling of winning a hotly contested checkers match, and a million more. These experiences are processed by the brain as bits of information. If the information is stored and retained, it may be retrieved and remembered. If it is not stored and retained, it cannot be retrieved and remembered: it is forgotten.

Characteristics of the information, of the individual, and of the environment determine whether or not the information is stored and retained. For example information that is frequently repeated is more likely to be remembered than information that is presented once or only a few times. Information that has an emotional impact is more likely to be remembered than information that leaves us cold. The people and books and pictures that interest us are more likely to be remembered than those that don't. An individual who is highly motivated and whose environment is free of distractions stands a better chance of being able to remember what is being said or shown to him than one who is preoccupied or worried, or beset by noise and turmoil.

The second step in the memory process, the retrieval of information, may be by either recall or recognition. In recall, the individual "brings back" information that has been acquired, stored, and retained. In recognition, he identifies information—a word or phrase of music, for instance—as having been experienced before.

Recall and recognition are quite different methods of retrieval, and it often happens that information that cannot be recalled can be recognized (though not vice versa). For example, a child may not be able to answer essay questions on a history test because he cannot recall the information. But he may have no trouble with multiple-choice questions on the same material because he can recognize the correct answer among the choices given.

Both recall and recognition may be either spontaneous or the result of an active, internal process called a memory search. An individual may spontaneously recall something that happened in the past, in a flashback. Or he may have to actively search his memory to bring back previously retained information, such as the directions he was given on how to get to his friend's new house. Similarly, he may spontaneously recognize a face in a crowded room as that of someone he has met before. Or, taking a multiple-choice test, he may have to actively search in his memory for the answer that "looks right."

———— MEMORY SYSTEMS

We tend to think of memory as a single entity. In fact, there are three distinct memory systems: the buffer, the short-term memory system (STM), and the long-term memory system (LTM). All information that is retained as long-standing memory goes from the buffer to the STM to the LTM. Other information is "lost"— forgotten—along the way.

The buffer. An image, a vivid reproduction of what was experienced, is formed in the buffer when a stimulus registers on the senses. The buffer holds incoming information for only a very brief period of time—a matter of seconds—after the experience stops registering. After the "holding" period, some information is passed on to short-term memory, and some is "lost." Although this selection process is not fully understood, it is known to be affected by characteristics of the individual (such as readiness to learn), of the information (such as relevance), and of the environment (such as freedom from distractions).

The short-term memory system. Short-term memory holds a limited number of items for immediate retrieval—that is, in adults, retrieval within thirty seconds or so. The length of time that information is held in the STM can be increased by maintenance rehearsal, in which the data are continually being "reinserted" into STM. Repeating to yourself the telephone number you're about to dial is an example of this. The ability to hold information in STM develops over time. A child of two and a half can hold only two or three unrelated pieces of information in STM, but the average adult can hold seven (plus or minus two).

Information held in the short-term memory may be processed to some degree. For example, a set of numbers may be grouped into the familiar telephone number pattern: three digits followed by four digits.

The long-term memory system. In contrast with short-term memory, the capacity of long-term memory is enormous. Moreover, this system retains information for considerable periods of time— back to early childhood in the case of some memories.

Information is believed to be transferred from short-term memory to long-term memory for storage and retention, but it is not clear how this happens. It is known, however, that, again, characteristics of the individual and features of the information and the environment interact to affect the transfer. This interaction by itself may be sufficient to explain why we have both pleasant and unpleasant memories in our long-term memory systems.

In the case of intentional long-term memory (for example, irregular verbs committed to memory in preparation for a test), incoming information is typically reorganized for storage and retention through active rehearsal. Active rehearsal involves further processing. This might entail tying the new information to a known format—for example, placing a string of unrelated words in sentence form. The old trick for remembering the order of the planets in the solar system is an example of this kind of further processing. (The initial letters of the words in the sentence "Mary's violet eyes make John sit up nights pondering" match those of the planets in order outward from the Sun—Mercury, Venus, Earth, Mars, Jupiter, Saturn, Uranus, Neptune, Pluto.)

FORGETTING

Memory failure, or forgetting, something we all experience many times every day, is part of the normal memory process. It occurs in each of the memory systems: information that is not passed on is "lost" from the buffer; information that is not reinserted in STM drops out; information that is not stored in LTM will not be recalled or recognized at a later time. We actually forget much of the information that we process, and this forgetting is adaptive. If we were to remember everything that we experience, our brains would be flooded with data, most of which would be of little interest or use.

Sometimes, however, an individual has difficulty remembering information that—either because it is of interest or because it has a useful application—is important to him. Forgetting of this kind is not adaptive, but problematic. Among other things, it interferes with the ability to learn. When we say that a child has difficulty with memory, or that he has a memory disorder, we are referring to problematic forgetting. (This is discussed further in the section on memory disorders.)

———— THE NEUROLOGICAL BASIS OF MEMORY AND FORGETTING

The neurological basis of memory is one of the most active areas of scientific research today. Scientists have learned a good deal about the brain's role in memory, particularly about the storage aspect. However, there still remains much about storage that is not well understood. Even less is understood about retrieval. For this reason we focus only on storage, highlighting a number of current understandings about the brain's workings in this memory process.

Storing information appears to involve at least three different biological processes. In the buffer and in short-term memory, storage is associated with the reverberation, or continuous activity, of the sensory pathways and the hippocampal circuit of the limbic system. In long-term memory, storage is believed to involve a process that produces a structural change in the neurons involved, or a process that produces a change in their chemical characteristics, or both. (These changes are sometimes referred to, collectively, as a memory trace.) Pieces of information in long-term memory are stored in multiple copies in many areas throughout the cortex. The presence of copies of memories in disparate brain regions explains why, short of massive and severe brain injury, long-term memory is so resilient.

Current thinking about forgetting suggests that brain changes that occurred during the memory storage and retention process undergo change. Thus, there are interruptions in the reverberations of the sensory pathways and the hippocampal circuit. There are also alterations in the previously changed structure or chemistry of the neurons, and the memory trace fades. Memory disorders may also occur as the result of the disintegration or "death" of neurons, as in the progressive and very significant memory losses suffered by people with certain dementias, such as Alzheimer's disease.

_____ THE DEVELOPMENT OF MEMORY ABILITIES

From his first day of life, an infant creates mental representations of his experiences. Very soon, he is able to tell whether an ongoing experience is related to his mental representations of earlier experiences—whether it is something new, something familiar, or something sort of familiar. This ability is known as recognition memory. We see it at work when a baby greets as an old friend the teddy bear he was given yesterday. Research suggests that a child's recognition memories last longer as he gets older.

At about six to eight months, recall memory begins to emerge. An infant is now able to recall previous experiences even when there are no relevant clues around. So, for example, an infant can remember a toy for a short period of time, though it has fallen out of sight off his high-chair tray or been covered by his blanket. At about the same time, he develops the related ability to "hold" incoming information while he compares and relates it to past experiences (this is sometimes called working memory). Take as an example an infant who has lost his toy over the side of a high chair and has been given a replacement. He will look back and forth between this new toy and the place where he last saw his lost toy, as if comparing the two.

The further development of memory abilities during childhood depends on maturing brain functions and practice in the use of the memory. Practice includes a child's growing awareness of how to make the most of his memory abilities. He finds out for himself that saying someone's name aloud helps him remember it, or that writing tricky spelling words is the best way to prepare for a quiz. From adolescence or early adulthood on, the development of memory skills rests almost entirely on practice in making the best use of one's memory abilities.

_____ MEMORY DISORDERS

Memory disorders exist on a continuum, from slight to severe. Most of them are very subtle and often go unrecognized. However, a child's memory abilities need only be somewhat compromised compared to those of other children his age, or even compared to his own abilities in other areas, to affect his learning adversely.

Both short-term and long-term memory disorders can be divided into three basic categories: those pertaining to the sense (modality) involved; those pertaining to the way the material to be remembered is presented; and those pertaining to the nature of the material itself.

_____ *Gail.* The quality of Gail's schoolwork had begun to slide in the second part of the third-grade year. Her greatest areas of difficulty were learning arithmetic "facts," especially the multiplication tables, and answering questions about material that her teacher had explained in class. Gail's performance on history and science tests was erratic, too. She did well with filling in maps and diagrams, but typically had a lot of trouble with short-answer questions and ended up with many incorrect answers. Things weren't going too well at home, either. Gail was the oldest child in her family and, far from being "a good example" to her siblings, she often seemed to be the most irresponsible of them all. When her mother asked her to run to the store for some groceries, Gail would come home with half the items asked for. And she had to be reminded over and over again that it was her week to walk the dog, set the table, or collect the newspapers for recycling.

_____ *Maria.* Maria, age nine, joined in class discussions with enthusiasm and seemed eager to learn. But her grades were poor and she was on the verge of having to repeat fourth grade. At a conference with her teacher, Maria's parents were told that their daughter was much slower than her classmates in doing her work —especially in arithmetic, since she still didn't know the sequence of steps for multiplication and division. Maria also had difficulty with spelling. She studied hard for class quizzes and typically did all right, but she often forgot the words the minute the quiz was over. History also presented difficulties. Although she had a good general grasp of the topic the class was studying—the discovery of North America—Maria couldn't remember such facts as whether Sebastian Cabot came before Henry Hudson or the other way about. At home, Maria often didn't do her share of the household chores, claiming that she had forgotten what she was supposed to do. Also, games with her siblings usually ended up with an argument about the rules and with accusations that Maria was cheating. All this was creating a lot of tension in the family.

_____ *Brendan.* Brendan was in the seventh grade in a highly competitive school. He was maintaining his grades only through what his parents thought was much too much time studying. During the past year, he was often still doing his homework at midnight. And sometimes even hours of study didn't help. When his parents reviewed notes with him for a test, they noticed that he often didn't remember the material. Science, French, and world history were the hardest subjects for him, with diagrams, vocabulary, and maps giving him the most trouble. Brendan's teachers considered him a fine student overall, but they did note that the writing he did in class tended to have little detail and a great deal of "filler." An essay he wrote about a film he saw in English class was only three lines long.

Disorders Involving Modality

Although a child's ability to remember information provided by all his senses is vital to his development, we'll focus on two modalities —sight and hearing—because of the central role they play in academic learning and a child's socialization and emotional development.

A memory disorder may be "modality-specific." That means a child may have difficulty remembering information that is presented through one modality but have no difficulty with material that is presented via another. He may, for example, be able to remember visual information with perfect clarity but be hazy about information that comes to him via the auditory route. Or his difficulty may be just the opposite: he can remember every word the teacher said in class but practically nothing about the map he studied for the history test.

Auditory memory disorders involving language are associated with inefficiency in the language-dominant cerebral hemisphere (usually the left hemisphere). Auditory memory disorders involving nonlanguage information, such as music, are associated with inefficiency in the right hemisphere. Visual memory disorders may be associated with either the left or the right hemispheres, or both, depending on the mode of presentation.

Disorders Involving Mode of Presentation

Material that is to be remembered may be presented either sequentially or spatially. Auditory information is, by its very nature, presented sequentially, and processed sequentially one bit at a time. In many cases, the sequence is crucial to the meaning of the message. The sequence of numbers makes a phone number or a date in history right or wrong. A child with an auditory-sequential memory disorder may be able to remember a number of verbal instructions, but he may not carry them out in the right order. This type of memory inefficiency is associated with left hemisphere dysfunction.

Visual information, on the other hand, may be presented and processed sequentially or in terms of its spatial features. In a television commercial, the images appear sequentially, whereas in a magazine advertisement the visual information is presented within a single block on the page. A child with a visual-sequential memory disorder may not be able to remember the order of letters in a word (he may spell "train" as "trian") but have no trouble filling in a map. The reverse may be true for a child with a visual-spatial memory disorder whose visual-sequential memory is fine. Visual sequential memory disorders are associated with left hemisphere dysfunction. Visual-spatial memory disorders are associated with right hemisphere dysfunction.

Disorders Involving the Type of Material

The material to be remembered may be either "meaningful" or "nonmeaningful." Early learning requires that a child remember information that has little meaning for him—such as the number series, when it is first taught. But as he develops and learns, more and more of the information he is presented with takes on meaning, since he can associate it with what he already knows. Throughout the learning process, however, a child must be able to remember both meaningful and nonmeaningful material to be an efficient learner.

A child may have fine recall of meaningful sentences or a string of numbers in a traditional order (1, 2, 3 . . .), but significant difficulty recalling a string of unrelated words or a set of random numbers. Similarly, a child may have difficulty recalling a sequence of geometric shapes, but no trouble with a series of shapes that outline drawings of a cup, a car, a house, a flower. Or he may have trouble recalling an abstract painting but remember vividly a representational one. A marked discrepancy in a child's ability to remember meaningful material and his ability to remember nonmeaningful material is not an uncommon pattern and it is one that parents often describe.

_____ ASSOCIATED EMOTIONAL AND BEHAVIORAL PROBLEMS

A memory disorder is often a source of special frustration and un-happiness for a child. Its impact on his psychological and emotional development may be considerable, and, as a result, he may have difficulty meeting developmental and social expectations as well as academic demands.

Early on, signs of a child's memory disorder may be seen in his seeming confusion about what is going on around him, or his apparent lack of interest in his world. Later, it may be noted that he can't remember his playmates' names, or what he had for lunch, or where he went in the afternoon. For all his efforts, he may have difficulty learning his address and his phone number, and he is likely to respond to such difficulties with anger or sadness or shame. He may also show a poor ability to tolerate frustration, be impulsive, or regress.

A child with a memory disorder may well have problems with his peer relationships. He may be hard pressed to learn the rules of the card games and board games that his friends play together. He may seem to disregard the rules of team games. He may have difficulty joining in conversations about professional sports teams because he can't remember who plays for what team, or talking about music because he can't remember who recorded which current hit song. His response to such difficulties may be to withdraw socially, or at least to become very quiet when he is around his peers. Alternatively, he may "tough it out" and take the consequences of making mistakes.

Family relationships may also be difficult. Chores not done or done incorrectly, telephone messages not delivered disrupt the smooth running of a family. They may also result in resentful siblings and annoyed parents. For his part, the child with the memory disorder, taking the heat from siblings and parents, may become defensive or argumentative. Or he may adopt the attitude that he simply couldn't care less.

Common Warning Signs of a Memory Disorder

Slow development of early memory abilities
A need for constant repetition and frequent reminders
Extra time taken in remembering factual information
Inconsistent performance on tests
Dislike (and avoidance, when possible) of subjects and
    activities requiring memory abilities—academic subjects,
    games, and even sports
Signs of emotional distress and behavioral problems

Once a child is in school, memory problems affect both academic and social development. This, in turn, may trigger emotional and behavioral problems. A child with a memory problem, for example, who is in the beginning grades is likely to lag behind his peers in mastering early academic skills. Because the role of memory increases throughout the school years, a child with a memory problem may fall further and further behind his classmates over time. He typically experiences great frustration, confusion, and anger in the face of his difficulties. In response to these feelings, he may react with behaviors ranging from withdrawal to acting out. How he reacts is a function of both his personality and his environment.

CHAPTER 14

Language and Speech

L anguage and speech are basic to a child's intellectual growth and his mastery of academic skills. They also play a central role in his social and psychological development. For example, they influence his ability to form relationships with other people.

A language problem is often very obvious. As a parent, you would notice if your seven-year-old couldn't name everyday objects such as a spoon or a television set, or familiar people such as a teacher or the next-door neighbor. You would notice if your ten-year-old spoke without regard for grammar. But language problems can also be subtle. Speech problems, similarly, may be noticeable or hard to spot. You'd notice if your baby never made any cooing or babbling noises, if your two-year-old never uttered a word, if your five-year-old always spoke with a high, monotonous pitch, or if your seven-year-old developed a serious stutter. But you might not recognize less striking problems—a five-year-old mispronouncing the letter-sounds *m* and *d*, for example, or a six-year-old failing to articulate *g* or *b*.

——————— THE NEUROLOGICAL BASIS OF LANGUAGE AND SPEECH

Language ability is commonly understood to involve the accurate reception, interpretation, and expression of words or symbols (for example, numbers), spoken or written. Reception is taking in words; interpretation is further processing the information and attaching meaning to it; expression is producing ideas, thoughts, and feelings in the form of a word or symbol message, either mental, verbal, or written. For a young child, language is an auditory affair: he deals only with words that he hears and speaks. As he gets older, his language involves written words and symbols as well. Speech—producing spoken words—involves correct pronunciation, or articulation, and expressing emotional tone. Language and speech are complex abilities requiring the intact functioning and coordination of many different brain regions. We can illustrate this by highlighting the neurological processes that go on during a conversation between two siblings, Jack and Emma.

Jack says, "Mine!" and the speech signal is transmitted, via the auditory nerve, to the primary auditory receiving area of Emma's brain, located in the left temporal lobe. (The process has been described, in part, in Chapter 11.) In the temporal lobe, the preliminary discrimination begun in the auditory nerve and auditory pathway is refined. The information is then further processed in other regions of the brain, with different regions handling different aspects of language. For example, the interpretation of the speech signal ("Mine!") involves Wernicke's area in Emma's left temporal lobe, while her right hemisphere is involved in understanding the tone of the message—evaluating whether Jack's voice sounds happy, angry, or sad. Following still further interpretation, Emma's response is framed. The frontal lobe region of her left hemisphere is responsible for her verbal response. Again, the right hemisphere becomes important, now in terms of the tone of the word-message that is produced, or expressed. "No, *mine!*" says Emma, crossly.

Processing written language (an essential part of reading, writing, and arithmetic) also entails coordinating a number of different functions in different brain regions. In addition to the many neurological underpinnings it shares with oral language, written language depends on several "special" brain functions. (We'll discuss these in Chapters 16, 17, and 18.)

Translating inner verbal messages into spoken words involves connections between the language and speech centers of the brain and the nerves, muscles, and organs responsible for speech. The movement of the muscles involved in producing the sounds of speech—in the chest, throat, mouth, and tongue—is controlled and coordinated by the peripheral nerves and the frontal lobes. The final product—speech—requires integrating these movements with information from additional brain regions. The parietal and temporal regions, for example, provide the somatosensory and auditory feedback that is crucial to proper speech.

_____ LANGUAGE DISORDERS

Language disorders—neurologically based language problems—are often divided into three general groups: inefficiency in the reception of language; inefficiency in the interpretation or "processing" of language; and inefficiency in the expression of language. It is, however, very difficult to categorize neatly a child's language difficulties. The fact is, they often fall into more than one group. For example, when the reception of language is compromised, so are its interpretation and expression.

Thus, although it is possible to describe three distinct types of language disorders, no one type typically exists in isolation in children. So we see children like Julie, Mark, and Margaret, referred to later, who have a mixed bag of language disorder symptoms and a mix of associated academic, emotional, and behavioral problems.

Disorders that involve reception or interpretation are usually associated with a disturbance in the dominant (usually the left) temporal lobe. A disturbance in the right temporal lobe may underlie problems understanding the rhythm and intonation of spoken language. Disorders that involve expression are usually associated with a disturbance in the dominant frontal lobe. A disturbance in the right frontal lobe may underlie problems with the tone and rhythm of a child's own speech.

Receptive Language Disorders

A disturbance in the reception of language may be seen in a child's difficulty in discriminating among the words he hears. As a result, he may have difficulty attaching meaning to these words. A child with a receptive language disorder usually appears not to be listening. Or, when he clearly *is* listening, he may be clearly not "getting it." He may not speak very much, and when he does, he may use single words to express his ideas. Or he may fall back on gestures. He is likely to respond inappropriately to what is being said—his words or behavior don't suit the moment. For example, if he is asked, "Where are you going to camp?" he may well answer, "June."

_____ *Julie.* Take the case of Julie, who was almost six years old. As a toddler and preschooler Julie had not talked much. She was a quiet child, something of a loner, who spent a lot of time drawing. Her parents were relieved by her behavior, since Julie's older brother was such a handful. They were pleased that she was well-behaved and self-contained. With the beginning of school, however, they started to become concerned. Julie had refused to become the slightest bit interested in learning to recognize or write letters and numbers. Although her kindergarten emphasized writing, she couldn't spell her name. Nor could she identify any of the letters in her name when someone else wrote it for her. When asked "Is 'B' a letter or a number?" or "Is '2' a letter or a number?" she had difficulty coming up with the right answer. When given a set of cards each with a written number or letter on it and asked to sort them according to category, she couldn't do it. Julie continued her great interest in drawing. In school, she insisted on perfecting her pictures instead of writing letters and numbers with the rest of the class. When her teacher gently offered to help her with the lesson, she declined in a way that was cocky, even fresh. Often, she just flat out refused to do anything other than what *she* wanted to do, even announcing that she hated the teacher and was ready to go home to her mother. Julie's unhappiness in the face of her classmates' achievements was not very well concealed.

Interpretive Language Disorders

These disorders involve a problem with the ability to understand or "process" language beyond the discrimination of individual words. The difficulty may be with attaching meaning to words, or with understanding the grammatical uses of words and the relationships between them. For example, a child may not understand prepositions and may use them incorrectly, mixing up "on" with "under" or "before" with "after." He may have trouble with verb tenses and with the plurals of nouns. Though he may understand simple sentences ("Mother and Father take the children to the zoo"), he may not understand sentences that contain more complex grammatical relationships ("At the zoo, there was a bear inside his cave. The cave was across the walk from where a monkey was climbing a tree"). He may have difficulty understanding the changed meaning when identical words in a phrase are rearranged ("the dress caught on the swing" as against "the swing caught on the dress").

Expressive Language Disorders

A child with this type of language disorder commonly says very little. When he does speak, he is likely to use very short sentences or no sentences at all but clipped phrases. His articulation tends to deteriorate in proportion to the complexity of the spoken message. As the content of the message becomes more involved, or the words become more sophisticated, or the grammatical structures become increasingly complex, the child may omit or distort speech sounds, or substitute one for another. Automatic speech—reciting the alphabet, for example, or rote counting—is, however, not affected. But even casual conversations are often marked by mispronounced or omitted or badly chosen words, or by poor grammar.

_____ *Margaret.* Nine-year-old Margaret had been plagued with social and academic difficulties ever since nursery school days. At that time, her teachers voiced concern about her comprehension of spoken language because, when asked a question or told to do something, her response was often "What?" or an action that was not appropriate. In first grade, she had unusual difficulty learning her classmates' names. She also tended to describe a person rather than giving him or her a name ("the woman who teaches in the art room" instead of "Ms. Smith, the art teacher"). She often spoke hesitantly, stumbling over words and saying, "Oh, you know what I mean." She misused pronouns and prepositions, saying "him" for "her," or "under" when she meant "over." Margaret's first-grade teachers were also concerned about her difficulty following directions and her slowness in mastering the basic reading and spelling skills. In second grade, her reports noted slow progress in reading and spelling. Math was also slow going. She was still struggling with basic reading and subtraction the following year. Now that she was in fourth grade, her spelling was still rudimentary and she was having trouble understanding what she read. Having finally mastered subtraction, she still struggled with multiplication and division, which many of her classmates had already mastered. Most of all, she hated having to express her ideas either orally or in writing.

_____ *Mark.* Mark's parents were astounded when his second-grade teacher called to ask for a special conference. School had been going well for him, they thought. He had enjoyed every minute of first grade, excited that he was beginning to read, write, and do arithmetic. But now, it seemed, Mark was having a hard time in several areas. In arithmetic, his earlier fascination with numbers was waning as he struggled to learn the meanings of the multiplication and division signs. And spelling was giving him a great deal of trouble. Mark had wonderful ideas and was clearly very verbal, yet he often sounded anything but intelligent. For example, if he couldn't come up with the word he needed, he would substitute a whole phrase—"the thing you eat dinner on," or "the thing you sit at with a chair," instead of "the table." Mark's teachers wondered whether something was going on at home that could explain his change in school performance. Perhaps some emotional stress was undermining his previously good attitude toward learning.

_____ SPEECH DISORDERS

There are several speech disorders, found in children, that are not related to language disorders. Among them are articulation disorders, fluency disorders, and voice disorders.

Articulation Disorders

Mastery of the basic speech sounds develops sequentially. A four-year-old may mispronounce "up" because he cannot articulate *u* and "sit" because he hasn't mastered *s*. A five-year-old may mispronounce "show," "love," and "this" because he can't articulate *sh, l,* or *th*. But by the age of six to seven, children have generally mastered all the speech sounds. (Table 3-3, in Chapter 3, outlines the developmental sequence and expected age of specific consonant articulation mastery.)

A child whose pronunciation of speech sounds lags significantly behind what is expected at his age is said to have an articulation disorder. So is a child whose pronunciation is "deviant"—that is, varying from what is considered normal in his language community. Sometimes specific speech sounds in a word are mispronounced ("weal") for ("real"). Sometimes pronunciation is incorrect because sounds are omitted ("wur" for "word") or substituted for one another ("bet" for "bed"). Sometimes extra sounds are added ("hadet" rather than "hat").

The underlying neurological problem in articulation disorders may be a disturbance in the brain's control and coordination of movements of the tongue and mouth. The articulation problem may simply be a reflection of inadequate muscle strength. Or the cause may be a hearing loss, either congenital or due to repeated ear infections. In this case, a child may also have difficulty with the rhythm and intonation of speech.

Fluency Disorders

Boys are more likely than girls to have fluency disorders—we don't know why. This problem with the rhythm of speech is often called stammering or stuttering. There may be long pauses between words, or whole words may be repeated, or syllables within words, or even whole phrases.

It is fairly common for children under six to stutter at one time or another, and this is no cause for concern. But stuttering that persists beyond six years is worrisome. And whenever a child's speech is characterized by frequent repetition of an initial consonant or the first syllable of a word, or the holding of a sound for longer than a second as he tries to get it out, it may not be normal dysfluency, even in a child under six.

Nearly 70 percent of stutterers come from families where at least one other person has had the same problem. This suggests that inherited neurological factors may have a role in this type of speech disorder. Emotional factors may also be involved, either alone or along with the neurological factors. Children who stutter often have trembling voices and taut neck muscles—signs of tension. Moreover, stuttering often grows worse under conditions of stress.

Voice Disorders

These disorders affect the quality of a child's voice. His speech may be noticeably soft or loud, too low or too high in pitch, monotonous, or harsh and nasal. The change of pitch that occurs during puberty in boys is totally normal, although it is sometimes referred to as a transient voice disorder.

————— *Tommy.* This eighth-grader and avid science buff, suddenly began to hate science. His parents were baffled by this sudden change. When they spoke to him, however, it became clear that Tommy's sudden change of heart was due to his embarrassment about his voice cracking when he gave the weekly oral reports on current events in science.

Like fluency disorders, voice disorders may be associated with neurological problems or emotional problems or both. One child may use a very loud voice because of a hearing loss. Another may speak in a monotone because he is depressed.

————— ASSOCIATED EMOTIONAL AND BEHAVIORAL PROBLEMS

Language and speech disorders are often a source of special frustration and unhappiness for a child. Children with such disorders are at high risk for developing emotional and behavioral problems. These problems may be observed in the school setting or at home. Sometimes, as in the case of subtle language disorders, a child's emotional or behavorial problems are the first or only sign of the language difficulty.

As a toddler, a child with a language or speech disorder may be reluctant to explore his world. He may appear extremely shy or infantile. As he gets older and starts school, he may be reticent about speaking and act out his feelings and wishes instead of talking them out. He may tend to become aggressive with other children. Alternatively, he may withdraw socially. Mastery of academic skills is likely to be slow, affecting his sense of himself as a competent learner. Speech is so much a part of everyday life, and a speech disorder may be so obvious, that a child with such a disorder is often the focus of his peers' unkind comments and teasing. As a result, he tends to develop a poor self-image and to become a loner. He not only avoids social situations, he also avoids new challenges. A child's emotional and behavioral reactions to his language or speech difficulties may also affect his relationships with his siblings. He may be aggressive at home or he may tend to withdraw.

Common Warning Signs of a Language or Speech Disorder

Slow or deviant development of language or speech
Problems with naming objects and people
Difficulty understanding the nuances of language
Difficulty or reticence in expressing thoughts
Difficulty following directions
Academic problems, including underachievement
Signs of emotional distress and behavioral problems

Adolescence is problematic for a child with a language or speech disorder. The very apparent difference between his communication skills and those of his peers and siblings, coupled with the cumulative effect of his disorder on his social development and academic progress, may impact profoundly on his ability to deal with the many new demands at hand. As a consequence, existing emotional and behavioral problems may be aggravated.

CHAPTER 15

Attention

From the earliest days, when a baby fixes his attention on the brightly colored mobile hanging over his crib, attention and learning are inseparable. In order to learn to sit, to walk, to talk, he must pay attention to what he is doing and to the people and objects in his environment. Later, when formal academic learning begins, attention is a clear prerequisite. Perhaps less obvious is the role that attention plays in a child's psychological and social development. His overall psychological growth—the development of basic trust, autonomy, self-definition, competence, and independence—depends heavily on his ability to pay attention to the "facts" of his relationships with his parents and the other people in his life. He must attend to the subtle aspects of his interpersonal experiences—his parents' proud smiles and the disapproval they convey through silence—as well as the hard-to-miss ones—words of praise and reprimands. It's the same with his peers: his ability to work and play cooperatively and to make friends hinges on his ability to attend to what he is doing and to what his friends and classmates are doing. He must be attentive to the cues that tell him how others are reacting to him. Do they seem annoyed, upset, pleased? He must be attentive to others' feelings. Does his friend need his support, or would he rather go it alone?

_____ *Alexander.* This unusually attractive and very verbal fourth-grader was not doing at all well at school. He didn't seem interested in his lessons; he had difficulty following instructions; he was generally disorganized; he was fidgety and restless and prone to getting into trouble. His teachers' dissatisfaction with his performance didn't seem to bother Alexander at all. In class discussions, he often came out with comments that were quite inappropriate, or at least off the mark, and would continue to expand on his topic until someone cut him off. He often answered questions in a similarly inappropriate way. At home, his parents said, Alexander frequently seemed to be immersed in his thoughts, and it was very hard to get his attention. Sometimes it was almost as if he were purposefully ignoring them or tuning them out—almost refusing to acknowledge their presence. He often didn't finish things he had started and would drift off in the middle of a game or a television show. His books and toys were usually in a terrible muddle.

Paying attention is no easy matter. At any given moment, there are literally hundreds of stimuli bombarding the senses. Take the situation of a seven-year-old in math class. The teacher is explaining multiplication, talking about the general number concept involved and about the specifics of the mathematical operation. Imagine the competing stimuli in the classroom: the whispering of another child, the passing of a note from desk to desk, the warmth of the sunlight streaming through the window, the sound of traffic going by outside, the smell of chalk and floor polish, and the child's own excited anticipation of his plans after school. Only after the child's brain has selectively "tuned in" to his teacher's words can it go about its business of processing the new information: analyzing it, interpreting it, and finally storing it.

Attention has at least two essential components. One is the degree to which an individual is available to stimulation in the first place. This is often called the arousal or alertness aspect of attention. The second essential aspect of attention is the degree to which an individual is able to select one particular stimulus to focus on, at the same time filtering out the other stimuli that impinge on his senses. This is known as the selective aspect.

An individual's arousal level determines the likelihood that he will register the presence of stimuli. A lethargic child who seems oblivious to your words may have a problem with his general level of arousal. So may an elderly person in deteriorating health, who sits with his eyes closed, occasionally responding to your voice or to the sound of the television. Adequate functioning of the arousal functions of the brain does not by itself ensure adequate selective attention to one particular set of stimuli and adequate screening out of others that are also present. Only when both the arousal and the selective aspects of attention are engaged and in balance will that seven-year-old in math class be able to attend primarily to what his teacher is saying, despite all the distracting stimuli that bombard his senses and register in his brain. Only then will he be able to award his teacher's words "special attention" status, award the other stimuli "ignore" status, and learn about multiplication.

_____ THE NEUROLOGICAL BASIS OF ATTENTION AND ATTENTION DISABILITY

Attention requires the efficient functioning and the interaction of a number of brain regions. These include the cortex; a number of deep structures, often referred to as subcortical structures; and the reticular activating system of the brain stem. Together, they determine the extent to which the brain can be aroused by incoming sensory information, and also the extent to which it can "tune in" certain stimuli and "tune out" others.

Nearly all the information coming in from our sense organs to the cerebral cortex, the highest level of our brain, travels there along two different routes—the "direct" and the "indirect" routes. Take, for example, a sound that impinges on the ear and thereby activates the auditory nerve in the inner ear. On the direct route, the nerve impulse is transmitted via the auditory pathway (which is routed through the brain stem and subcortical regions) to the temporal lobe, the primary auditory reception area of the brain. Simultaneously, the same information is traveling toward the brain via a second, indirect, route. On this route, the nerve impulse is first transmitted from the ear to the brain stem, as on the direct route. But there, some of the information is routed to the cortex by way of the interlocking, looping structures of the reticular activating system (RAS) of the brain stem. This indirect route transmits the nerve impulse to brain regions that include the auditory association areas as well as the auditory reception area. Sometimes the impulse is sent to the whole cortex. The information transmitted by the indirect route serves as an excitatory signal. The excitation of the cortex by the indirect route, namely the ascending pathways of the RAS, is referred to as cortical arousal. It is this that lays the groundwork for our readiness to respond to stimulation.

Feedback pathways between the cortex, the brain stem, and the subcortical region make it possible for us to ignore some stimuli and attend to others. While the *ascending* RAS pathways arouse the cortex, the *descending* RAS pathways and the frontal lobe play a central role in the screening out of sensory information, enabling us to select some of the sensations impinging on us and ignore the rest. The cortex transmits both inhibitory and excitatory impulses back to the descending RAS—as it were, censoring or endorsing the information that reaches it. (Thus, you are able to sit and read a book while the rest of the family is watching a TV show in the same room.) Modulating cortical arousal and filtering sensory input are intimately connected, mediated by reciprocally related brain systems.

The neurological basis of the haphazard, disorganized, and random motor activity often associated with attention disorders is not well understood. The disturbance may be in the frontal lobes, which would interfere with the ability to set in motion, evaluate, and modify or inhibit motor behavior. Or it may be in the RAS, which would affect arousal. Or it may be in some other, as yet unidentified region of the brain.

_____ THE DEVELOPMENT OF ATTENTION

As a newborn, a child has a few rudimentary attention abilities. For example, he pays attention to things that move within his field of vision. He notices changes and contrasts in the pitch and rhythm of sound, and changes and contrasts in the size of objects and their orientation—beside him, above him, to his left or right. He doesn't yet see colors, but he does pay attention to the difference between dark and light.

By the time he is two or three months old, a baby begins to be a little less attentive to experiences that are completely familiar and to those that are completely novel. Instead, he gives extra attention to those that lie in the middle range—for example, the sounds and sights that are moderately familiar, moderately novel.

These relatively undeveloped attention abilities provide the basis for the more mature attention abilities that develop as the baby grows. In turn, his growing ability to attend is crucial to his development across the board—to his language abilities, his social behavior, and his ability to make ever finer discriminations among the things he sees, hears, and touches.

As the child's brain continues to mature, and as abilities and experiences of the world accumulate, a new kind of attention begins to unfold. Increasingly, the child can focus on some particular aspect of his environment because he *wants* to do so, or because it is important to him to do so, and not because of some special physical feature it has. For example, a toddler will pay attention to a favorite toy despite the competing sounds and pictures on the television.

From childhood through adolescence, attention continues to develop as a function of the developing brain and of increasing experience. The child becomes able to sit and sustain a good focus on what he is doing for longer and longer periods of time. Increasingly, he can stay with tasks and carry them through with a consistently high standard of performance—both those tasks that seem meaningless or unimportant to him and those that have intrinsic value. His ability to focus grows, so he can keep his attention on what he is doing equally well in group situations and on his own.

—————— ATTENTION PROBLEMS

A child with an attention problem has much more difficulty than other children his age keeping his mind on what he is supposed to be doing. He is often restless. A seven-year-old with this problem may not be able to sit in his chair for a thirty-minute classroom activity—even when he *is* sitting he squirms and wriggles. Another child, though able to sit still, can't tell you much about what the teacher is saying. A third child may be described as a nonstop talker. A thirteen-year-old with attention difficulties can't sit long enough to read through the chapter assigned for history homework. He is up and about, into the refrigerator, fooling with his siblings. Even on the rare occasions that he manages to get through the chapter, he ends up with a very sketchy idea of what it was about.

A child with an attention problem tends to be easily distracted; he has trouble following directions and completing activities. Since he is easily "pulled" by competing events in his environment, he is likely to have difficulty organizing himself and his things. At the behavioral extreme, a child with a serious attention problem sometimes seems to be "climbing the walls."

_____ *John.* Nine-year-old John is such a child. From the moment he awakens until the end of a long day he is in perpetual motion. He dresses in such a hurry that he always looks disheveled. He can't sit down long enough to eat his breakfast. His parents get weekly notes from his teacher that he is disruptive—out of his seat, talking out of turn. Once home from school, he creates havoc. He does not walk in the house, he runs. He does not sit to do his homework, he stands. At dinner he gulps his food and talks nonstop. He drops his napkin and fork on the floor. He wiggles in his chair.

A significant attention problem is very likely to interfere with a child's school performance, with his home life, and with his social life. A mild attention problem can easily go undetected. Nevertheless, it may subtly undermine a child's overall well-being, both in school and out.

Causes of Attention Problems

Attention problems may be due to a number of neurological problems: inefficient workings of and communication between the RAS, areas of the cortex, or a number of subcortical structures. When attention problems are neurologically based, they are properly referred to as an attention disability. (Over the years, many different "labels" have been given to the combination of behaviors that we now refer to as an attention disability. Among them are minimal brain damage or minimal brain dysfunction, the hyperactive syndrome, and hyperkinesis.)

But this isn't the whole story. Attention depends not only on intact neurological underpinnings but also, very importantly, on the individual's personality, his overall state of emotional well-being, and his environment. In addition, the importance of *physical* well-being should not be underestimated. Good health, adequate sleep, and a nutritious diet all contribute to good attention.

Personality clearly affects a child's attention—or inattention. One child's introspectiveness, his natural sensitivity, his vigilance, his curiosity, his think-first-act-later approach, all contribute to his attention to what is happening around him and to his behavioral style. By contrast, another child's domineering style, his overall gutsiness, his brashness, his act-now-think-later attitude, all make him vulnerable to being less than adequately attentive and to his active behavioral style.

Further, for both of these children, with their very different personal styles, the ability to pay attention is affected by emotional well-being. There may be a particular emotional stress in a child's life that interferes with his attentiveness. In one child, this may result in sluggishness; in another, increased activity. Perhaps it is his parents' divorce, an illness (either his own or that of someone he's close to), a traumatic experience such as getting lost or having a bad accident. Or maybe there is some special excitement, such as an upcoming birthday or a trip to Disney World. Or there may be no single stressor but, rather, a general emotional fragility that leaves a child open to inattention. Such a child may be preoccupied by his ongoing thoughts, or by worry about poor grades, or by anger about persistent failures, social or academic.

Attention problems have also been associated with certain features of a child's environment. More precisely, they have been associated with a mismatch between a given child's environment and his personal style. A particular classroom or school may be too unstructured, or too stimulating, or too crowded for a particular child. Similarly, a mismatch between a child's personal style and his home environment can lead to problems there—and these may not surface when the child is at school, where the match is better.

Attention is always a balance between a child's working brain, his personality, and his environment. It is important to remember that every child is likely to have greater difficulty with attention some days than others. When a child's brain functions, personality, or environment make him particularly vulnerable to attention problems, his difficulty is likely to be ongoing and interfering.

———————— *Nancy.* Five-year-old Nancy impressed her nursery school teachers as being a gifted child, with basically good ability to hold her own in school. But they were concerned about her behavior in the classroom. She tended to be impulsive and had a terribly hard time sitting still. Once she was in motion, it seemed that she really couldn't stop by herself—it took her teacher's firm hand, directing her to her chair or her spot on the floor. During story time, she was all over the place, so it was no surprise that she couldn't join in the discussion about the story or answer questions about it. She would ramble on and on until the other children insisted that she'd had her turn and now it was theirs. There was another problem, too. Although at the beginning of the year Nancy was often sought out by her classmates for activities in the doll corner, or for drawing a class mural, by midyear she was usually rejected by them.

———— ASSOCIATED EMOTIONAL AND BEHAVIORAL PROBLEMS

In a child with an attention disorder, good focus is short-lived and behavior may be a problem, too. As a toddler, he may float—or dash—from one activity to another, losing interest in even a favorite toy after a minute or two. It is hard for him to sit and listen while you read to him, and he may not tune in carefully when you are telling him something. You may often find him doing the wrong thing, at the wrong time, in the wrong place.

In preschool, such a child is likely to be easily discouraged if his preliminary attempts at new games and new materials do not work out. He moves from activity to activity, disrupting his classmates and often failing to follow his teacher's directions. He has a difficult time staying with his teacher's reminders about the day's program and will be getting ready to go outside when the others are lining up to go to music, still working at the paint table when the others are busy cleaning up.

In first grade, he is likely to fall behind in the mastery of basic academic skills because he is always "missing" key points that his teacher explains in class. The more he falls behind, the more frustrated, disorganized, and angry he becomes. His teacher may assume that he is unmotivated when it comes to school work, or just plain lazy. Meanwhile, he has probably decided that school is just plain boring. Peer relationships may also suffer. He may begin to act out, perhaps by constantly trying to disturb his classmates' attention to the lesson. During recess, he may show his muscle rather than his gifts for verbal persuasion when dealing with misunderstandings with his friends. He may not be sought out by other children.

As he moves beyond first grade, a child with an attention problem is vulnerable to ever-increasing emotional and behavioral problems. His teachers may note that he seems to daydream in class. Or they may report that, although he seems to be paying attention, he can rarely answer when called upon or make meaningful contributions to class discussions. He may start refusing to participate in class, knowing that what he says will be wide of the mark. In middle and high school, he is likely to be described as preoccupied, fidgety, careless, and an underachiever. His sloppy homework, and his poor and typically unprepared work in school, will probably be taken by his teachers as clear statements that he doesn't take school seriously. All the while, his attentional difficulties, key to his academic failings, are feeding a growing sense of self-doubt. He is likely to continue to have poor peer relationships.

For a child with an attention problem life is not easy at home either. Relationships between him and his siblings and parents are likely to be strained. His behavioral style and the emotional consequences of his difficulty dealing with academic, social, and developmental demands are disruptive to family life.

Common Warning Signs of Attention Problems

Undue fidgeting and restlessness
Difficulty following directions
Excessive difficulty waiting while others take their turn
Inattention to what others are saying
Lack of ability to organize personal belongings, schoolwork, or time
Sometimes appears lost in own thoughts
Impulsiveness
Signs of emotional distress and behavioral problems

CHAPTER 16

Reading

R eading is often considered the basic academic skill a child must master. It is an important accomplishment in itself. Beyond that, it is the major vehicle of the learning process during the school years.

In the earliest grades, the focus is on a child's ability to decode written words—that is, to translate printed or handwritten words into words that he can say aloud, or "say" silently in his head. As the school years progress, the emphasis gradually and steadily shifts to comprehension: the child's ability to grasp the message, or meaning, of what he reads. In the middle grades, and on through junior high and high school, reading is used increasingly as the means by which a child is exposed to academic content areas: science, social studies, literature, foreign languages. Clearly, a child will be hard pressed to progress academically if he has not adequately mastered the decoding of the written word, or has difficulty understanding what he reads.

———— *Jessa Ann.* Jessa Ann is in the second grade at a competitive school and is finding it hard to keep up with her classmates. Even though she is in the lowest reading group, she is still floundering. Her reading vocabulary is small, and when she comes across a word she doesn't know, she can't sound it out. Her teacher is concerned not only with Jessa Ann's slow progress but also with her emotional state: Jessa Ann, so enthusiastic and full of life at the start of the academic year, is now quiet and withdrawn. More than likely, this change is related to the girl's difficulties with reading. Jessa Ann's parents have noticed a similar change and have begun to wonder whether she wouldn't do better in an academically less rigorous school environment.

_____ *Patrick.* Nine-year-old Patrick, unlike Jessa Ann, doesn't have difficulty decoding the written word. His problem is understanding what he reads. He can read with ease, but when it comes time to put what he's read into his own words, or answer questions about it, he's at a loss. As a result, he is doing very poorly in most of his subjects. Social studies and science are especially problematic, but he also has difficulty tackling arithmetic number story problems since he doesn't understand how the "story" translates to the computations he has learned. He often daydreams in class.

To better understand why children like Jessa Ann and Patrick are having trouble with their reading, let's consider what reading is, what the brain's job is in reading, and how reading skills develop.

_____ WHAT IS READING?

There are two kinds of reading tasks: single-word and sequential. In single-word reading a child is presented with one word by itself (the STOP sign at an intersection) or with several isolated words (the words in the list he must study for a spelling test). In sequential reading, he is presented with a string of words in the form of a sentence or a group of sentences. In the early grades, sequential reading might be the sentence on the blackboard giving directions for that night's homework assignment. In middle school, it might be a chapter from a history book describing the writing of the Constitution.

Every reading act, whether single-word or sequential, occurs in two steps. First, a child must decode the written word, translating it into a word that has a sound that can be "said." Decoding can be done in two different ways. Using one approach, a child forms an association between the whole written word and the spoken one. He labels the written word. This is called sight reading or the "look-say" approach. Alternatively, decoding can be done by breaking the written word down into its component letters, then associating the written letters with their corresponding sounds, and finally blending the individual letter-sounds to produce the word. This is phonetic reading. To read proficiently, a child must be able to use both approaches with ease. To read efficiently, he must also be able to add words he has analyzed phonetically to the list of words he knows by sight.

The second step of the reading act has to do with comprehending the "message." Comprehension means that a child obtains information from what he reads; it is, in fact, the goal of the reading task. Broadly speaking, there are three different types of comprehension: literal comprehension, inferential comprehension, and critical comprehension. Literal comprehension is the grasp of information explicitly stated in the text—for example, the boiling point of water or some important reasons why America declared independence from Great Britain. Inferential comprehension involves going beyond what is explicitly stated and generating new ideas—or, at least, ideas new to the reader. Inferences may be arrived at by relating several concepts presented in the text or by combining concepts from the text with previously acquired knowledge. A child who reads about the Pilgrims' troubles with crops and the weather and concludes that life was no picnic in Massachusetts in those days is reading inferentially. Critical comprehension requires the reader to evaluate the writer's viewpoint or come up with his own interpretation of the information presented. A child who reads Rev. John Williams's account of the Deerfield massacre of 1704 and figures the story would be different if told by a Native American is reading critically.

THE BRAIN'S JOB IN READING

Reading is a complex task. It depends upon varied abilities that require the efficient working of a number of different brain regions, as well as good communication between those regions within and across the hemispheres. We'll describe some of these abilities and the important brain areas associated with them.

First, several "core" abilities must be in place. Clearly, a child must be able to attend to his reading, so the brain regions involved in attention—notably, the frontal lobe and the reticular activating system—must work smoothly. Equally clearly, his senses and perceptual abilities must be intact. He must be able to see the written word accurately and make the necessary discriminations (this is mediated by the occipital lobes). He must be able to hear and discriminate the sounds of speech (handled by the temporal lobes). Fine motor functioning, based principally on the motor regions of the frontal lobes, is needed: a child must be able to move his eyes purposefully across and down the printed page. Motor systems essential to speech must also be intact in order to read aloud.

Both the decoding and the comprehension aspects of reading require good memory abilities, which are associated with the workings of cortical and subcortical regions. "Sight" words must be remembered; the letter-sound associations needed for phonetic reading must be remembered; the phonetically analyzed words incorporated into the "sight system" must be remembered. Literal comprehension of a written passage requires that a child be able to recognize or recall the information presented. And both inferential and critical comprehension build on a child's ability to remember the information given in the material he is reading currently, together with his ability to recall facts and concepts that he has been exposed to previously.

A child's language abilities are also central to his comprehension. He needs to understand the grammar of his linguistic community, and also the significance of punctuation and capitalization. Equally important, he must master the semantics of his language: the meaning of words and the significance of word-forms (for example, "play," "to play," "playing," "played," and so on). As we saw earlier, language abilities are associated with the dominant hemisphere, usually the left hemisphere.

Given that "core" abilities and the workings of all the brain areas involved in them are intact, reading also requires some "special" abilities to be in place.

To highlight some of them: One is the ability to form the letter-sound associations needed for the phonetic approach to decoding a word, and the word-label associations needed for sight-reading. Research suggests that the ability to form these associations is mediated by the occipital-temporal association region in the dominant hemisphere (usually the left). An ability peculiar to reading is blending letter sounds and syllables together to make a word. This ability relies, in part, upon the dominant temporal and frontal lobes.

Another "special" ability has to do with the switching back and forth that goes on constantly during the decoding of words. The child must be able to shift between the visual image (the word or letter) and the sound (the label or the phonic association, respectively), and also between the "sight" and the phonetic approaches to decoding. The prefrontal region of the left frontal lobe is central to this switching.

While most "special" abilities involved in reading are mediated by areas of the dominant hemisphere, efficient working of the right hemisphere is also crucial. A child's appreciation of the role of inflection in spoken language—and, consequently, in reading aloud —is mediated by the right temporal lobe. His ability to put this understanding into action and read aloud with appropriate phrasing and changes in pitch and tone (for example, raise his voice at the end of a question) is among the jobs of his right frontal lobe.

THE DEVELOPMENT OF READING COMPETENCE

The foundations of a child's competence in reading are laid long before he reads his first word, long before he enters school. As we saw in earlier chapters, "core" abilities—sensory-perceptual abilities, the motor system, memory, language, attention—begin their development very early on and continue to develop dramatically throughout the first years of life. Reading, as such, can be said to begin when a child says the letters of the alphabet by rote, names the letters, knows some letter-sound associations, and identifies familiar words in his environment (for example, STOP). He also learns to read his name. This stage is usually reached when he is somewhere between three and five years old and is in nursery school or kindergarten. By the time he is six and enters first grade, "core" abilities and "special" abilities have developed and formal instruction in reading is well on its way.

The initial focus is on decoding. Instruction takes the child's ability to link speech sounds and visual objects (demonstrated early on in his language development) one step further. Usually, the child is taught to associate a speech sound in the form of a label with a visual image in the form of a whole written word—for example, the label *no* with the written "NO." Letter-sound associations and blending are also taught. The child learns, for example, to associate the written letter "c" with the sound *c,* "a" with *a,* "t" with *t,* and then to put the sounds of *c* and *a* and *t* together to make the word *cat.* By the end of first grade, most children have the ability to blend sounds together and are learning to decode using both sight and phonetic approaches. Around second grade, children master phonetic skills. By third grade, they are expected to be able to use syllabication as an aid in decoding unknown words. Instruction in decoding continues, but for all intents and purposes a child is expected to be a proficient decoder by the end of third grade.

For beginning readers, literal comprehension is all that is usually expected. A first-grader should understand and remember factual information given in a simple, straightforward way in his reader. But as his mastery of the grammar and semantics of his language increases, and as he builds up his knowledge base, he will also be expected to draw inferences and formulate opinions based on what he has read. Work of this kind is usually introduced toward the end of first grade, definitely in the second, and is stressed increasingly as the school years progress, gradually overtaking the earlier focus on decoding.

Accompanying reading is instruction in the areas often referred to collectively as communication arts. For example, a child's teacher will help him develop skills in understanding spoken language and in expressing himself both verbally and in writing. He will be exposed to a wide range of reading materials—prose and poetry, newspapers, periodicals, and books—to develop a critical appreciation for and ability to write in a variety of literary forms. Appreciation and enjoyment of nonprint media, such as film, will also be fostered. He will be shown how to find the books he wants in the library and will be initiated as a borrower. Communication arts are typically taught as part of an integrated curriculum, beginning as early as preschool. Highlights of the development of reading skills are seen in Table 16-1.

Table 16-1

Highlights of the Development of Reading Skills

Kindergarten

Match and identify upper- and lowercase alphabet letters
Recognize familiar words in the environment—e.g., stop
Begin to develop phonetic skills—e.g., letter-sound associations
Start to develop literal reading comprehension skills—e.g., match a word with its picture

First Grade

Match words and sentences
Continue development of sight vocabulary
Continue to develop phonetic skills
Develop awareness of structural features of words—e.g., plural endings
Continue to develop literal reading comprehension skills—e.g., identify main facts of a story
Begin to develop inferential and critical reading comprehension skills—e.g., identify main idea of a story

Second Grade

Master phonetic skills
Increase reliance on structural features of words
Begin to develop syllabication skills
Refine reading comprehension skills
Begin to develop appreciation of literature

Third Grade

Begin to apply syllabication skills to reading
Change focus from decoding to comprehension in reading
Identify and discuss different types of literature—e.g., poetry, plays

Fourth Grade

Continue to develop reading comprehension skills
Continue to study different literary forms
Begin to develop different reading styles depending on purpose—e.g., skimming to find specific bits of information

Fifth Grade

Continue to develop reading comprehension skills
Formally study characteristics of different types of literature
Master use of varying reading rates depending on purpose

Sixth Grade

Refine reading comprehension skills
Refine skills in analysis of literature

Seventh Grade and On

Refine reading comprehension skills
Continue to study different literary forms

—————— COMMON READING ERRORS

Reading involves decoding the written word and comprehending the "message." Errors may occur at any point in the act of reading, from the perceptual analysis of the printed word to the ability to answer questions about the material that has been read. Significant difficulty in any aspect of reading due to brain inefficiency is commonly referred to as dyslexia.

The types of errors that reflect a reading disability are varied. Some of them are described below.

Common Error Patterns in Reading

Letter confusions
Errors involving work patterns
Insertions and substitutions
Errors involving letter-sound associations
Problems with blending sounds
Problems involving the "sight" vocabulary
Problems with syllabication
Problems in understanding the "message"
Problems with reading aloud

Letter confusions. The first step in reading is the accurate reception and discrimination of letters and words. It goes without saying that a child's sight must be adequate to the reading task. But, beyond that, he must be able to appreciate the difference between letters and words that are visually similar and attach distinct meaning to this difference. A child may confuse letters that differ only in detail. Karen, for example, often fails to distinguish "n" from "h" and "e" from "c." She has the same kind of trouble with "b" and "d," which are mirror-images of each other, and "u" and "n," which are the same shape but face in opposite directions. She also confuses similar-looking words, like "them" and "then," or "cat" and "eat."

Auditory discrimination errors may also affect a child's ability to learn letter-sound associations and word labels. A child may confuse the sounds *f* and *v*, for example, and so misread the words "fat" and "vest."

Errors involving work pattern. Both phonetic analysis and sight-reading in English require the reader to scan individual words from left to right. Justin has difficulty with this and frequently scans in a right-to-left fashion. Consequently, he often reads words backward—"was" as "saw," "top" as "pot." The left-right work pattern sometimes breaks down in the middle of a word, too, so that he reads "form" instead of "from" or "bluk" instead of "bulk."

In sequential reading, the reader must maintain the scan of words across the printed line and then, at the end of the line, drop to the next line to begin the scan again. A child who has difficulty maintaining this kind of control over his eye movement may read words and phrases twice over, reverse the word order or omit words altogether. When reading paragraphs, he may skip whole lines.

Insertions and substitutions. Sometimes a child's sequential reading is characterized by inserted and substituted words (usually small words) or word endings. The impact of the error on his ability to understand the material varies with the word or word ending that is inserted or substituted. For example, if "a" is read as "the" there may be no major change in meaning, whereas there is when "and" is read as "but." Similarly, the addition of "ed" to a verb stem changes the meaning significantly.

Errors involving letter-sound associations. Perhaps the most common reason for poor reading is a child's problem "sounding out" unknown words. Phonetic analysis is complex, so a child may have difficulty with this skill for a number of different reasons, but the most frequent one is difficulty learning the letter-sound associations. This is Naomi's problem. She is in the second grade and, though her teacher has focused throughout the year on phonetic skills, she still "doesn't get it." She finds the letter-sound associations for the vowels particularly difficult to master and often confuses the "short" sound (as in "fat" or "hop") with the "long" sound (as in "fate" or "hope"). The result is that many of her attempts to read unfamiliar words are off the mark.

Problems with blending sounds. Most children are able to "blend" by the age of five or six. But Lowell, in the same class as Naomi, just can't manage it, try as he may. His reading is based on a "sight" system, with the occasional lucky guess when he is confronted with a word he doesn't recognize. The majority of children do eventually master blending, but a few don't. Because these children are unable to decode unfamiliar words, their reading vocabulary is limited to words that others have read to them and tends to be very small.

Problems involving the "sight" vocabulary. Some children who are able to "sound out" an unfamiliar word seem to be unable to learn the words on an automatic level—that is, a word that has been analyzed does not become part of a "sight" vocabulary. As a result, these children must reanalyze the word every time they encounter it. This clearly makes reading very laborious, as it is for Caroline. She has learned to sound out words, but she is exceptionally slow at building her sight vocabulary. Though some lag time might be expected, Caroline is in the last months of first grade and is still stumbling over words that were first introduced the previous fall.

Phonetically irregular words present a similar problem. These words do not look the way they sound, and there is nothing for it but to memorize them. There are a great many words of this kind in the English language—"was" and "said," for example, as well as the notorious "-ough" words.

Problems with syllabication. Children usually begin work in identifying the syllables in an orally presented word in the second grade. By the third grade, they are beginning to be able to divide up unfamiliar multisyllable words to help decode them. Many children have trouble with this last step—ten-year-old Glen, for one. Faced with a word more than two syllables long, he tends to "break" it in the wrong place. He reads "encyclopedia" as "ensy-clop-edja," for example. It often seems that he has forgotten all the rules he learned for decoding shorter words, and he inserts or omits sounds and confuses letters as he stumbles through the syllables. So he reads "specific" as "spikifik," and "demonstrate" as "delmanstrat."

Problems with understanding the message. Broadly speaking, there are three types of questions that may be asked about material that has been read, corresponding to the three different types of comprehension. One type of question draws on the reader's ability to grasp information presented in the text. Jeremy, who is in the second grade now, has difficulty with this type of task. At the beginning of first grade, because he was great at decoding, Jeremy was considered by his teachers to be the best reader in his class. This changed, though, as comprehension became an increasingly important part of reading. Now, more and more, Jeremy is expected to be able to answer questions about the material he has read, not just decode the words, and he has a hard time with it.

The second and third types are questions that tap the reader's ability to go beyond a literal reading of the text. Louise's difficulty isn't so much understanding what she has read as using the information to generate new ideas and evaluating it. She can grasp the meaning of a string of facts in a simple, concrete way. But if called on to make inferences based on something she has read, or give her opinions about it, she falters.

Problems with reading aloud. Disregard for punctuation, or poor phrasing, or lack of expression may be noted when a child reads aloud. Reading aloud, given adequate speech abilities, requires a degree of proficiency in decoding. It is also based on a child's ability to understand the meaning of words as he's reading them, on his understanding of the significance of punctuation marks, and on his grasp of the message.

_____ CHECKING YOUR CHILD'S READING PROGRESS

The ability to develop into a skilled reader depends to a large extent on "core" abilities. So the earliest sign of a possible reading disability is the compromised development of abilities such as memory or attention, or of perceptual, motor, or language abilities. Perhaps your child's development in one or more of these areas is slow, compared with the expected developmental timetable. Or perhaps his development is compromised compared with that of a child of any age. Sometimes the signs of a reading disorder are seen not so much in inadequate development as in the effort that reading requires. A child in kindergarten who has to struggle long and hard to master the letter sounds may have a reading disability in later years.

With the introduction of formal reading instruction, "academic" signs of a reading disorder may show up in your child's schoolwork and homework. Or "nonacademic" signs of a disorder may manifest themselves in his behavior in and out of the classroom. We'll discuss some of the academic signs first.

Common Warning Signs of a Reading Disability

Preschool Age

Compromised or slow development of any "core" abilities
Lack of interest in written symbols such as letters or numbers

School Age

"Academic" Signs

Presence of common error patterns (see box on page 191)
Undue effort expended on reading; excessive time spent on
    reading assignments
Slow progress, in comparison with classmates, in learning
    "sight" words and mastering phonetic analysis
"Careless" errors in word reading and in reading
    comprehension
Inconsistent performance on tests requiring reading
Underachievement in subjects that require fine reading skills

"Nonacademic" Signs

Avoidance of reading, or lack of pleasure in it
Acting out or disruptive behavior associated with time given
    to reading
Daydreaming
Signs of emotional distress and behavioral problems

Assuming that "core" abilities and "special" abilities for reading are in place, children are expected to learn to decode words at a fairly similar rate. The first sign of a reading disability may be that a child is taking longer than his classmates to learn sight words, to grasp letter-sound associations, and to master the process of sounding out unfamiliar words. Or he may be slow in adding words he sounds out to his sight vocabulary.

Another sign of a disability is lack of improvement. No child reads with proficiency and ease at the beginning, but, over time, he can be expected to become more adept and faster. Reading should not be laborious, a matter of hesitations and numerous false starts. By the end of the first grade, he should have developed a sight vocabulary and the ability to analyze words phonetically without strain. (One sure way of knowing whether a child is able to decode words by letter-sound analysis is to have him read nonsense words such as "tev" or "bome.") By second grade, all the basic letter-sound associations and many of the more complex ones should be mastered. In third grade, he should be using syllabication to help in the decoding of words he hasn't seen before.

Although young readers are focusing on the decoding aspect, it is also important that they understand what they are reading. A second- or third-grader, reading aloud, should read with correct phrasing, with expression, and with regard to punctuation. He should be able to grasp the information presented in the text. As he gets older, he should be better able to handle questions that go well beyond the simple "spitting back" of information. Forming inferences and opinions based on what he has read should present no problem.

Since a child's reading may vary somewhat from day to day, it is important that you check his progress several times during the academic year. Have him read aloud to you. You may notice that he makes some of the errors noted earlier. You may find that even an older child has a problem with decoding. Students are usually not required to read aloud once they reach the middle grades, because it is assumed that the decoding aspect of reading has been mastered. So no one may be aware that a child hasn't in fact developed his decoding ability adequately. Have him read different kinds of material, single-word and sequential. Some children with weak decoding skills handle sequential material quite well, because the decoding process is helped along by the general flow of the meaning. They have comparatively greater difficulty with reading isolated single words or nonsense words.

It is also important to compare your child's reading with his performance in other academic areas. Does his ability to read lag behind his ability to compute? Does he participate eagerly in class discussions but seem unable to tell you much about the book he is reading? Are reading assignments a greater burden than other kinds of homework? If the answer to any of these questions is yes, then you should question whether or not his reading skills are adequately developed.

The nonacademic, or behavioral, signs of a reading disability show up in a child's behavior at school or at home, or in both places. One such sign is avoidance. Most children are excited by learning to read. And, even if only a few go on to become voracious readers, reading is not usually responded to as if it were a chore to be gotten out of. A "problem" reader, though, often does no reading other than what is demanded of him. He reads only those sections of a chapter that are necessary for answering the assigned questions. The idea of reading for pleasure is completely foreign to him. And, typically, a child with a reading disability has little ability to tolerate the frustrations involved in reading, either in school or out.

In more extreme cases, when a reading disability is severe, a child may respond by more dramatic behavior. During times set apart for reading, he may act out or behave disruptively. Or he may become withdrawn, both at home and at school, in response to his anger and frustration.

CHAPTER 17

Writing

U sing symbols of his own devising, a three-year-old puts his mark on his drawings and in his books. He is writing, as he will tell you if you ask. He is right: he is communicating something—in this case, ownership—by forming graphic symbols on paper.

Writing often begins before a child enters kindergarten—for example, the experimenting with writing letters of a four-year-old. In the early school years, the emphasis is on the graphomotor aspects of the skill: a child learns to form the letters correctly and easily, first in print and then in script. By the time he is in third grade, writing comes to be more than a mechanical skill. Now it is a major way for a child to express himself. He communicates in writing his ideas and his understanding of information presented in his classes and in the books he reads. From this point on he is expected to produce stories and reports with increasing skill and ease. And this written work should show that he can choose and use words that accurately convey the message he wants to get across, knows the rules of grammar, punctuation, and capitalization and that he can spell correctly.

_____ *Nathaniel.* In kindergarten Nathaniel lagged behind the others in his ability to copy and write the letters of the alphabet. Vertical lines leaned sideways, diagonals were erratic, rounded shapes were tight and spiky. Letters were often formed with the different strokes widely separated or placed at strange angles to one another. Nathaniel also had trouble writing his name. Although he could spell it aloud easily enough, when he came to writing it he ran the risk of leaving out a letter, writing a letter backward, or writing several letters in the wrong order. In the first grade he began to insist that he be called Nate. Both his mother and his teacher suspected that this choice was largely triggered by his desire to cut down on the error-potential of his full name.

Spelling tests were introduced and short writing assignments increased in second grade. Nathaniel floundered on both. Words he knew by heart the night before were misspelled on tests. He responded to writing assignments with nervousness and reluctance, putting them off until the last minute. Now, at the end of the school year, writing work in class is done sullenly and he flatly refuses to do any writing homework at all. He has also begun to act out in school. Seeming to have a hard time sitting still and keeping quiet, Nathaniel not only fails to get on with his own work, he also disturbs the other children.

In order to understand why a child might be having trouble with writing, it is necessary to appreciate what writing is, what the brain's job is in writing, and how writing skills develop.

_____ WHAT IS WRITING?

There are three kinds of writing tasks: copying, writing from dictation, and spontaneous writing. In copying, a child is reproducing an original model, using paper and pencil. The model might be a letter in his penmanship workbook or the sentence the teacher has written on the blackboard about that night's homework assignment. In writing from dictation, a child is reproducing with pencil and paper the words that someone else is saying. A teacher may dictate a poem that is to be memorized or the study outline for a science test. Spelling tests are, necessarily, dictated. In spontaneous writing, a child is his own motivator: his writing reflects his own thoughts and feelings, not someone else's. Spontaneous writing might be a book report, an essay answer on a history test, or a creative writing assignment. Or, at home, it might be the note he leaves saying that he has gone to play at a neighbor's or the letter he writes his grandparents.

Writing acts can be thought of in terms of three hallmarks: letter neatness, layout, and message. Letter neatness depends on how well a child can make his letters. Layout—how the writing is arranged on the paper—encompasses such things as the spacing of letters within individual words, spacing within words, even margins, and the extent to which writing is on a line. The expression of the message calls on word-choice, grammar, punctuation, capitalization, and spelling. All three writing tasks—copying, writing from dictation, spontaneous writing—involve letter neatness and layout. But only spontaneous writing reflects a child's ability to communicate a message as well.

_____ THE BRAIN'S JOB IN WRITING

Writing is a complex task. It is based on the efficient working of various brain regions as well as good communication between these regions, within and across hemispheres. We will highlight some of the abilities involved in writing and note the important brain regions associated with them.

First, several "core" abilities we have discussed must be in place. A child must pay attention. Whether copying, writing from dictation, or writing spontaneously, he must focus on the task. This, as we have seen, requires the efficient interplay of various regions of the brain—notably, the frontal lobe and the reticular activating system of the brain stem. His senses must be intact: he must be able to see the model and make the necessary distinctions among the letters; he must be able to hear the words that are dictated; he must be able to feel the pencil in his hand, so as to grip it. These sensory-perceptual abilities are mediated by the occipital, temporal, and parietal lobes, respectively.

When writing from dictation a child must be able to remember what is being dictated and what the "target" letters or words look like. Spontaneous writing also requires remembering "target" words. And in all three writing tasks, a child must have a memory of what it "feels like" to write the letter or word that he is about to write again. This memory is crucial to the figure and hand movements needed to write a given letter or word. Memory functions depend on the workings of both cortical and subcortical regions of the brain. The smooth execution of commands pertaining to finger and hand movements is largely the responsibility of the motor region of the frontal lobe opposite the writing hand.

Writing often aims at communicating a message—thoughts and ideas and feelings—by means of the written word. The message is conveyed by the words that are used, by grammatical construction, and by punctuation and the appropriate use of capital letters. A child's language skills, mediated by the dominant hemisphere, usually the left, play a central role in this important aspect of writing.

In addition to "core" abilities, writing skills depend on many "special" abilities. Let's highlight some of them. In copying, for example, the letter or word copied must be properly positioned on the paper. Otherwise, it will not be easily read, or it will be read to mean something other than what was intended. So, not only must the "target" letter or word itself be noted accurately, its position on the line and on the page also must be correctly noted. This information, in turn, must be integrated with the motor system, so that the copied figure is both correctly formed and correctly oriented in space—that is, in relation to the line and the page. The cooperative efforts of the right occipital and both parietal lobes, and the motor region of the frontal lobe, which controls the child's preferred hand, are central to the integration of visual-spatial information and motor function.

A more complex skill peculiar to writing is spelling—writing letters (or saying them aloud) in a specific order, to form a word. Spelling is crucial, since the misspelling of a word may interfere with the message getting across to the reader. There are two approaches to spelling. A proficient speller uses both.

One way is by breaking down a word into its component sounds. This is called phonetic spelling, and it is a very complex act. The speller must be able to hold the target word in his memory while at the same time segmenting it into its individual sound components—one by one, in the correct sequence—and linking each of them to a graphic image (a letter that is to be written). These skills require efficient working of various reception and association areas in the temporal, parietal, occipital, and frontal lobes. The phonetic approach to spelling also involves remembering and applying appropriately special spelling rules, such as " 'i' before 'e,' except after 'c.' " Thus, there is a constant integration of "core" memory abilities with special phonetic spelling skills.

The second way of approaching spelling is by recalling from memory the full string of letters that make up the target word. This is called sight spelling and it, too, requires fine memory as well as the constant integration of memory and language abilities. Integration is needed as the child shifts back and forth between the spoken word (or the word that is thought about) and the written one. Without it, errors will be made—for example, a child will write "there" when the sentence calls for "their," or "are" when what he means is "our."

_____ **THE DEVELOPMENT OF WRITING COMPETENCE**

As we saw in earlier chapters, "core" abilities start their development very early in life. Actual writing behavior can be said to begin at a little over a year, when a child starts to imitate simple drawn strokes. By eighteen months, he is scribbling spontaneously and enthusiastically; by age two, he can imitate a circular stroke. He is still holding his crayon in his fist, but about six months later he gets a grip on it with his fingers. At about age three, he gives his drawings names—"This is a fire truck. This is my dog, Kipper"— and he can copy a circle. At about four, he can draw a primitive human figure and can copy a cross. At about four and a half, he can copy a square. He may begin to write letters, even his first name. Alongside these growing skills with crayon and pencil, a child's ability to understand what is said to him and to express his thoughts and desires is increasing dramatically—especially between three and four years of age.

At about five years of age, in most children, "core" abilities and requisite "special" abilities have developed sufficiently that additional progress in writing can be made. In kindergarten, a child copies shapes, single letters, and words, and practices writing his name. In first grade, he is writing simple words and sentences without the aid of a model. Script is typically introduced by the third grade. The stress in these early years is on the first two hall-marks of the writing act: letter neatness and layout. He learns to write neatly and evenly and on the lines, to keep his margins straight, and to maintain an even spacing between letters and words. There is also work on the "message" aspect of writing.

By the third grade, a child is expected to have mastered the mechanics of writing, and the emphasis shifts. Now his ability to communicate his thoughts and ideas takes center stage. Writing exercises become more complex, and he is expected to focus increasingly on vocabulary, grammar, punctuation, capitalization, and use traditional spelling. How much stress is put on accurate spelling varies from school to school and from teacher to teacher. In some schools, "invented spelling" for unfamiliar words is permitted in an effort to promote a child's confidence in his ability to express himself in writing. Typically, though, a second- or third-grader under-stands the difference between "good" and "bad" spelling, whether or not this is something his teacher emphasizes.

Building on the foundation laid in the early grades, later in-struction emphasizes written composition and proofreading skills (checking for errors in word usage, grammar, punctuation, capital-ization, and spelling, as well as for the adequacy of the message). A child will also refine his ability to write in different literary forms and for different audiences, composing poetry and prose, business letters, news reports, and content reports. These skills are usually taught as part of an integrated curriculum that includes reading, listening, and speaking skills. Highlights of the development of writing skills are seen in Table 17-1.

Table 17-1

Highlights of the Development of Writing Skills
Kindergarten
Develop and improve ability to hold and use pencils
Trace, copy, and write letters, names, and words
First Grade
Continue to copy and write letters, names, and words
Begin to develop layout and composition skills
Begin to write various literary forms—e.g., poetry, invitations
Use invented as well as traditional spelling

Second Grade

Master all manuscript letters using legible and appropriate letter form and size
Continue to develop layout skills—e.g., margins
Continue to develop skills in the composition of written work—e.g., combine sentences into short paragraphs
Develop additional spelling skills as well as continue to use invented spelling
Begin to develop proofreading skills

Third Grade

Use both manuscript and script writing
Use appropriate layout
Refine composition skills—e.g., write passages that express a central idea and reflect an expanding vocabulary
Learn to identify and use different types of sentences—e.g., declarative, interrogative, etc.
Use different types of written productions—e.g., poetry
Improve spelling skills
Continue to develop proofreading skills

Fourth Grade

Use script writing
Continue to refine composition skills
Use variety of sentence types in written work
Continue to improve spelling skills
Develop sense of writing as "a process," requiring prewriting activities, such as outlining as well as proofreading

Fifth Grade

Continue to refine composition skills
Continue to refine spelling skills
Continue to develop prewriting and proofreading skills

Sixth Grade

Continue to refine composition skills
Continue to refine spelling skills
Continue to develop prewriting and proofreading techniques

Seventh Grade and On

Continue to refine composition skills
Continue to refine spelling skills
Demonstrate understanding of "writing as a process"

_____ COMMON WRITING ERRORS

A child's difficulty with writing may be due to a number of different areas of difficulty. When a child's poor writing is the result of inadequate visual-spatial abilities or compromised language abilities, he is said to have dysgraphia, or developmental writing disability. When his poor writing is the result of inadequate muscle strength or muscle tone, or inadequate coordination of the hand or fingers, he is said to have a motor disability, rather than a writing disability.

It is important to remember that writing disabilities range from the very obvious to the very subtle. Clearly, a child will be seen as having a problem if his written work looks as though a chicken had tracked across the page. But it may not be so easy to catch a writing disability due to subtle inefficiency in the brain functions that underlie the language features of written expression. Take just one example, a child whose spontaneous writing is full of spelling mistakes. This child has a writing disorder, but it is likely that he will be seen as lazy or careless. He may even be seen as having an attention disorder.

Common Error Patterns in Writing

Problems with letter formation
Rotations
Mirror writing
Problems with layout
Errors in word usage and grammar
Repetitions and omissions
Errors in punctuation and capitalization
Phonetically correct spelling errors
Phonetically incorrect spelling errors
Spelling errors involving sequence
Spelling errors involving repetition
Spelling errors involving substitution
Spelling errors involving omission

What kinds of errors can we expect to see in the schoolwork of a child who has difficulty with writing? Errors typically show themselves in a mix of difficulties with the three hallmarks of writing—letter neatness, layout on the page, and message.

Problems with letter formation. Some children have difficulty

with writing letters. Producing acceptably neat work is truly beyond them. Nick, now ten, had difficulty learning to print. He
never became adept at it. The switch to script was torture, and
every term his teachers noted on his report card that his writing was
"terrible," "a disgrace," "almost completely illegible." Now in fifth
grade, Nick is taking advantage of his teacher's willingness to let
him use print. And though his print is not good, it's better than
his script. A look at Nick's written work shows that the letters are
poorly formed. Lines don't join up as they should, especially in
letters like "v," "k," and "y." Pressure on the page (you can feel
the letters on the reverse side of the paper) suggests how laborious
writing is for him. Keith, a third-grader, also has trouble writing
neatly. His letters are nearly illegible. Letters such as "a" and "o"
tend to have angles where they should be rounded, and lines are
shaky.

Rotations. Young children learning to write often rotate letters, writing "b" as "d," for example, or "u" as "n." After about
the age of six, however, the tendency to turn letters around in this
fashion typically ends. This was not the case with Lou. He is in
fourth grade and his written work still shows rotation errors. The
letters "b" and "d" are very problematic, and though he doesn't
make the error every time, he makes it often enough for it to be a
noticeable pattern. At this point, he handles it by writing "b" and
"d" as capitals. A sentence of his might look like this: "The Boy
Dug through layers of Dirt and found the pirates' treasure Box."
Lou's solution flouts all the rules of capitalization, but at least it
solves the "b"/"d" rotation problem.

Mirror writing. Mirror writing is usually seen only in very
young children. In this striking error, letters are correctly formed
and words are correctly spelled, but everything is written backward.
The writing is correct only if held up to and viewed in a mirror.

Problems with layout. In a typical school day, a child's writing assignments may include filling in blanks in his workbook,
taking a spelling test, and writing short answers to social studies
questions. Each task requires the child to organize his writing on
the page. He must fit his answers into the blanks, stay on line, line
up his written words in columns, and keep the spacing of letters
and words uniform. Some children have great difficulty negotiating
the writing space—Judy, for one. She is in the fifth grade and is

generally considered to be a bright girl and a satisfactory student, except for her disorganized written work. In spelling tests, where the children are supposed to write the words in a column down the left side of the page, Judy's list snakes all over the place, with only the first word anywhere near the margin. It is impossible for her to write without lines. In fact, if she is given an unruled sheet of paper, Judy will painstakingly draw horizontal lines down the length of it before starting her work. Even so, her written work is poorly aligned: letters rarely touch the line, but are typically a bit above it or a bit below. Spacing between one word and the next is also very erratic. The stories Judy writes are nearly illegible.

Errors in word usage and grammar. Errors in word usage or grammar or both may appear in a child's spontaneous writing, even though they aren't evident when he speaks. Roger, a sixth-grader, speaks well and his command of language is impressive. But his written work is often full of poor word choices and grammatical mistakes. For example, in a recent book report he used the phrase "effective allergy" when what he meant was "effective strategy," and wrote "The general telled his men . . ." rather than "The general told his men. . . ." Nothing like this ever appears in his spoken language.

Repetitions and omissions. Sometimes words are repeated or omitted altogether. David often makes such errors in his reports and on written tests. A word is inappropriately repeated in a sentence—"They were were sailing north along the Maine coast," for example. Or crucial words are left out, making his writing seem "telegraphic": "They reached harbor sunset." It's usually quite easy to understand what he is trying to say, though it can seem that his grammar is poor. With very careful proofing, David is sometimes able to find his errors.

Errors in punctuation and capitalization. A child's spontaneous writing may show all kinds of errors in punctuation and capitalization. He may leave out the period at the end of a sentence, fail to use a capital letter when starting a new sentence or writing the name of a person, omit quotation marks altogether or put in only the first set or the last. Adam tends to make such errors though he can tell you all about the rules of punctuation and capitalization and sometimes he can pick up his mistakes when he rereads his work.

Phonetically correct spelling errors. Sometimes a child's misspelled word can be understood by the reader because his spelling is phonetically correct—that is, it contains all the sounds heard when the word is spoken. Chris, a fourth-grader, often makes this kind of error. Chris's spelling of phonetically irregular or "sight" words is poor. His written work is full of misspellings of these words that one would expect a child his age to spell correctly without giving the matter a second thought—"giv" for "give," "sit" for "sight," and so on. The problem here is that the correct spelling of these words requires a child to remember what the word looks like, not just what it sounds like. If a child's disability makes it difficult for him to do this, simply giving more time or attention to these words will not be very helpful.

Phonetically incorrect spelling errors. Unlike Chris's, Sophie's written work is characterized by spelling errors that are *not* phonetically correct. Many of the words she writes are just a jumble of letters. For example, she writes "nature" as "neghr" and "result" as "refst." If you try to read through one of her sentences, you are likely to come up with nonsense.

Spelling errors involving sequence. A different kind of spelling pattern, which at first looks like Sophie's, is one in which the letters or syllables in a word are written in a mixed-up sequence. All the correct letters are there, but they are in the wrong order. Mary makes this kind of error, whether copying, writing from dictation, or writing spontaneously. She spells "train" as "trian," "insider" as "indersi," "bigger" as "bigerg."

Other spelling errors. Other spelling errors involve the repetition of a letter in a word ("run" spelled as "runn") or the substitution of an incorrect letter for a correct one ("gist" instead of "gift") or the omission of letters or groups of letters from a word ("lat" for "latch," "soid" for "solid"). Errors like these are often seen as carelessness, but they may actually be signs of a true writing disorder.

_____ CHECKING YOUR CHILD'S WRITING PROGRESS

Perhaps the earliest sign that a child may have a writing disability later on in his life is the slow development of "core" abilities. Some of your baby's hand or finger motor abilities may be slow in developing and he may be late in learning to hold his spoon, for example. Or his speech development may be delayed. Another sign of potential difficulty is the poor quality of performance of skills dependent on "core" abilities. Sometimes, even when performance is adequate, a child may take much longer to carry out a task or may seem to have to try much harder than other children do. For example, a toddler may be able to hold a crayon, but only after a long struggle to get his fingers around it. Another early sign of a possible writing disorder may be a young child's lack of interest in scribbling, or an older child's ignoring his coloring books and crayons.

With the beginning of instruction in writing, signs that a child has difficulty with writing will show up in his schoolwork: what it looks like and how well it is done. Parents can easily observe these "academic" signs in the work a child brings home from school and in his homework. They may also be the main focus of the teacher's comments.

One such sign of difficulty with writing is an excessive amount of time taken to master some aspect of writing, like learning to copy the letters of the alphabet or making the switch from print to script. Compare your child's learning timetable with that of his brothers and sisters and classmates. You may see that there is a significant lag.

To get a good picture of your child's total writing ability, you have to look carefully at all three of the hallmarks of writing—letter neatness, layout, and message. This means checking the quality of his work on a number of different tasks (perhaps his copy of the homework assignment, the poem he has written from dictation, and the book report he has just finished) because, while all written work reveals a child's ability to form the letters neatly and negotiate space, not all written work reveals how well he can express his ideas. When you look at his copying and his writing from dictation, focus on how well he has formed the letters, how well he has spaced the words and the letters within the words, and how well he has organized his writing on the line and page. When you look at a spontaneous writing task, like a book report, focus as well on his language abilities: his choice of words, his understanding and use of good grammar, as well as his use of correct punctuation, capitalization, and spelling.

It is important to bear in mind that a child with difficulty writing may falter in one kind of task and not in another. He may do fine on spelling tests but make a hash of spontaneous writing assignments. You should be alert for unevenness of this kind in your child's work.

Be sure to check your child's writing progress several times in the course of the school year, looking for some of the common writing errors described earlier. Every child's writing performance varies somewhat from day to day. Moreover, even a true "problem writer" may at times produce work that is acceptable. A child whose written work is usually characterized by sloppy letters, numerous erasures, and faulty grammar and misspellings can occasionally come up with a couple of sentences that look just fine. Sometimes the quality of the work varies even within one task—for example, words that are spelled correctly on one line are misspelled on the next. Looking at work like this, it is easy to think, "He can do it if he really tries." But lack of effort is rarely the problem here.

You should also compare your child's written work with his performance in other academic areas. You may see that, whereas he does his math homework with relative ease, he spends hours agonizing over a book report. And that the report, when it is finally done, falls far short of his verbal explanation of what the book is about. His teacher, also, may comment that his written test performances in science and history don't equal his oral participation in class, either in quantity or quality.

As well as "academic" signs like these, there may be "nonacademic," or behavioral, signs that your child has a writing disability. These indicators appear in his overall behavior both at school and at home. Such signs include a lack of interest in writing and everything to do with writing. Typically, children are excited about learning to write, thrilled when they begin to write in script "just like the grownups," proud of the first story they write, or the first letter to their grandparents that they compose on their own. Lack of interest is often a sign that the task is difficult—that there is a problem.

Often, also, a child with a writing disability will show little tolerance for the frustrations that are inevitable in learning this new skill. Mastering new skills and applying "old" ones to new areas are what the learning process is all about. Most children respond eagerly to the challenge and can deal with the frustrations. This may not be the case with a child for whom writing presents major difficulty.

Disruptive behavior in school, and battles about any or all homework that involves putting pencil to paper, may also signal a writing disorder. So might distractible behavior or daydreaming during class or homework that involves writing. Alternatively, a child may become withdrawn in response to his anger, frustration, and confusion. As time goes on and writing becomes more central to the educational process, these signs may worsen.

Common Warning Signs of a Writing Disability

Preschool Age
Compromised or slow development of any "core" ability
Lack of interest in scribbling or drawing

School Age
"Academic" Signs
Common error patterns in writing (see box on page 205)
Slow acquisition of writing skills
"Careless" errors or errors that seem to show lack of effort
Poor or inconsistent performance in academic areas
   requiring writing
Excessive time taken to complete writing assignments
Poor written expression

"Nonacademic" Signs
Lack of interest in and avoidance of writing tasks
Poor frustration tolerance with writing tasks
Overall disorganization when it comes to writing
Signs of emotional distress and behavioral problems

CHAPTER 18

Arithmetic

Arithmetic ability begins to develop early. Toddlers learn to count a few numbers by rote, and by the time they are in nursery school children are using some basic number concepts—for example, the ideas that numbers can be used to label things ("This is cubby number three") and count them ("two raisins"). During the early school years, a child builds on his previous ideas about numbers. He also learns to perform the basic calculations: addition, subtraction, multiplication, and division. At the same time, he learns how to apply his knowledge about number concepts and calculations to solve story problems that involve numbers. Beginning in third and fourth grades, more complicated concepts, calculations, and applications come to the fore. Most of these are advanced versions of the basic calculations and concepts that a child has been exposed to previously; some, like decimals, are new introductions.

For many children, basic arithmetic is a breeze. But for others, arithmetic skills are very slow in coming. Some of these children, by the time they reach middle school, simply say they cannot do arithmetic, period.

_____ ***Lisa.*** In nursery school, Lisa learned to count by rote to 10. In kindergarten, she extended her range to 15 and learned to recognize all the written numbers up to 15. Moreover, she was really excited about numbers: she loved to count her toys and read off numbers on license plates. Not surprisingly, her parents assumed that arithmetic would be her strong suit. They couldn't have been more wrong. Now in first grade, Lisa was utterly lost. Simple addition and subtraction calculations, both written and oral, baffled her. Unable to grasp what the calculations meant, she dealt with her difficulties by memorizing the "facts" ($2 + 4 = 6$, $8 - 5 = 3$, and so on). Number story problems also seemed insurmountably difficult. Again, it didn't make any difference whether the problem was presented in the textbook or posed orally by the teacher in class. Either way, she was at a loss. Somehow, though, Lisa stumbled through first grade.

In second and third grades, things got worse. Never having understood simple calculations, Lisa, not surprisingly, "didn't get" the more complex calculations she was now facing. With poor addition and subtraction skills, she was unable to learn how to do the calculations involved in multiplication and division. Without good computation skills, working with decimals and fractions was impossible. And all the time, number story problems grew increasingly complicated. These problems assumed an understanding of the meaning of arithmetic calculations and a mastery of the specific operations involved. But Lisa had neither the understanding nor the mastery.

Now in fourth grade, Lisa has given up trying to figure out what the problems are about and what she is supposed to do. She is lost in class and sits staring out a window. She is unable to do her arithmetic homework. She consistently fails math tests.

To appreciate why a child such as Lisa struggles with arithmetic, let's consider what arithmetic is all about, what the brain has to do to enable us to master arithmetic, and how arithmetic skills develop during childhood and adolescence.

———— WHAT IS ARITHMETIC?

Arithmetic is the science or art of computing numbers. It involves the ability to understand number concepts, to master certain operations used to manipulate numbers, and to apply these concepts and operations to the solution of problems and to special topics, such as handling money, that have to do with numbers. A child's mastery of number concepts, operations, and applications in arithmetic is a gradual, step-by-step process. And each of the three arithmetic areas mastered gives meaning to the others. The concept that counting is a way of describing objects gives meaning to an operation: for example, addition. Number concepts, operations, and applications are usually introduced in the early grades—even before then, in some instances—and are built on gradually over the years. For example, a preschooler learns to recognize the difference between a circle and a square, and to count how many sides a square has. These are concepts at the core of geometry, which is not usually taught as the focus of the arithmetic curriculum until high school.

Number concepts are ideas about numbers and about the relationship among numbers. They are learned in a hierarchical fashion, with mastery of the more complicated concepts depending on previous mastery of the simpler ones. For example, a child learns that each object in a group can be assigned its own number label—perhaps "1," "2," or "3." This idea must be mastered before the child faces the next one: that each of the objects in a group can also be counted and that "3" applies to the number of items in the group as well as to one particular item *within* the group. These two skills —labeling and enumeration—must, in turn, be thoroughly understood before a child can go on to such ideas as "more-less," "bigger-smaller," as these are applied to numbers.

Arithmetic operations are used to manipulate numbers. Mastery here involves learning how to carry out calculations, such as addition, subtraction, multiplication, and division. A child learns what the steps in the calculations are, the significance of the position of the numbers, and so on.

Ideas about numbers and number calculations can be applied to solve problems and special topics involving numbers. A relatively simple application would involve figuring out the final height of a block tower that has two floors when one more is added to it. A more complicated application would entail finding the original price of a jacket that is now on sale at a 40 percent reduction. Another would be figuring out how long it will take you to drive from Boston to Baltimore at an average speed of 55 miles an hour. The special topics deal with measurement. For example how many quarters make a dollar or how many minutes in 1½ hours. A child's developing ability to solve problems such as these depends not only on his grasp of number ideas and his calculation skills, but also on his understanding of how these ideas and calculations should be applied to the given circumstances—real or hypothetical.

_____ THE BRAIN'S JOB IN ARITHMETIC

Arithmetic competence depends upon a number of crucial abilities. These, in turn, depend upon the efficient workings of a number of different regions of the brain, and on smooth communication between these areas within and across hemispheres. We will highlight some of these critical abilities and the key brain regions associated with them.

First, several "core" abilities must be intact. In order to develop good arithmetic skills, a child must pay attention. He must listen carefully as the teacher explains a number story problem to the class; he must focus on the page of calculations. These attention abilities depend heavily on the workings of various brain areas; the frontal lobe and the reticular activating system are especially important. A child must also have unimpaired sensory and perceptual abilities. He must be able to make the necessary distinctions among written and orally presented numbers, and feel the pencil he holds when writing numbers. These sensory-perceptual abilities depend on the occipital lobes, the dominant temporal lobe, and the parietal lobes, respectively. For counting objects and writing numbers, a child's finger and hand motor abilities must also be in place. Motor skills depend especially on the frontal lobes.

Arithmetic requires a great deal of memory work. For example, the number sequence, the number "facts" (such as the multiplication tables), and the correct sequence of steps for complex computations must be committed to memory. So an unimpaired memory is crucial. Memory abilities depend on the workings of subcortical memory circuits and on the cortex. A child must also have intact language abilities. He must be able to associate verbal labels with visual patterns, such as the word "addition" with the plus sign, to write an arithmetic computation problem from dictation. He must have adequate knowledge of word meaning, so that he knows what "addition" means. He must have good language abilities, so that he can grasp the fine points of a number story problem. Language abilities depend particularly on the dominant, usually the left, temporal lobe.

As well as these "core" abilities, good reading and writing skills are essential for arithmetic. A child must be able to read a number story problem before he can solve it; his writing skills must be in place before he can do a written computation. The skills and brain regions involved in these two academic areas were described in the previous two chapters. Among the brain regions crucial to the special abilities required in reading are the dominant occipital and temporal reception areas and occipital-temporal association area (required for correct letter-sound and word-label associations), and the dominant temporal and frontal lobes (for adequate blending of sounds). Among the brain regions involved in writing skills are various reception and association areas in the occipital, temporal, parietal, and frontal lobes, working cooperatively.

Given adequate working and communication among the brain areas involved in "core" abilities and in reading and writing, certain "special" abilities are also crucial for arithmetic. To highlight some of them:

The left frontal lobe is critical in the planning, switching, and maintenance of appropriate work strategies in multistep problems, such as: "What is the sale price of a pair of skis when the original price was $350 and they have been marked down 20 percent?"

An appreciation of the spatial organization of written numbers is very important in arithmetic. The numbers 3/5 and 5/3 are not the same. A child must note the position of numbers—their spatial relationships—and be able to place numbers in the correct spaces when he writes them. These abilities depend on the right hemisphere, especially the right occipital and parietal lobes. A child must also understand the significance, or value, of number placement—the 1's column versus the 10's column versus the 100's column and align numbers accordingly. This is associated with the workings of the left hemisphere.

Consistent and appropriate work patterns are essential in arithmetic. Work patterns are important in such relatively simple tasks as reading and writing numbers correctly—for example, reading 1 followed by 2 as 12, not as 21. They are also crucial in more complex arithmetic tasks, such as addition problems that involve carrying, where, if you start in the wrong place and work the wrong way, you get the wrong answer. The ability to deal with work patterns is particularly dependent on the left parietal lobe.

Sequencing ability underlies a child's mastery of the number series. It is also involved in calculations that have several different steps—for example, in division. A child must know that he divides, *then* subtracts, *then* brings down. The workings of the left-hemisphere parietal region are particularly important here.

A skill that is peculiar to arithmetic is the putting together of information about numbers so a child can understand relationships among them. In this way, he develops number concepts, such as the ideas of more-less and bigger-smaller. This putting together of information pertaining to numbers depends on higher association areas of the left hemisphere.

───────── THE DEVELOPMENT OF ARITHMETIC COMPETENCE

The foundations of arithmetic competence are laid early. As a child grows and develops, he is increasingly able to process sensory information, to coordinate his hand and finger motor abilities, to understand language, to remember, and to pay attention. The development of "core" abilities during the early years, described in previous chapters, is truly impressive. On that development hinges the mastery of arithmetic.

Clear indications of developing arithmetic competence can be seen in a toddler counting by rote to 2 or 3 and learning how many fingers he has, how many eyes, and how many noses. His evolving speech and language comprehension skills parallel his growing ability in the rote-counting department and also his growing understanding that numbers can be used to count objects. A child of four can usually count by rote to 10. In addition, his eye-hand coordination now permits him to count things by touching them one at a time. For example, as he checks on his collection of cars or walks along a picket fence, he will touch and enumerate. Reciting numbers and counting objects are of great interest to young children—and the ability to do these things is a source of considerable pride.

By the time he is five, a child will probably be able to recite the numbers up to 15. He is also adding to his earlier knowledge about number concepts. He will be able to answer some simple number questions, such as: "Which is more, two or three?" or "Which comes first, nine or four?" Before he enters first grade, he may be able to recognize numbers to 15.

In first grade, the reading and writing of numbers moves right along with other reading and writing skills. Simple addition and subtraction are taught. In the second grade, a child learns multicolumn addition with carrying, and multicolumn subtraction with borrowing. Carrying and borrowing are sometimes referred to as exchange or regrouping. A beginning is also made on multiplication and then on division. During third grade, he practices these written computations and, by fourth grade, it is expected that he will be secure in all of the basic computation skills.

All along, in these early grades, applications become more and more complex, keeping pace with the child's growing knowledge of basic number concepts and his improving calculation skills. For example, a simple number story problem, suitable for a kindergartner, might be: "If I give you two pieces of candy and then I give you one more, how many would you have altogether?" A first-grader might be asked, "If you have eight cents and you find nine more cents, how many will you have?" By the third grade, the problems become harder—for example, "If each of three boys had nine cents, how much money would they have if they put all their money together?" Here, the child must know that the calculation is either addition $(9 + 9 + 9)$ or multiplication (9×3). If his knowledge of the multiplication tables is sound, the problem is easily solved. But if he is shaky on the multiplication tables, he may come up with the wrong answer (perhaps $3 \times 9 = 21$). Or he will have to get the answer through the more laborious multistep addition.

During the early school years, also, arithmetic curricula include number application topics: making measurements, for example, or reading tables and graphs, and handling money. These topics will be built on, step by step, in middle school and high school.

From fourth grade on, a child is expected to have mastered the basic calculation skills. Beginning in fifth grade, less time is spent on them. Topics such as positive and negative numbers, exponents and bases, among others, build on the basics. There is continued elaboration of the groundwork of topics such as fractions, algebra, and geometry (in the early grades children learn, for example, that a triangle is a three-sided figure). Some children go on to trigonometry and calculus. The teaching of the calculations involved at this level—for example, solving quadratic equations and using logarithms—assumes, as at each earlier level, an automatic facility with the calculations taught previously. Highlights of the development of arithmetic skills are seen in Table 18-1.

Table 18-1

Highlights of the Development of Arithmetic Skills

Kindergarten

Count number of objects in a group and make comparisons between
    groups, using basic arithmetic "vocabulary"—e.g., "more" and "less"
Recite, read, and write numbers 1 through 15
Understand concepts of addition and subtraction
Add 1 through 9 objects
Recognize difference between whole and part of a whole (fractions)
Recognize basic geometric shapes (geometry)
Begin to learn about basic concepts of measurement—e.g., weight, time,
    and money
Begin to work with graphs

First Grade

Recite, read, and write numbers up to 100
Count by twos
Identify even and odd numbers
Perform simple addition and subtraction not requiring exchange
Learn simple addition and subtraction facts
Continue work on basic concepts in fractions, geometry, measurement,
    and graphs
Recognize number sentences as true or false (algebra)
Begin to work with number story problems

Second Grade

Read and write numbers to 1,000
Count by tens and fives
Round numbers to nearest ten
Read and write Roman numerals I through XII

Add and subtract numbers with and without exchange
Learn concepts, symbols, and basic facts of multiplication and division
Continue to explore basic concepts in fractions, geometry, measurement, graphs and algebra
Continue work with number story problems

Third Grade

Identify and write four-digit numbers
Count by twos, threes, and fours
Develop understanding of and begin work with negative numbers
Continue to learn Roman numerals
Continue to develop skills in addition, subtraction, multiplication, and division
Learn multiplication and division facts
Begin to work with decimals
Refine understanding of fractions, geometry, measurement, graphs, and algebra
Continue work with number story problems

Fourth Grade

Learn to read and write numbers through hundred millions
Begin work with prime and composite numbers
Continue work with positive and negative numbers
Continue work with Roman numerals
Master addition, subtraction, multiplication, and division
Refine understanding of fractions, geometry, measurement, graphs, algebra, and decimals
Continue work with number story problems

Fifth Grade

Begin work with exponents and bases
Continue to learn Roman numerals
Continue work with positive and negative numbers
Refine understanding of fractions, geometry, measurement, graphs, algebra, and decimals
Continue to develop number story problem-solving skills

Sixth Grade

Continue work with exponents and different number bases
Continue to develop skills with Roman numerals
Continue work with prime and composite numbers
Refine understanding of and computation with positive and negative numbers
Continue work in fractions, geometry, measurement, graphs, algebra, and decimals
Continue to develop number story problem-solving skills

Seventh Grade

Work with squares and square roots
Continue work with positive and negative numbers

Develop understanding of and computational skills with percents
Continue work in fractions, geometry, measurement, graphs, algebra, and
   decimals
Continue to develop skills in solving number story problems

Eighth Grade and On

Master previously introduced skills
Begin work in and master new skills—e.g., calculus

————— COMMON ARITHMETIC ERRORS

A child who has difficulty in arithmetic due to inefficiency in brain
function is said to have dyscalculia. What types of errors turn up in
his work? You are likely to see one or more of the error patterns
we'll describe.

Common Error Patterns in Arithmetic

Problems with counting
Errors involving enumeration
Errors involving basic number concepts
Errors involving reading and writing numbers
Rotations
Problems with alignment
Difficulty learning calculations
Errors involving spatial organization
Errors involving work patterns
Language-based errors
Difficulty with measurement
Perseveration

Problems with counting. Number counting is first taught to
toddlers, in an informal fashion. For most children, running
through "One, two, three, four . . ." becomes second nature. But
some just can't keep the sequence in their heads and at the age of
eight or nine still can't count with ease. For example, Ann, who is
in the third grade, can count only to 100 and only with considerable
effort. She has most of her difficulties at the "corners"—29–30,
49–50, and so on.

Errors involving enumeration. Some children don't seem able to grasp the one-to-one correspondence (i.e., one object—one number) or the fact that the last number said when counting a group of objects is the number value of that group of objects. Alexandra, now in first grade, has finally learned to say the numbers aloud at a steady rhythm and pace while she moves her fingers along the objects to be counted at the same rhythm and pace. But she still doesn't understand that the last number provides a number label for a particular object *and* a number value for the size of the group of objects. And so she can't answer the question, "How many blocks are there in this group?" although she has just labeled each one: "One, two, three . . ."

Errors involving basic number concepts. Understanding quite basic number concepts is a problem for some children. Vivian can't answer the question "Which of these two boxes has more dots?" because she doesn't understand the relationship between the numbers she comes up with when she counts the dots, four in one box and six in the other. Frank doesn't understand the concept of position and order and so can't answer questions like "What number comes first, four or six?" He also has trouble with tasks involving the concept of size, such as identifying the smaller group of blocks and the larger group of blocks.

Errors involving reading and writing numbers. Sometimes an arithmetic problem shows itself in a child's difficulty with learning to read or write the numbers or both. Danny, a first-grader, still doesn't recognize or write many of the numbers. While his classmates are beginning work on the numbers up to 100, he is struggling with those beyond 20.

Rotations. It is quite common for children under the age of six to rotate numbers (turn them upside down or back to front) when writing or reading them. This tendency is of little concern at that age. However, it *is* of concern to Tim, who is nine. Because at times he still rotates numbers, reading 6 as 9 and writing 2 as 6, written calculations are a real struggle. He tries hard to get the numbers on paper the right way, but it is very slow going. What looks like 6 + 5 in his copy may well have been 9 + 5 when the teacher wrote the calculation on the blackboard.

Problems with alignment. Some children have trouble aligning numbers vertically, which affects written calculations that involve columns of numbers—for example, multidigit addition and subtraction, multiplication, and long division. When carrying and borrowing, Betsy tends to put numbers in the wrong column. She understands the concepts of carrying and borrowing and she can tell you the steps involved in a particular calculation, but she often can't carry them out accurately.

Difficulty learning calculations. Some children have difficulty learning one or more of the basic calculations. Tom, a second-grader, had no problem mastering addition and subtraction. Faced with multiplication and division, however, he was at a loss. He was unable to learn the steps involved in multiplication and division. Knowing the basic facts (for example, $2 \times 4 = 8$) did not get him very far when he was confronted with a written computation problem.

Errors involving spatial organization. Organizing numbers in space is a problem for some children. Ten-year-old Hope tends to misplace decimal points (.01 becomes 0.1) and write fractions incorrectly (⅔ becomes ½). Although she was a good arithmetic student in the earlier grades, she is now having difficulty.

Errors involving work patterns. Keeping the correct work pattern when doing calculations is often a problem. Brent can't remember whether to work right to left or left to right when he's doing multidigit addition, subtraction, multiplication, and division.

Language-based errors. Children with relatively weak language skills may sail along just fine in first, second, and third grades. But once the language demands of number story problems increase—typically, in the fourth grade—they run aground. Nine-year-old Hannah, for example, can read the "story" of the word problem, but she can't figure out what computations are needed, and in what order. Recently, she was presented with the following problem: "How many cartons of soda will you have to buy for a party, given that there are six cans to a carton, and each of your fifteen friends will want two cans?" Hannah was at a complete loss.

Difficulty with measurement. "Practical" skills involving measurement may be a stumbling block. Allison, for example, is having the worst time learning how to apply her number skills to the handling of money. Jane is finding it hard to figure out where the hands of the clock will be in one hour and fifteen minutes from now. For Brian, figuring out how much water will fit into his teacher's pitcher, is next to impossible.

Perseveration. "Getting stuck"—perseverating—can result in work that looks as though a child hadn't made any effort at all. Heather tends to "get stuck." In a series of written addition and subtraction problems, she may correctly add on the first problem then continue to do addition on the second though the computation sign has changed to subtraction. When number story problems are read to her, it is not uncommon for Heather to incorporate the answer to a previous problem into the problem that follows. Sometimes, she merely repeats a number from a computation problem as the answer. For example, $4 - 1 = 1$. At first glance, it seems as though she has produced numbers at random. But when her work is scrutinized carefully, you can see a clear pattern of perseveration in it.

_____ CHECKING YOUR CHILD'S ARITHMETIC PROGRESS

With arithmetic, as with reading and writing, the earliest sign of a possible disorder is the compromised development of "core" abilities, or slow development in these areas. Perhaps your child is very late in picking up small objects or saying his first words. Perhaps he has noticeable difficulty keeping his attention on what he is doing or remembering the names of things. Sometimes, though, an early sign of a possible disorder is not so much inadequate development as excessive effort—in the case of an arithmetic disorder, the excessive effort that a child must put into anything having to do with numbers. A toddler who must struggle and strain to count to two may later turn out to have an arithmetic disability.

Lack of interest in numbers, and things involving numbers, is another early sign of a possible arithmetic disability. Young children are usually fascinated by the idea of counting and very proud of their early efforts in that direction. So a toddler or preschooler who seems indifferent to the finger- and toe-counting games his parents play with him, or one who has no interest at all in numbers, or one who never even tries to count, may later be found to have a disorder.

When a child starts school, signs of an arithmetic disability may show themselves in his work—how it is performed, how it looks on paper. One such sign of difficulty with arithmetic is an excessive amount of time taken to master skills. This may be evident as early as kindergarten, with a child taking much longer than his classmates to learn about adding objects, or to recognize and write the numbers. From first grade on, check your child's arithmetic workbooks. They will provide tangible evidence of his progress— or lack of it. You can compare his work with that of his siblings and classmates, to see if he is learning at about the same pace.

In arithmetic skills are built stepwise, one on another. A child must be secure in basic skills before going on to more complicated ones. Check your child's skills against those outlined in Table 18-1, which highlights the development of arithmetic skills for each grade. If you notice that your child is shaky on an "old" skill at the time when a "new" one is being introduced—for example, if he is unsure about addition when instruction in multiplication is beginning, in second grade—you should not hesitate to point this out to his teacher.

Another sign of a disability is extremely untidy or messy work. In arithmetic, neat work is essential. If numbers are not written clearly, they will not be read clearly, and so will not be computed correctly. If numbers are not aligned in their proper columns, a computation may be off by hundreds, if not thousands. While every child has days when his work is less tidy than it usually is, persistently messy arithmetic papers may well indicate the presence of a disability.

It is important to bear in mind that a child with an arithmetic disability may do just fine with basic concepts and calculations but may flounder when applications of arithmetic skills are involved. You should be alert for this kind of unevenness in your child's performance.

It is also important to compare your child's work in arithmetic with his work in reading and writing. You may find that his ability to compute is far behind his reading ability. You may notice that he takes much longer to do his arithmetic homework than his writing assignments, and complains about it more. Such unevenness in performance is often a sign of disability.

In addition to such "academic" signs of an arithmetic disability, "nonacademic" signs may surface in your child's behavior. He may, for example, avoid games and activities that have to do with numbers. He may shy away from card games, board games, and the counting games that are part of most children's play repertoire. He may make a guess when asked to say what time it is, rather than figure it out from the clock, and find excuses not to handle money. He may have no interest in measuring and weighing things—projects that enthrall most children.

Common Warning Signs of an Arithmetic Disability

Preschool Age
Compromised or slow development of any "core" ability
Lack of interest in counting and numbers

School Age
"Academic" Signs
Presence of common error patterns (see box on page 232)
Careless errors
Slowness in arithmetic skill mastery
Inconsistent performance on arithmetic tests
Arithmetic performance that falls behind performance in
    other academic areas

"Nonacademic" Signs
Avoidance of anything having to do with numbers
Complaints that arithmetic is "boring" or "horrible"
Consistent acting out in arithmetic class or when
    arithmetic homework is to be done.
Consistently misplacing or forgetting arithmetic homework
Poor frustration tolerance with tasks involving numbers
Signs of emotional distress and behavioral problems

Take the case of Bill. His parents made it a point to make Saturday night family night. After dinner, they would all sit around and play card games and board games. Bill's mother began to notice that he often said he didn't feel like playing. He used such excuses as having too much homework or wanting to read or watch TV.

When she put Bill's reluctance to play together with his poor math grades, she began to suspect that the real reason for his lack of interest in joining the family was really his lack of confidence in his ability to handle the number requirements of the games.

Other behavioral signs that suggest an arithmetic disability include disruptive behavior in class—especially arithmetic class—and reluctance to do arithmetic homework, which may reach the extreme of "losing" the assignment to be done. Some children, however, do not act out in this way in response to their frustrations but, rather, become apathetic and withdrawn. Some daydream during arithmetic class.

Putting It All Together

INTRODUCTION

In Part One you have gained the necessary basic knowledge to understand your child's learning disability. In Part Two you have been provided with an action program to help your child. The core abilities and basic academic areas, with special emphasis on their neurological underpinnings, were presented in Part Three. In this section, Part Four, we put it all together. Perhaps the best way of doing this is to share with you the story of Deborah, a child with a learning disability, and what Deborah's parents did to help her. Deborah's story illustrates in many ways how it should be done.

We can also use Deborah's story to highlight what we can say about the future of a child with learning disabilities. The question of what the future holds for their child is never far from the minds of parents, and it appears that the question is all the more pressing for parents of a child with a learning disability. In this final section we end the book as it begins, with a look at a child who is having trouble at school and with some answers to questions that her parents are likely to be asking as they continue to educate themselves about learning disabilities in their ongoing effort to help their child.

CHAPTER 19

Today and Tomorrow

As a way of summing up much of what we've been discussing, we will tell you about Deborah. If any child's situation is illustrative, Deborah's is. Her story brings everything together: parents' understanding what a learning disability is and what it is not, the first signs of a learning problem, the search for professional help, the evaluation process, and the treatment. It also gives a glimpse into the future of a child with learning disabilities. Reading about Deborah will provide you with a "dry run." Before you actually embark on your own journey with your own child, you'll have seen another child go through it all.

_____ DEBORAH: A SUCCESS STORY

Deborah was seven years old. Her family had moved to a new house during the summer, and Deborah started second grade in unfamiliar surroundings. Up to now she'd enjoyed school and had done well there. But early in the first term at her new school, she asked if she could attend an extra class for children in her grade who were having difficulty reading. Her parents, concerned about this, requested a conference with Deborah's teachers. They were told not to worry: Deborah was doing fine. She had scored in the lower part of the average range on a recent reading test, but her performance was considered satisfactory. Deborah's teachers assured her parents that if there really was a problem, next year would be soon enough to intervene and refer her to the school psychologist for an evaluation.

Still, Deborah's request had put her parents on the alert and they began to watch her schoolwork and her general behavior more carefully. She seemed to have a hesitant quality about her on school mornings that had not been there before. Of course, this could be because she was starting in a new school. The last few months had been rough on the family all around. But they began to wonder whether Deborah's behavior could be related, instead, to her concern about reading.

They noticed that although Deborah was able to read in her workbook, when the same words appeared somewhere else she frequently hesitated or stumbled in her efforts to read them. Also, she still wrote a number of her letters and numbers backward—and they knew that by age seven most children outgrow this tendency. Talking with other parents, they learned that Deborah was behind many classmates in academic skills.

Confused and concerned, Deborah's parents decided not to wait for next year and the school's referral. Something just wasn't right, and it was time to explore the possibility that their daughter's new behavior and her slowness in learning were connected. They asked Deborah's pediatrician how to go about having Deborah evaluated to determine why she was behind her peers. Various options were discussed regarding the types of professionals who do such evaluations and where the evaluation could be done—for example, the public school or a local clinic. Deborah's parents then made a number of calls and asked some key questions. Finally, they made an appointment to see a psychologist, with special training in the factors that affect learning, who was in private practice.

At the initial meeting, they were asked to describe Deborah's problems and their own concerns. They told the psychologist about Deborah's school background, the family situation, and their goals in going forward with the evaluation. More background information was reviewed and arrangements were made for Deborah to be tested.

By the end of the meeting, the parents felt relieved that something was finally being done, although their relief was tempered with great concern about what the testing might show.

Deborah's mother brought her in for testing. She relaxed when she saw the warmth with which the psychologist greeted Deborah and ushered her into the office. Though a bit shy in general, and certainly timid about showing others what she could do, Deborah seemed to enjoy her meetings with the psychologist. On the way home after each session, she talked cheerfully about the "games" she had enjoyed playing. Her mother found this reassuring and she also appreciated the psychologist's willingness to talk to her for a few minutes at the end of each session.

The results of the evaluation were explained to Deborah's parents at a follow-up session. Though the initial concern was about her difficulty in reading, Deborah's academic difficulties were of a more global nature. Deborah had a number of weak areas that were hindering her ability to learn when taught by traditional methods. However, she was a bright girl and, if taught in a way that minimized or bypassed the underlying weaknesses, she had a good shot at learning and progressing academically. Her disabilities did not warrant special class or special school placement. Deborah's hesitancy seemed to be a sign of distress about her learning difficulties. Her request for help—the extra class in reading—was an attempt to get relief.

Deborah's parents told the school about the testing and signed release forms authorizing school personnel to call the psychologist to discuss the test results. In terms of treatment, Deborah's parents decided to use remedial services at a local clinic recommended by the psychologist. They talked to a remediator there whose work the psychologist was familiar with, someone who could translate the results of the evaluation into specific teaching strategies and techniques for Deborah. Deborah's parents signed a release permitting ongoing communication between the remediator and school personnel.

Remediation on a twice-a-week basis was started right away. The first order of business was prioritizing Deborah's learning needs, since a number of areas were affected. Initially, in part because of Deborah's concern about her poor reading performance, reading was the focus. Basic letter-sound associations had to be mastered before she could learn to "sound out" whole words or tackle her difficulties with spelling. The strategies and techniques that were used capitalized on Deborah's strengths; also some gimmicks were designed to get around her areas of difficulty. For her problem with learning the letter-sounds, the gimmick was this: Deborah would be shown a letter embedded within a picture of a familiar object whose name began with that letter. She would be taught to "peel off" the first sound from the name of a picture. Gradually, she moved to the letter in isolation and by remembering the original picture and its name, and by "peeling off" its initial sound, she was able to come up with the correct letter sound. For example, the hard *c* sound was embedded within a drawing of a cat (Figure 19-1), and so on. Additional strategies and techniques were devised as they were needed. They were designed specifically for Deborah and changed in response to her ability to use them. Her approach to reading was different from her classmates', but the end result was the same. Spelling skills began to improve as decoding skills were mastered and as sight vocabulary began to expand.

Once reading was under control, the remediator began to focus on math skills. Progress was slow but steady. At home, Deborah's parents began to notice an encouraging change in her behavior and in her overall sense of well-being. By the end of the school year, her academic skills had improved dramatically.

———— QUESTIONS PARENTS ASK ABOUT THE FUTURE

What about the future? What can we predict for Deborah? There is much that we *can't* say for certain. But there are some things that we can be relatively confident about. As a way of discussing these, let us try to answer some of the main questions that Deborah's parents are likely to ask?

What about her chances of a bright future? We can say that Deborah should have a very good shot at a bright future, in part because she received help when she was still young, before years of failure had left their scars. Her parents recognized her struggles early on. A comprehensive evaluation and appropriate help were put in place early, too. She was in the second grade, rather than in the fourth grade or beyond, when help came her way. There was never

FIGURE 19-1

Cat
C

The child is presented with a picture in which a letter is embedded. He is taught to "peel off" the initial sound of the picture label, which is the correct letter-sound association.

At the next stage the child is taught to come up with the picture and its label upon presentation of the letter in isolation. From the label of the picture, he is able to "peel off" the initial sound. Gradually the need to come up with the picture and its label drops out as the letter-sound association is established.

a great gap between her performance and that of her classmates. In addition, her parents and school understood her problem. She had excellent support all around—at home, at school, and at the remediator's office. For her part, she seemed to meet her special learning challenges with a positive outlook and much energy. Her sense of self, pretty shaky at the beginning, was increasingly nourished by her improved academic skills and growing self-esteem.

Are her difficulties over? When thinking about Deborah's future, it is important to remember that, although her remediator developed good strategies and techniques, as the years go by and demands on the brain change, many of the learning strategies that worked so well for Deborah when she was seven will not work so well anymore. As with all children she will have many ups and downs, successes and disappointments—then much hard work and more success. The fact that Deborah has a learning disability may make her more vulnerable than many of her peers to such fluctuations but not necessarily less able to deal with them successfully.

What hurdles lie ahead? We can be certain that, along with the challenges that face all children as they grow to adulthood, there are a number of hurdles along the way that are likely to be especially difficult for Deborah. Each school year, of course, brings new learning demands, new academic topics, new adjustments to new teachers. But the transitions between major school divisions—lower school to middle school, middle school to high school, and so on—are likely to pose significantly more academic problems for Deborah than for her peers. In turn, these major school transition times are characterized by major changes in social demands. These, too, are likely to be more problematic for Deborah than for her classmates.

What are her long-term schooling options? Will Deborah go to college? A learning disability does not shut off a child from a higher education. Many children with learning disabilities go to college. Some go to a college that specializes in educating individuals with learning disabilities. Many others take advantage of special programs and services for students with learning disabilities within traditional colleges. Some attend traditional colleges and receive no external support. They rely on their own strengths, their motivation, and their by then well-developed learning skills to see them through. And there are many different types of institutions of higher learning, besides the liberal arts colleges. For a youngster with special visual abilities, a school that specializes in graphic design might be the perfect choice; for a promising actor, one that specializes in the performing arts. Or, having tested the waters in high school—having performed with the school chorus, for example, or been a member of the photography club or the auto mechanics' club—a youngster may decide to pursue some special interest or talent where the traditional higher education route isn't needed.

Will she be able to make it on her own as a young adult? For every horror story of a young adult who doesn't make it because of a learning disability, there is a success story. Although there are no guarantees here, we frequently hear from young adults with learning disabilities that their struggles with learning have been key to their development in some areas that are especially valued in adulthood. Often, these have gone unrecognized during earlier years. They say, for example, that learning to get around a learning disability provided them with far more than their fair share of practice in developing and implementing innovative work strategies. Perhaps most important, they say, is the true appreciation they have of their own individuality, having been so aware of their own strengths and weaknesses for so long. This often makes them champions of their own rights and of the rights of others, too. As people with creative approaches to the tasks at hand, with the highest respect for individual rights, and as experienced advocates for these rights, they are young adults who can make a very valuable contribution to society.

Finally, a few more things to remember: some key words. These apply to every aspect of everything that parents—as advocates and allies, today and tomorrow—can do to help their child.

UNDERSTANDING the basis of your child's trouble
    at school is your first priority.
KNOWLEDGE is imperative.
FLEXIBILITY is the rule.
PATIENCE is not only a virtue but a must.

APPENDIX 1

*Checklist on Preparing for the Background Meeting of a
Comprehensive Evaluation*

1. Presenting problem(s)
   a. onset
   b. associated emotional or behavioral changes
   c. possible triggering factors
2. General description of the child
   a. personality traits
   b. general style and level of functioning at home
   c. adjustment to significant life events
   d. special abilities and interests
   e. noteworthy attitudes or behaviors
3. Developmental history
   a. prenatal, perinatal, postnatal
      (1) mother's care and health during pregnancy
      (2) duration of pregnancy, type of delivery
      (3) mother's and newborn's health
   b. childhood
      (1) place in family
      (2) developmental milestones
      (3) sexual development and adjustment
      (4) significant medical illnesses
      (5) previous evaluation or treatment

4. Academic history
   a. age of first school experience
   b. past and present level of academic performance
   c. nonacademic performance
   d. relationships with teachers and classmates
   e. behavior in school
   f. extra help in academics
   g. school reports, past and present
   h. recent work sample
5. Family history
   a. family composition and relationships among family members
   b. significant events in family—death, divorce, remarriage
   c. current living arrangements and support systems

APPENDIX 2

Some Tests Commonly Administered in a Comprehensive Evaluation

Boston Right-Left Discrimination Test
Children's Apperception Test
Cognitive Education Screening Test
Developmental Test of Visual-Motor Integration
Draw-a-Person Test
Finger Agnosia Test
Graphesthesia Test
Gray Oral Reading Test, Revised
Key Math Diagnostic Arithmetic Test
Neurosensory Center Comprehensive Examination for Aphasia
Ravens Coloured (Standard) Progressive Matrices
Revised Test of Visual Retention
Rorschach
Test of Written Language
Thematic Apperception Test
Wechsler Intelligence Scale for Children, Revised
Wepman Test of Auditory Discrimination

APPENDIX 3

National Organizations That Provide Information on Learning Disabilities

Children with Attention
Deficit Disorder
499 N.W. 70th Avenue,
Suite 308
Plantation, FL 33317
Tel. (305) 587-3700

Council for Exceptional
Children
1920 Association Drive
Reston, VA 22091
Tel. (703) 620-3660

Higher Education and Adult
Training for People with
Handicaps
1 Dupont Circle, Suite 800
Washington, DC 20036
Tel. (800) 544-3284

Learning Disabilities
Association
4156 Library Road
Pittsburgh, PA 15234
Tel. (412) 341-1515

National Center for Learning
Disabilities
99 Park Avenue
New York, NY 10016
Tel. (212) 687-7211

National Information Center
for Children and Youth
with Handicaps
P.O. Box 1492
Washington, DC 20013
Tel. (800) 999-5599

Orton Society
724 York Road
Baltimore, MD 21204
Tel. (800) 222-3123

APPENDIX 4

Highlights of Public Law 94-142

1. All children with handicaps, including children with learning disabilities, have a right to:
   a free education and appropriate education;
   an education with nonhandicapped children to the maximum extent appropriate;
   an education based on a determined assessment of their special needs; and
   an individualized education plan that documents the special services a child is to receive.
2. Children with handicaps, including children with learning disabilities, and their parents have a right to:
   a due process hearing when they disagree with the identification, assessment, or placement of their child.
3. Theoretically, a school's negligence in serving handicapped children can result in a loss of federal funding.

GLOSSARY

Acquired Brain Dysfunction   Brain dysfunction that is the result of damage to the brain after birth.

Articulation Disorder   A speech disorder in which basic speech sounds are not mastered as expected.

Attention has at least two components: arousal and selection. Arousal is the degree to which an individual is available to stimulation. Selection is the degree to which an individual can select one particular stimulus to focus on, at the same time filtering out other impinging stimuli.

Autonomic Nervous System   A functional division of the nervous system that sends commands to the glands, smooth muscles of the skin, blood vessels, and internal organs (heart and stomach, for example).

Brain Stem Auditory Evoked Potentials (BAEP)   A technique that measures very tiny electrical signals in the brain as a sound is processed. It uses earphones and electrodes placed on the scalp.

Basal Ganglia   A group of centers located deep within the brain that functions as a bridge between sensory and motor systems. They influence our movement and are essential in maintaining normal posture and motor control.

Blending   A special ability needed in reading in which letter sounds and syllables are blended together to make a word.

Brain   The structure that is snuggled in the skull. It runs on oxygen and glucose supplied by the bloodstream. It has four main regions: the cerebrum, cerebellum, deep structures, and brain stem.

Brain Stem   The part of the brain that lies below the deep structures at the top of the spinal cord. It contains most of the nerves branching out of the brain, called the cranial nerves, and the reticular activating system.

Central Nervous System   A part of the nervous system that consists of the brain and spinal cord.

Cerebellum   A part of the brain, next in size to the cerebrum. It lies beneath the cerebrum and behind the brain stem. It is responsible for the control of body balance, muscle tone, and the precision and coordination of movements.

Cerebral Hemispheres   The two very similar halves of the cerebrum.

Cerebrum   When people speak about the human brain, they usually mean the cerebrum, the part of the brain that is especially highly developed in humans. It has four lobes: the occipital, temporal, parietal, and frontal.

Comprehensive Psychological Evaluation   The evaluation that is used to identify a learning problem and its primary source: emotional, environmental, or biological. It assesses an individual's intellectual functioning, emotional well-being, academic skills, and strengths and weaknesses in brain functions.

Computerized Tomography (CT scan)   An X-ray procedure that takes a 3-dimensional picture of the brain or body.

Contralateral   A term that refers to the relation between one cerebral hemisphere and the opposite face and body side from which it receives certain sensory information and to which it sends certain motor information that activates our muscles.

Cortex   The outer layer of the cerebrum. One of the most important parts of the human brain.

Critical Comprehension   One of three types of reading comprehension. It requires that the reader evaluate the viewpoint of the writer or come up with his own interpretation of the information read.

Decoding   The first step in the reading act in which the written word is translated into a word that has a sound that can be said.

Deep Structures   Structures located deep within the brain in what is known as subcortical regions—for example, the thalamus and hypothalamus.

Developmental Brain Dysfunction Brain dysfunction with which a child is born.

Dominant Hemisphere Because of its control of language, considered by many to be our most important intellectual possession, the left hemisphere is known as the dominant hemisphere. The left cerebral hemisphere is specialized for language in all right-handers and most left-handers.

Dyscalculia Developmental arithmetic disability.

Dyslexia Developmental reading disability.

Dysgraphia Developmental writing disability.

Electroencephalogram (EEG) A procedure that measures the brain's ongoing electrical activity. It uses electrodes placed on the scalp.

Expressive Language Disorder A language disorder that involves inefficiency in the expression of language.

Extrapyramidal System One of two motor systems that carries information to our muscles.

Frontal Lobes The part of the brain that plans, sets in motion, evaluates, and modifies our motor performance and also behaviors that do not involve movement—for example, solving a number story problem.

Gray Matter Regions of the nervous system where most of the neurons do not have myelin sheaths—the outer layer of the brain, for example.

Hippocampal Circuit A subcortical circuit that is especially crucial in memory.

Hypothalamus A deep structure that regulates appetite, sexual arousal, and emotions such as anger.

Inferential Comprehension One of three types of reading comprehension. It requires that the reader generate new ideas by relating several concepts presented in the text or combining concepts from the text with previously acquired knowledge.

Interhemispheric Commisures The large bundles of nerve fibers that connect the two hemispheres of the cerebrum allowing communication between them.

Interpretative Language Disorder A language disorder in which there is a problem with the ability to understand or "process" language beyond the discrimination of individual words.

Ipsilateral   A term that refers to the relation between one cerebral hemisphere and the same face and body side from which it receives sensory information and to which it sends motor information that activates certain muscles.

Learning   The ability to put skills and concepts into long-term storage in a form that allows them to be used later, as the situation requires.

Learning Disability   A learning problem that is attributable to inefficiency in the workings of the brain.

Learning Problem   A difficulty learning which may have its primary roots in emotional factors (for example, depression), environmental factors (for example, a teacher-child mismatch), or biological factors (for example, brain dysfunction).

Limbic System   A group of deep structures whose complex circuits are especially important in memory and emotion, feeding and reproduction.

Literal Comprehension   One of three types of reading comprehension. It requires that the reader grasp information explicitly stated in the text.

Long-Term Memory   One of the memory systems. It has enormous capacity and retains information for considerable time periods.

Magnetic Resonance Imaging (MRI)   A procedure that uses magnetic fields to take a three-dimensional picture of the brain or body.

Memory Trace   The biological changes in the nervous system that are believed to underlie long-term memory.

Myelin   A white fatty material that sheaths the axons and dendrites of many nerves. It speeds up the transmission of nerve impulses.

Mirror Movement   An associated movement disorder, also called overflow, in which intended movement on one side of the body is mirrored on the opposite body side.

Mirror Writing   Writing, usually seen in very young children, in which letters are correctly formed but written backward.

Neuropsychological Testing   Part of a comprehensive psychological evaluation that assesses strengths and weaknesses in brain functions that affect learning.

Neuron   The basic unit of the nervous system. A neuron is a cell with a cell body, axon, and dendrites. Communicating among themselves, neurons do the work of the nervous system.

Occipital Lobes   The part of the brain that is responsible for receiving and interpreting visual information.

Parietal Lobes   The part of the brain that is responsible for receiving and interpreting somatosensory information (temperature and touch, for example).

Peripheral Nervous System   A part of the nervous system that consists of the nerves branching from the brain and spinal cord and parts of the autonomic nervous system.

Perseveration   The repetition of motor activity when it is no longer appropriate.

Phonetic Reading   One of two ways to carry out the decoding step in reading in which the written word is broken down into its component letters, and associations are made between the written letters and their corresponding sounds. The sounds are then blended to produce the word.

Pyramidal System   One of two motor systems that carries information to our muscles.

Remediation   The individualized treatment of choice for a learning disability. It follows a comprehensive evaluation. It utilizes specifically designed teaching strategies and techniques that recruit adequately developed or strong brain functions to do the work that less developed or weak ones cannot manage very well.

Receptive Language Disorder   A language disorder in which there is a difficulty discriminating among the words heard.

Reticular Activating System (RAS)   A group of complex interlocking nerve pathways, located in the brain stem, that is concerned with attention and arousal.

Short-Term Memory   One of the memory systems. It holds a limited number of items for immediate retrieval within thirty seconds or so.

Sight Reading   One of two ways to carry out the decoding step in reading in which the whole written word is associated with a spoken word.

Somatic System   A functional division of the nervous system that conveys and processes sensory information and mediates voluntary muscle movements.

Syllabication   A reading skill in which the reader is expected to identify syllables within words. It is used in the decoding process.

Synapse Gap   An infinitesimally small gap between neurons across which neurons communicate via a chemical messenger.

Temporal Lobes   The part of the brain that is responsible for receiving and interpreting auditory information.

Thalamus   A deep structure that acts as a relay station for all sensory information (except smell) transmitted to the cerebrum.

White Matter   Regions of the nervous system where most of the neurons are sheathed in myelin.

INDEX

ABOUT THE AUTHORS

BARBARA Z. NOVICK is a psychologist specializing in the evaluation and treatment of children who are struggling in school. She has published a number of articles in professional journals, and she and Dr. Arnold have co-authored a widely used textbook in clinical child neuropsychology. She is on the staff of Lenox Hill Hospital, consults with schools, and has a private practice. She is the mother of two grown daughters and lives in New York City with her husband.

MAUREEN M. ARNOLD, with degrees in psychology and education, specializes in the diagnosis and remediation of learning disabilities. In addition to having co-authored a textbook with Barbara Novick, she is on the staff of Bronx Children's Psychiatric Center and is a faculty member at Albert Einstein College of Medicine and Yeshiva University's Ferkauf Graduate School of Psychology. She also has a private practice in New York City where she lives.